FUTURE-PROOFING THE NEWS

FUTURE-PROOFING THE NEWS

Preserving the First Draft of History

KATHLEEN A. HANSEN
NORA PAUL

ROWMAN & LITTLEFIELD
Lanham • Boulder • New York • London

Published by Rowman & Littlefield
A wholly owned subsidiary of The Rowman & Littlefield Publishing Group, Inc.
4501 Forbes Boulevard, Suite 200, Lanham, Maryland 20706
www.rowman.com

Unit A, Whitacre Mews, 26-34 Stannary Street, London SE11 4AB

British Library Cataloguing in Publication Information Available

Library of Congress Cataloging-in-Publication Data

Names: Hansen, Kathleen A., author. | Paul, Nora, author.
Title: Future-proofing the news : preserving the first draft of history / Kathleen A. Hansen, Nora Paul.
Description: Lanham : Rowman & Littlefield, [2017] | Includes bibliographical references and index.
Identifiers: LCCN 2016043888 (print) | LCCN 2016057283 (ebook) | ISBN 9781442267121 (cloth : alk. paper) | ISBN 9781442267145 (electronic)
Subjects: LCSH: Journalism—United States—History. | Journalism—Technological innovations—United States. | American newspapers—History. | Newspapers—Conservation and restoration—United States. | Newspaper publishing—United States—History. | Press law—United States.
Classification: LCC PN4855 .H26 2017 (print) | LCC PN4855 (ebook) | DDC 071/.3—dc23
LC record available at https://lccn.loc.gov/2016043888

∞™ The paper used in this publication meets the minimum requirements of American National Standard for Information Sciences—Permanence of Paper for Printed Library Materials, ANSI/NISO Z39.48-1992.

Printed in the United States of America

For tomorrow's seekers of yesterday's news

CONTENTS

PREFACE

News coverage is often described as the "first draft of history." From the publication in 1690 of the first colonial newspaper, *Publick Occurrences*, to the latest tweet, news has been disseminated to inform its audience about what is going on in the world. But preserving yesterday's news for possible future use has been neglected in the day-to-day work of newsmaking. *Future-Proofing the News* examines the technological, legal, economic, and organizational challenges faced by those concerned with preserving the news.

Over the centuries, as new means of finding, producing, and distributing news were developed, the methods used to ensure access for future generations changed, and new challenges for news content preservation arose. *Future-Proofing the News* covers the history of news preservation (or lack thereof), the decisions that helped ensure (or doom) its preservation, and the unique preservation issues that each new form of media raised.

All but one copy of *Publick Occurrences* were destroyed by decree. The wood pulp–based newsprint used for later newspapers crumbled to dust. Early microfilm disintegrates to acid, and decades of microfilmed newspapers have already dissolved in their storage drawers. Early radio and television newscasts were rarely captured, and when they were, the equipment for accessing the content has long been superseded. Sounds and images stored on audio and videotapes fade and become unreadable. The early years of web publication by news organizations were lost by changes in publishing platforms and a false security that everything on the Internet lives forever.

In fifty or one hundred years, what will we be able to retrieve from today's news output? How will we tell the story of this time and place? Will we have better access to news produced in 1817 than news produced in 2017? These are some of the questions *Future-Proofing the News* aims to answer.

Chapter 1 asks "Who Needs Yesterday's News?" Chapters 2 through 8 tell the story of how the content from each form of news delivery—newsprint, photojournalism, newsreels, radio, television, and digital news—was or was not preserved, with a detour to describe the news industries' "digital turn" in chapter 7. Chapter 9 delves into the challenges news archive seekers face in gaining access to the materials they need. Chapter 10 lays out some of the technological, legal, and economic issues that must be addressed if we are to have any hope of avoiding historical amnesia.

Future-Proofing the News is written in an accessible style but with thoroughly researched and documented sources. We mined archival and manuscript collections that have not been used for this topic before. In reviewing the key books of media history, it was clear that little attention had been paid to what happened to those news products once they were published, aired, or broadcast.

This book is written to appeal to the general public. It will be surprising to them to learn how at risk the first draft of history really is. We hope that those who rely on access to news as part of their professional activities will understand after reading this book just how tenuous their ongoing access might be. Librarians, archivists, and journalists—whether actively engaged in the work of news preservation or unaware of the issues at stake—will develop a greater appreciation of those issues. Genealogists, media historians, legal scholars, business historians, and others who use news archives for research and scholarship will understand the factors that affect their access to the materials they need.

The idea for *Future-Proofing the News* grew out of several concerns. The first was the attrition in the ranks of news archivists. With news organizations' declining revenue, hard choices have been made about staff reductions. Over the past decade the number of newspapers and broadcast stations with news researchers or librarians has shrunk. In many cases, newsrooms that had robust research and archiving staff now have no one. Who, we wondered, still cares about the newsroom archival assets?

Our second concern was the growing problem of disappearing web content that we encountered as researchers and teachers. We wrote the e-textbook for a course on information strategies for communication professionals. Each semester we had to check the sites we cited and clean out the dead and missing links. The notion that "once on the web, always on the web" was clearly a fallacy.

Over our professional and academic careers, we had kept our focus so set on the information usage and preservation issues of today that it hadn't occurred to us to look in the rearview mirror. Were news resources ever so highly valued that their preservation was an institutional priority or has news preservation always been an afterthought? How was reporting preserved as new forms of production and distribution arose?

Learning about the varied, inconsistent, sometimes accidental, sometimes obsessive ways that yesterday's news products have been collected has taken us deep into organizational archives and introduced us to colorful characters and dedicated guardians of the past. We have learned about inspiring efforts to preserve certain slices of media history. And we have gained a greater understanding of why the effort to create today's first rough draft of history often precludes attention to adequately preserving yesterday's.

We also quickly realized that we would have to narrow the scope of the topic. Therefore, we deal exclusively with news preservation issues and efforts in the United States. Though we honor the many initiatives undertaken in institutions elsewhere around the world, they are not discussed in this volume. Also, although we cite many useful finding guides for news archives, this book is not intended to serve that function.

As do all authors who become enthralled with their topic, we found much more material than we could include. Each of our chapters could be its own book. As a result, the preservation issues of mainstream, larger news organizations is our focus. To our regret, the preservation challenges for local, ethnic, and niche publications or broadcasts—in many cases more dire than those of larger, mainstream organizations—are not specifically addressed.

Our conclusion is that inattention to preserving news content is a classic example of history repeating itself. *Future-Proofing the News* provides background on the challenges to news preservation in the past and going forward. If the efforts of the archivists, librarians, and technologists trying to ensure ongoing access can be supported through a greater general knowledge of the challenges they face, we will consider our work here rewarded.

ACKNOWLEDGMENTS

We owe many debts of gratitude to the individuals and institutions that made this book possible. Hansen received a faculty sabbatical leave with supplement and a grant in aid of research, artistry, and scholarship from the University of Minnesota that provided the time and funding to visit the organizations that are doing news preservation work around the country. Paul's travel and time was funded by the School of Journalism and Mass Communication. We deeply appreciate the support our university and school have provided.

We interviewed many, many individuals during the course of our work. The list here represents the bare minimum in acknowledging their contributions. Each one offered his or her time, expertise, insights, and candid views. Many also generously allowed us to photograph their work spaces, photocopy their archival materials, and record their voices. We are most grateful to all of them.

The staff at the American Antiquarian Society provided invaluable help in using the priceless Isaiah Thomas manuscript collections for chapter 2. Thank you to Thomas Knoles, Vincent Golden, Kimberly Pelkey, Jacklyn Penney, and Daniel Boudreau for their hospitality and expertise. Curator Carrie Christofferson at the Newseum in Washington, D.C., offered a backstage view of that institution's work in raising public awareness about the importance of journalism history. Professor David Copeland at Elon University helpfully described his experiences as a journalism historian using archival news collections.

Hal Buell and Claudia DiMartino offered their insights into the history of the Associated Press photo service and its transition to the digital environment for chapter 3. AP special projects manager Chuck Zoeller and AP archivist Francesca Pitaro provided additional help in understanding the valuable role the wire service has played through its long and storied history.

Curator Greg Wilsbacher in the Moving Image Research Collections at the University of South Carolina led us to archival documents that explained the origin story of the Fox *Movietone News* collection for chapter 4. Mark Quigley and Blaine Bartell at the UCLA Film and Television Archive provided insights and access to their collections of archival documents about the history of the Hearst *Metrotone News* collection. Artist and filmmaker Bill Morrison generously devoted time during his attendance at the 10th Orphan Film Symposium in Culpeper, Virginia, for an interview about his work with archival nitrate film. Library of Congress (LOC) staff members Mike Mashon, George Willeman, and Rob Stone offered many anecdotes about film preservation efforts. Janice Allen provided candid testimony about her father's work as the compiler of one of the largest personal collections of newsreels in the country.

Chapter 5 was greatly enhanced by the contributions of interviewees Professor Michael Stamm of Michigan State University; Professor Josh Shepperd of the Catholic University of America; Patrick Loughney, chief of the Packard Humanities Institute; and Executive Director Jim duBois of the Minnesota Broadcasters Association. Karen Fishman, research center supervisor in the LOC Motion Picture, Broadcasting and Recorded Sound Division helped us gain access to the National Broadcasting Company history archives, with so much inside information about the Press-Radio War of the 1930s. Matthew Barton, recorded sound curator at the LOC, answered a number of in-depth questions about the LOC's radio collection.

CBS News archives manager Roy Carubia devoted a full morning to a tour and a candid interview that filled in many blanks for chapter 6. Staff at the Paley Center for Media in New York, including visitor services manager Mark Ekman, helped us locate the historical materials about the Vanderbilt Television News Archives in their collection. Amy Ciesielskii at the USC Moving Image Research Collections eloquently described the challenges in working with archival television news film, as did Daniel Einstein at the UCLA Film and Television Archive. Nancy Mate and Ken Rees, former WCCO-TV staffers in Minneapolis, helped us understand the efforts of individuals to save local television public affairs content.

Chapter 7 could not have been written without the substantial help of the staff at the New York Public Library Brooke Russell Astor Reading Room for Rare Books and Manuscripts. Their collection of the *New York Times* company records from a pivotal time period provided unparalleled insights into the challenges and (many missed) opportunities for news organizations as the digital age dawned. Librarian Kyle Tripplet and reference archivist Tal Nadan were particularly helpful in making sure we took best advantage of that treasure trove of archival documents.

Former journalists-turned-academics David Carlson and Rich Gordon provided rare screenshots of early videotex and digital news sites from their personal collections when none could be found elsewhere for chapter 8. Staff at the LOC, including Abbie Grotke, Michael Neubert, Roslyn Pachoca, Amber Paranick and Jennifer Gavin, were most generous with their time in describing the LOC's efforts in archiving website content. EidosMedia Client Solutions Manager Rob Schmitt gave us an insider's view of the challenges facing legacy news organizations trying to reform their work flows for the digital environment. *Washington Post* Research Editor Alice Crites described the many issues she faces in doing news archive research across different internal systems and collections for the journalists at the *Post.* Mark Graham and Roger Macdonald at the Internet Archive provided valuable details about current and planned future efforts to archive television news and news websites.

The National Endowment for the Humanities (NEH) has played an outsized role in funding many news preservation efforts. Senior program officer Joel Wurl in the NEH Division of Preservation and Access helped us understand the mission of the NEH and some of its future plans, as described in chapter 9. An early discussion with Center for Research Libraries President Bernard Reilly encouraged us to move forward with the book project as a way to shed light on the many challenges raised in chapters 9 and 10. University of Minnesota School of Journalism alum and award-winning visual journalist for the *Washington Post* McKenna Ewen gave us an insider's tour of the *Post*'s new facilities that presage the future of legacy news organizations with the vision to look forward.

Finally, we would like to thank a number of colleagues, friends, and family members who read early drafts and provided helpful feedback. The Rowman & Littlefield team has been a joy to work with. University of Minnesota Mass Communication PhD candidate Chelsea Reynolds did a superb job copyediting the chapters before we submitted them to the publisher and offered many invaluable suggestions for improvements. Albert Tims expertly photo-edited the images used here. Matt Achor and Nancy Doig assured us that non-specialists would find the content interesting. We hope others agree.

1

WHO NEEDS YESTERDAY'S NEWS?

> In spite of its name, the chief function of the newspaper is not to give the news, it is not even exclusively to reflect public opinion—important as this is—but it is to record all contemporaneous human interests, activities, and conditions and thus to serve the future.
>
> —Historian Lucy Maynard Salmon, 1923[1]

Sharing and spreading news about the interesting, unusual, and important events in a community has always been a key aspect of human communication. The oral tradition of storytelling was based on what happened on the battlefields, among the rulers, or in the affairs of state. The town crier carried news of these happenings through the streets at the pleasure of the king, reading proclamations to a mostly illiterate populace. Without a written record, the original news item would morph and change over time.

Early efforts at capturing and recording the news of the day date back to 59 BC when papyrus news sheets, called *acta diurna*, gave the early Roman government a vehicle to make notification possible for "imperial decrees, senate resolutions and general information that the government wanted people to know. They also included miscellaneous news."[2] Eventually the *acta* came to chronicle changing political alliances, conspiracies, battles by sea and land, marriages, divorces, and court proceedings.[3]

There are no recordings of the town crier's news updates, and no copies of ancient Roman *acta diurna* have survived the ages. These voices and scrolls announcing the news of the day have been lost, and with them, a record of the important and mundane daily occurrences within the community.

The introduction of the printing press in the West starting in the mid-1400s provided new avenues for creating and capturing contemporary news. The first acknowledged newspaper, *Relation aller Fürnemmen und gedenckwürdigen Historien* (translated as "Account of All Distinguished and Commemorable News"), was started in Germany in 1605. The earliest surviving issue is from 1609.[4]

As the means and methods for generating news reports changed over centuries, there has been a consistent pattern. With an emphasis on accurately, thoroughly, and engagingly finding and reporting the news, archiving that news output for future reference has been an afterthought—if it has been thought about at all. With the introduction of each new news format or change in the technology used to produce and distribute the news, obstacles such as institutional neglect, natural disasters, material deterioration, and budgetary shortfalls have challenged the future-proofing of news content.

In the following chapters, we tell the story of how each form of news (newsprint, news photos and graphics, newsreels, news radio, television news, and digital news) evolved in terms of its production. We talk about the curators of these forms of news and, in many cases, all that was lost because there were no curators. The specific preservation challenges posed by different formats used for news content is detailed. And we share stories of obsessive collectors, tragic losses of collections, technological doomsdays, and preservation heroes who helped save news content for future generations.

LOSING THE NEWS

Early newspapers are only available by chance, collected and preserved by hobbyists. The news organizations that created them rarely considered preservation in the early days of publication.

The record of news illustration through engravings and photography is best seen on the printed pages of preserved newspapers. The original wood cuts, metal cuts, and negatives were rarely archived.

As the movie industry matured and grew, journalists saw the opportunity to create newsreels to inform audiences with motion pictures of news events. Newsreel companies kept stock footage libraries but few preserved the newsreels as they were exhibited in the theater each week.

The first U.S. radio newscast, which sent out election results to the Detroit area, was on August 31, 1920.[5] This earliest news program was not saved. We only know about its content from the newspaper report about it the following day.

Television news as we would recognize it was launched in 1940 when Lowell Thomas appeared in the first network televised news broadcast (a simulcast of his NBC radio program). The Lowell Thomas archive at Marist College in New York does not include any of the simulcast content.[6]

As we've entered the digital age where a previously unimaginable scale and scope of information is readily accessible, attention to the preservation of digital content is only now being addressed. As with the early days of American newspapers, news photographs, newsreels, radio broadcasts and television news content, the early days of digital news publication are either lost or only sporadically preserved. As digital archivist Howard Besser noted in 2001, "While the default for physical artifacts is to persist (or deteriorate in slow increments), the default for electronic objects is to become inaccessible unless someone takes an immediate pro-active role to save them. Thus, we can discover and study 3,000-year-old cave paintings. . . . But we are unable to even decipher any of the contents of an electronic file on an 8-inch floppy disk from only 20 years ago."[7]

NEWS USERS

> What is "news" today will be history tomorrow. . . . The newspapers are making morning after morning the rough draft of history. Later, the historian will come, take down the old files, and transform the crude but sincere and accurate annals of editors and reporters into history, into literature.
>
> —*The State*, Columbia, South Carolina, 1905[8]

Why does it matter that yesterday's news is available tomorrow, next week, next year, or next century? Though some might argue that "old news" is an oxymoron and that the usefulness of news is temporal, for many others, access to news reporting from the past is essential.

Journalists require access to past reporting from both their own publications and other news outlets to provide context and comprehensive coverage. In an industry where fact checking is an essential step in creating the product, the admonition to "check the clips" presumes those clips are readily accessible. Stock footage of images and sound have been essential storytelling resources for broadcast organizations since newsreel days. Newsrooms don't have the resources to recapture sound or images of familiar locales over and over each time they are needed in the day's news. A well-organized and readily available archive is essential.

The use of news as a historical resource has been widely debated. Broadcast historian Donald G. Godfrey framed some of the issues: "[Broadcast sources] are primarily media of information and art. They do not fit easily into the tests of critical, legal, or historical evidence. They are affected by economies of law, technology and science, audience and entertainment, and public trust and politics." But even with these issues, he concludes, "nevertheless, they deserve serious historical analysis."[9]

Historians rely on contemporaneous news coverage as a key source for understanding past events and social trends. Sociologist Michael Schudson reminds us that "the media are a central institution—one might even claim *the* central institution—in the cultural construction of American nationhood and cityhoods and communityhoods across the land."[10]

As such, the media provide a window into a time and place that historians find useful not because news accounts are free from error, but because they provide an interpretation of the life and interests of a community as revealed unconsciously through that content. Text, photos, moving images, recorded sound, and advertisements all might contribute to a historian's understanding of an era.

Journalism historians are particularly reliant on comprehensive access to news archives. For these scholars, the news content itself is the subject of study, along with records of the processes, economics, and technologies of news production. Communication historian Garth Jowett explains, "The central problem confronted by communications historians is what takes place when a new medium of communication is introduced into a society?"[11] Obviously, such questions are difficult to answer without access to the actual content of that new medium from that time period.

For law professionals, access to news archives is not only an important research resource, it also is the evidentiary record they may need in a legal action. If the digital version of a news story that included a potentially libelous statement can "disappear" from the archived record, how does a plaintiff prove something libelous was published?

Then there are the news hobbyists, such as genealogists. Perhaps the best record of the milestones in a person's life—their birth, marriage, death—are found on newspaper pages. Although many communities might have genealogy research libraries that include the local newspapers, the lack of indexing that allows lookup by name or the gaps in the availability of all issues of the newspaper makes it difficult to ensure thorough coverage.

Filmmakers and artists using archival footage, novelists looking for authentic representations of a period of time, students writing research papers, policy makers trying to understand the progression of awareness and sentiment about particular issues over time—these are just some of the other types of people for whom access to yesterday's news is essential today.

NEWS PRESERVERS

> America is the only country in the history of the world where the production of the major popular culture is outside the responsibility of the government. The production of media has been done by individuals and companies and so there never was a consistent national policy for any of the media on who had a responsibility to preserve that material.
>
> —Patrick Loughney, director,
> Packard Humanities Institute, 2016[12]

Though one might expect that the news *producers* would also be its chief *preservers*, that has not, for the most part, been the case. Over the centuries different entities have taken on the role of news preserver, some with great consistency, and others sporadically or with very narrow special preservation interests. This preservation patchwork makes for a challenging environment for news users, and it makes a wide range of news research needs more—or less—difficult. The types of organizations that have taken on news preservation come to the role for a variety of reasons and through different paths of news acquisition.

News Organizations

News organizations preserve the news content they create both to satisfy copyright needs and as an internal research resource to support the creation of the next round of news. News organizations also understand that reselling access to their news products can be lucrative, which has led to partnerships with those in the information retrieval business. By providing digital versions of their current news stories to database vendors or by working with vendors to scan and make available back files of their publications, news publishers improve their own access to past news and create a new revenue stream from previously published news.

When newspaper publishers added websites to the mix of news delivery options in the mid-1990s, website content was primarily "shovel ware." The same news story that appeared on the printed page appeared on the computer screen. As digital news content matured and new features were added, the challenge of archiving all versions of the news product grew. News organizations fell far short as preservers of all of the output of the print and digital newsroom.

Broadcast stations focus on resource needs for tomorrow's show, not archiving yesterday's. Radio journalists log their sound files (interviews, natural sounds captured during reporting, etc.) and may reuse those when reporting on a developing story. The interview from years ago with a newsmaker may be an important piece of the reporting when that newsmaker dies. Television videographers log the images and sound they capture every day, but only a small proportion makes it into the story that actually airs. Television news operations run images from the archive ("file tape") when they cover a story that has developed over time. Stock footage and internal resources are not part of the content that is offered to commercial vendors and the public.

With the growing recognition of the monetary value of yesterday's news, companies increasingly offer their archival content to the public directly through their websites. Again, however, these archives do not offer everything that the news organization generated, and most do not offer content from before electronic news archiving systems became widespread in the mid- to late 1980s. In fact, there is an ongoing discussion in the news industry about how to do a better job of monetizing the news organization's own archive, with limited success so far.

Commercial Database Vendors

Those in the commercial database vendor business have a profit motive for preserving news. When news organizations partner with vendors, they get a share of the revenue from subscription access to their news archives. Database vendors compete to have the most complete array of news sources to make their service more appealing to researchers than their competitors'. Some provide specialized resources for specific types of users and try to preserve news content that would most appeal to those users. As copyright for print news publications expires, vendors rush to make old newspapers now in the public domain accessible to users for a fee. Most broadcast content is still under copyright protection, but commercial firms have made licensing arrangements to offer this content to the public as well.

Commercial news vendors also purchase back files of news content, even when they may not have any immediate intention to offer that content to the public. Of the vast collections in the vaults of news vendors, less than 2 percent has been digitized and offered for sale, primarily because the cost-benefit calculation tells them they could not generate enough revenue to offset the cost of digitizing the content.[13] Ultimately, commercial vendors operate to serve the needs of researchers, customers, and shareholders, not the needs of cultural heritage, which makes their acquisition and preservation decisions problematic for those who care about news as a cultural artifact.

Libraries

One category of news preservers has always been motivated by cultural heritage rather than a bottom line. Librarians serve as the custodians of a community's memory. In their mission to help citizens satisfy their information needs, librarians have long collected, indexed, microfilmed, and made accessible those newspapers deemed to be of the highest value to their constituents. Members of the American Library Association called for creation of a national newspaper index as early as 1893.[14]

Local libraries have accepted the bound editions and, in some cases, the clip files and photos from newspapers that have closed, merged, or moved. They are the grateful recipients of materials that news organizations weed and would have relegated to the trash can. In many communities, librarians are responsible for generating the only index to the local newspaper that exists. Unfortunately, indexing efforts are rarely consistently supported, which results in large gaps and sporadic coverage.

As commercial vendors of news databases have grown, their profit motive has been a challenge for public libraries with a service motive. The costs of providing free, public access to local news archives sold by commercial vendors sometimes exceeds a local library's budget.

At the national level, the Library of Congress has been able to preserve many television programs because networks deposited tapes for copyright protection. It also has attempted to salvage early examples of newsreels and broadcasts (radio and television) when they have been found. But on the local level, libraries are less likely to collect and index broadcast news archives because they are difficult to house and make accessible. It is more likely that these types of early collections are part of an archive rather than a public or university library collection. Nevertheless, libraries have always played a role as preservers of news content and will continue to do so.

Archives

Archivists are concerned with preserving collections of material that have enduring value. In many cases, an archive contains both published and unpublished material, one of the key characteristics that distinguishes an archive from a library. The American Antiquarian Society was established in 1812 with a gift from printer and historian Isaiah Thomas. The society's archive included Thomas's huge collection of colonial and early American newspapers as well as biographical information about the colonies' early printers, many of whom Thomas had known personally.

Archives focused on news companies attempt to collect not just the news productions themselves, but also the original documents and papers that help explain how that news was generated, the business dealings of the media organization, biographies of key figures, and related details. Archives also are charged with attempting to preserve and restore collections that have suffered from decades of neglect: deteriorating paper, nitrate film that has turned to powder, broadcast tapes that have demagnetized. But the scope of those collections is usually limited by source or date range.

News archives exist in academic institutions, historical societies, museums, and other similar memory institutions in a community. Professional associations such as the Association of Moving Image Archivists are responsible for some of the most important research being done on news preservation practices. And news archives have helped publicize the cultural heritage value of news collections through their festivals, public screenings, and exhibitions of early news content.

Hobbyists

Individuals with specific interests have collected original materials for centuries. Such individual-level archives of news and media content and the equipment needed to hear or view the stories are scattered across the country in basements, outbuildings, and in digital form. Hobbyists serve specialist audiences with deep and highly specific interests in a time period or a format of delivery. Nicholson Baker, author and activist for the preservation of printed material, acquired large runs of newspapers being discarded by the British Library as they replaced newsprint with microfilm. Baker initially stored the volumes in an abandoned mill in New Hampshire but eventually donated his collection of original printed publications to a more traditional news preserver, the Duke University Library.

Hobbyist groups are key players in the preservation of a particularly focused use or type of news. Gordon Skene started his collecting career as a boy in 1963 when he was home recovering from surgery, playing with his parents' tape recorder while fiddling with the radio dial. Skene captured live radio reports of President Kennedy's assassination, and he was hooked.[15] He continued to build his collection, even scouring through dumpsters behind radio stations to retrieve discarded program tapes.[16] Skene's website, PastDaily.com, is the result of his efforts. But although hobbyists and individual collectors may provide good samples of news, most are not archivists concerned with complete and carefully preserved runs of content.

Some individual collectors turn their passion into a business. A number of entrepreneurs buy, sell, and trade old news as profit-making ventures. The Old Time Radio Catalog, which sells CDs of thousands of radio programs, began with Jon Folk's personal collection of recordings of classic radio programs. Folk established a website to network and trade with other collectors. Some of these programs are classics of the radio news genre, including Edward R. Murrow's "Hear It Now," which dates back to 1939.[17] Websites such as RareNewspapers.com, HistoricPages.com, HistoricalNews.com, and MitchellArchives.com are just a sampling of the vendors who make old newspapers accessible. The same types of sites can be found for each of the other forms of news we discuss in this book.

Just as the African proverb states "it takes a village to raise a child," it also takes a number of players—professional, institutional, and interested amateurs—to preserve the news. The complexities of providing continuity of access start with the raw materials used in creating the news product and continue with the news producers' internal processes and policies for preservation. Preservation is aided when there are local and national institutions interested in collecting, cataloging, and making news resources consistently accessible. Preservation is imperiled by lack of foresight or funding by the organization that creates the news to ensure it is available for future researchers, journalists, and others.

ACCESS TO PRESERVED NEWS

In addition to understanding who needs yesterday's news and who is preserving it, the challenge of locating the news of interest is compounded when one considers the wide variety of potential news research needs. For instance, is news from a specific date in a particular locale needed? Is tracking the evolution of a news story over time (a trial or natural disaster or political campaign) required? In these cases, access to the relevant publications or newscasts will be sufficient for the research conducted.

More difficult is the need to determine whether and where a specific person, company, or event had been covered in the news. In this case, access to the full publication or newscast won't be helpful. What would be needed is an index to the news contents or a searchable version of the full text.

Sometimes a researcher simply needs access to the text of a news story or to a broadcast transcript. In content analysis research, however, the actual placement within the newspaper of an individual story might be needed, which requires access to the full news package, not just the individual news components. Understanding how words interacted with photos, video, sound, page layout, or other presentation elements might be as important as the textual content itself.

Copyright restrictions also affect access. Material published before 1923 for which copyright was not renewed is generally in the public domain. Anything after that date is likely to be more difficult and costly to access. The archiving format used for capturing the news poses further challenges. Researchers tell tales of frustration about trying to find the equipment to play a two-inch format videotape of a television news broadcast, for instance.

In some regions of the country with strong institutional support for libraries and archives, local news resources might have been gathered and preserved with care, while in other locations those resources have been lost. The commercial information industry's priorities dictate that well-known, high-demand news publications or broadcasts are likely to be preserved while news output from local, small-circulation, or limited-reach entities (such as the ethnic media) is neglected.

Every individual news research need will pose a challenge in determining where local news resources have been stored, in what form they are preserved, to what level they are indexed, and in what ways they are accessible. In many cases, the path followed to find the needed news will lead to a dead end.

FUTURE-PROOFING THE NEWS

Over the past three centuries of American news production, the preservation and disappearance of news content has had a consistent storyline. Saving previously published, projected, or broadcasted content is an afterthought. Changes in technology that might herald an improvement in the news product often brought challenges to those concerned with archiving.

As reporting about the wholesale loss of digital content and disappearing websites grows, some proclaim the information age is devolving into a digital dark ages. Vint Cerf, an early Internet pioneer, warned, "We are nonchalantly throwing all of our data into what could become an information black hole without realizing it."[18] As we illustrate in the following chapters, it has ever been thus. When a new news channel came along, the lack of attention, technology, personnel, and/or budget for preserving the output of the newsroom has resulted in black holes of access.

One definition of "future-proofing" is "to make or plan something in such a way that it will not become ineffective or unsuitable for use in the future"[19] In the case of news, unsuitability is subjective. For a genealogist looking for references in the news to his great-grandfather, a political reporter searching for background on the early statements of a new candidate, or a historian looking for a description of an epic forest fire in the 1890s, old news is exceedingly relevant and its value is dependent on its accessibility. As a growing proportion of the population gets news digitally, the issue of future-proofing is even more pressing if we are to know anything about today's news in five, fifty, or five hundred years.

Perhaps the goal of universally preserving news is unreasonable, impossible, and even—as some have argued—unnecessary. Decisions about what, how, and where to store the output of human creativity have always been complicated and costly. In the case of news preservation, complications have existed since the first news page was taken off Gutenberg's press. The following chapters provide some insight into these challenges.

NOTES

1. Lucy Maynard Salmon, *The Newspaper and the Historian* (New York: Oxford University Press, 1923), 470.

2. C. Anthony Giffard, "Ancient Rome's Daily Gazette," *Journalism History* 2, no. 4 (1975): 106.

3. Giffard, "Ancient Rome's Daily Gazette," 106–9, 132.

4. Jeremy Norman, "Johan Carolus's 'Relation,' the First Printed European Newspaper," *History of Information*, last revised January 17, 2015, http://historyofinformation.com/expanded.php?id=45.

5. The Radio Staff of the Detroit News, *"WWJ—The Detroit News": The History of Radiophone Broadcasting by the Earliest and Foremost of Newspaper Stations; Together with Information on Radio for Amateur and Expert* (Detroit, MI: Evening News Association, 1922).

6. "Lowell Thomas Papers," Marist Archives and Special Collections, http://library.marist.edu/archives/LTP/LTP.xml.

7. Howard Besser, "Digital Preservation of Moving Image Material," *The Moving Image* 1, no. 2 (2002): 39–55.

8. Tony Pettinato, "Newspapers: 'The Rough Draft of History,'" *Readex Blog*, October 4, 2014, www.readex.com/blog/newspapers-rough-draft-history.

9. Donald G. Godfrey, "Broadcast Archives for Historical Research: Revisiting the Historical Method," *Journal of Broadcasting & Electronic Media* 46, no. 3 (2002): 493–503.

10. Shannon E. Martin and Kathleen A. Hansen, *Newspapers of Record in a Digital Age: From Hot Type to Hot Link* (Westport, CT: Greenwood Publishing Group, 1998), 79.

11. Martin and Hansen, *Newspapers of Record*, 82.

12. Patrick Loughney (director, Packard Humanities Institute), interview with authors, June 7, 2016.

13. Center for Research Libraries, "Framing a Common Agenda for Newspaper Digitization and Preservation: An ICON Summit Report and Outcomes," April 14, 2015, www.crl.edu/events/framing-common-agenda-newspaper-digitization-and-preservation-icon-summit.

14. Martin and Hansen, *Newspapers of Record*, 90.

15. Gordon Skene, "An Accidental Commitment to History," *LinkedIn Pulse*, September 22, 2014.

16. Mark Quigley (director, UCLA Film and Television Archive, Research and Study Center), interview with Hansen, February 19, 2016.

17. "Old Time Radio," https://archive.org/details/oldtimeradio.

18. Ian Sample, "Google Boss Warns of 'Forgotten Century' with Email and Photos at Risk," *The Guardian*, February 13, 2015.

19. "Future-Proof—Definition from Longman English Dictionary Online," Pearson-Longman ELT, www.ldoceonline.com/dictionary/future-proof_1.

2

NEWSPAPERS

> If all the printed sources of history for a certain century or decade had to be destroyed to save one, that which could be chosen with the greatest value to posterity would be a file of an important newspaper.
>
> —Clarence Brigham, *History and Bibliography of American Newspapers*, 1947[1]

THE NEWSPAPER INDUSTRY

The history of newspaper publishing in the United States is intimately tied to the development of political, social, and commercial life in the fledgling British colonies. Early colonial newspapers were published weekly or monthly by postmaster/printers, who received lucrative government printing contracts to reproduce official proclamations, laws, assembly session

The *Rocky Mountain News* in Denver was going under. Colorado's first newspaper published its final edition on February 27, 2009. When parent company E. W. Scripps officials asked *News* editor John Temple what should be done with story clips, bound volumes, photos, negatives, editors' documents, reporters' notes, and projects that had been produced by the nearly 150-year-old newspaper, he suggested giving the collection to the Denver Public Library. After several years of negotiations, the newspaper turned over to the library everything except the newspaper's logo and its web IP address. The copyright to all of the *News*'s content was part of the deal.[2]

The *Grand Forks Herald* banner headline on April 21, 1997, read: "Come Hell and High Water." North Dakota's Red River had overrun its banks and flooded downtown Grand Forks. When fire then engulfed downtown, it delivered the death blow. The weekend fire gutted many buildings, including the *Herald*'s newsroom, and the printing press was submerged under floodwater. The staff put together the next day's newspaper from a borrowed press more than three hundred miles away. Among the losses they detailed were 118 years of photographs, news clippings, and historic books and documents from their own news library. "It makes me feel like I want to cry," said Jenelle Stadstad, manager of the newspaper's library. "I feel helpless. I can't even imagine all of the files we lost."[3]

records, and related government materials. Postmaster/printers were among the literate elite in colonial communities and required special government licenses to print. Three-quarters of the master printers in the colonies between 1700 and 1765 printed newspapers, while their contracts for other types of printing such as legal forms, religious tracts, and hymnals provided a measure of economic stability for them.[4]

The first newspaper published in the colonies was *Publick Occurrences both Forreign and Domestick* issued by the printer Benjamin Harris in Boston on September 25, 1690. Authorities suppressed the publication after one issue because they objected to some of the content and because the paper was printed without a license. The first paper to be continuously published was John Campbell's *Boston News-Letter*, which appeared in April 1704 and ran until 1776. Many newspapers up and down the East Coast were established and then went out of business in the years before the Revolutionary War.

By 1775, there were forty newspapers being published in the thirteen colonies.[5] Subscribers received newspapers via mail. Early newspapers had hundreds of readers, rather than thousands or hundreds of thousands common in much later decades. Publishers targeted the literate population with the means to subscribe. Taverns and public houses also made newspapers available so their patrons who didn't subscribe could peruse and discuss the news.

Post–Revolutionary War Newspapers

Newspaper publishing proliferated after the Revolutionary War. Citizens of the new republic were expected to stay informed in order to fulfill their duties as members of the electorate.[6] The first daily newspapers were published in Philadelphia and New York in 1784 and 1785. The Bill of Rights, ratified by the United States in 1791, codified protection of press freedom and further encouraged development of the newspaper as a major form of communication. From 1790 to 1810, the United States saw explosive growth in the number of newspapers, from 90 titles to 370. By 1830, there were roughly 1,000 titles.[7] However, the growth of the industry was not well-recorded at the time. The 1884 "census" of newspapers produced by the Government Printing Office stated bluntly, "It is impossible to trace the growth of newspapers during this second period [1783 to 1836] with anything like statistical accuracy, owing to the failure of the journals of this era to record this development in their columns and of any one else to make record of it."[8]

The development of the postal system, the Pony Express, railroad route expansions, and related transportation improvements also allowed newspaper publishers to establish elaborate systems of news exchanges. Editors made sure they reprinted news items, columns, commentaries, and information from like-minded publishers around the country whose papers they regularly received in exchange for sending their own.[9]

As in colonial times, newspapers during national expansion were still generally intended for literate audiences that had the financial means to subscribe. Single-copy sales were not the norm. But with the adoption of the steam-driven press in the 1820s and 1830s, publishing economics began to change. On September 3, 1833, Benjamin Day began publishing the *New York Sun*, later recognized as the first penny press newspaper (which cost one cent whereas others cost six). When James Gordon Bennett issued the first edition of the *New York Herald* in 1835, it firmly established the advertiser-supported mass market for news.

The penny papers also were early adopters of the newest technology for news gathering, the telegraph, introduced in 1844. The Associated Press, founded in 1846, was a cooperative venture in news collection that used the telegraph to distribute content to member newspapers. When the Atlantic telegraph cable was laid in 1866, news transmission from Europe was greatly accelerated.[10] News accounts began to reflect some of the influences of the telegraph, with short, concise stories that emphasized the essential facts at the start of the story. Between 1870 and 1890, the population of the country doubled, the number of dailies quadrupled, and the number of copies sold each day increased sixfold.[11]

Newspapers in the Twentieth Century

The first half of the twentieth century was the heyday of newspaper publishing in the United States. Most literate city dwellers read several newspapers a day, and most large cities had multiple competing morning and afternoon papers. However, the spectacular financial success of newspaper owners led to industry consolidation, with major newspaper companies buying up adversaries and merging with or shutting down their competitors for readership and advertising dollars. Major chain newspaper companies such as Hearst, E. W. Scripps, Ridder, Gannett, and others dominated the scene. As they purchased competing newspapers, some combined those papers' news library archives with their own, though it typically was not a crucial element of the business transaction.

As the news market expanded with the introduction of radio, television, and eventually the Internet, newspaper readership fell off. By the close of the century, most observers understood that the newspaper industry was in the throes of major, permanent change. Hundreds of newspapers ceased publication, thousands of journalists were laid off, and centuries of back files and news archives were endangered.

WHY NEWSPAPERS WERE LOST

Despite the fact that newspapers have been published in the United States for more than three hundred years, news organizations themselves did precious little to guarantee their long-term availability for posterity. Early colonial publishers, as mentioned, also were printers, bookbinders, and postmasters. Among their many activities, they no doubt kept an in-house file of their own newspaper issues. A large source of news for these early publishers came from the issues of other newspapers that they exchanged through the mail. Some publishers no doubt kept those exchange issues as well, but unless they also bound them and then made an effort to store them properly, their survival was hit or miss.

There is no copy on U.S. soil of the aforementioned *Publick Occurrences both Forreign and Domestick*, the first domestic newspaper, and it was all but lost until 1845. Reverend J. B. Felt was conducting research in the Colonial State Paper Office in London while preparing the second edition of his history of the settlement of Salem, Massachusetts. He came across the only extant copy of *Publick Occurrences* in that London office.[12] Presumably all other copies of the publication in the colonies had been confiscated and destroyed.

Early publishers printed just a few hundred copies of their title each week. Paper was scarce, many subscribers were slow to pay, and the finances of those early efforts were precarious. As newspaper enterprises came and went, it was not unusual for the failed proprietor to sell the back files he may have had for scrap.

After its founding in 1846, the Associated Press (AP) eventually had bureaus all over the United States and the world. But the AP itself has no back files or records of dispatches from 1846 to the 1930s. Memos in the AP's corporate files included instructions to bureau chiefs stating, "Keep the past ten years of stuff and throw out the rest."[13] The only record of that content is in the articles that member newspapers ran from the wire service, if back files of those newspapers survive. As AP bureaus shut down, moved, or ran out of space, the general practice was to simply throw out old files containing records of wire dispatches and clippings from newspapers that ran AP stories or printed AP pictures.

Much later, if or when a memory institution collected newspapers, the papers soon became a storage and space problem of monumental proportions. Librarian of Congress Ainsworth Rand Spofford used the growing newspaper back file collection at the Library of Congress (LOC) to argue on behalf of a new building in 1875. The New York Public Library's newspaper collection had so overrun its storage space that the entire collection was relocated to a warehouse in 1933. Newspaper organizations' internal libraries collected and bound their own titles, but as space ran out, these were typically relegated to sub-basements, outbuildings, or individual editors' personal collections. These collections often were lost to posterity.

Wars also took their toll on newspaper collections. As Revolutionary-era printers were threatened by advancing troops, they often packed up their types and presses but could not take along any newspaper back files as they fled. Federal government officials did not approve funds for a library to serve congressional needs until 1800 after Washington, D.C., was named the capital city. In 1801, the first books and maps purchased for the new library were stored in the office of the Secretary of the Senate.[14] Although the 1812 catalog of the holdings of the new library included scattered issues of nine newspaper titles,[15] none appears to have survived the fire that destroyed the library in the 1814 British attack on the Capitol.[16] Similar losses attended the Civil War as cities, along with their newspaper offices and libraries, were overrun, sacked, or burned in the conflict.

As the *Grand Forks Herald* example from the beginning of this chapter demonstrates, fires, floods, and other natural disasters often were the cause for newspaper losses. Thomas Jefferson sold his personal collection in 1815 to rebuild the burned federal library, and his newspaper files included approximately fifty titles.[17] But another fire in 1851 destroyed much of that reconstituted collection, including the newspapers. A historian quoted in a

Deteriorating bound volumes of the *Des Moines Register* found in a storage room. *Courtesy Nikki Usher/George Washington University*

1924 issue of the *New York Times* said, "In the short while that I have been interested in such matters I have seen three newspaper files, uniquely valuable for the antebellum period of Georgia, destroyed by fire—the *Augusta Chronicle*, dating from 1785; the *Macon Telegraph*, from 1826; and the *Columbus Inquirer*, from about 1828. Nothing can make good these losses."[18]

Teri Hayt, executive editor of *The Repository* in Canton, Ohio, tells a more recent disaster story. In 2014, she was preparing for the newspaper's two-hundredth anniversary, which would be celebrated the following year. She asked about old, bound volumes of the newspaper that might be mined for content as part of the retrospective edition the newsroom was putting together. She was told that the bound volumes were in a sub-basement of the building, a room no one had visited for a very long time. She got the key and ventured below. What she found was any archivist's nightmare. The sub-basement had flooded at an unknown point in the past and the bound volumes of the newspaper's history had turned to paste. In addition, the newspaper had to hire a hazardous waste removal team to come in and scour the room because it was covered in dangerous mold that had taken advantage of the mess.[19]

Newspaper consolidation and fallout from a shrinking industry in the twentieth century led to many losses. Some files of closed or merged newspapers would be incorporated into surviving papers' news libraries; others might make their way to historical societies, public libraries, or other memory institutions. That's what happened with the *Rocky Mountain News*. In countless other cases, however, the material was simply tossed.

HOW NEWSPAPERS WERE PRESERVED

In the twenty-first century, where the value of newspaper collections is well understood, it may be difficult to comprehend that the only reason we have collections of early colonial newspapers is because individual collectors were busy squirreling away copies in barns, attics, and outbuildings. There were no formal efforts to collect those early papers as they came off the presses. Subscription libraries, coffeehouses, taverns, and similar gathering spots provided early access to newspapers for their patrons but didn't archive them.[20] It was more than a century before news organization libraries, academic and public libraries, historical societies, and the LOC started collecting newspapers as a valuable addition to their holdings. Before that, newspapers were generally considered to appeal only to the lowest common denominator among the literate public and were not seen as fit material for safeguarding by the high-minded institutions of learning and historical responsibility.

Individual Collectors

Without the efforts of individual collectors, it is safe to say that many fewer newspapers would be preserved than we now have. Harbottle Dorr

Jr. (1730–1794), a Boston hardware dealer and selectman, collected, annotated, and indexed thirteen different newspapers published in Boston and surrounding towns during the pre-Revolutionary and early Revolutionary period. The four bound volumes of these newspapers ended up in the collection of the Massachusetts Historical Society, acquired over the span of 213 years from other local historical societies or museums.[21]

The newspaper collection of the LOC was enriched in 1867 when Congress appropriated $100,000 for the purchase of a large personal library from Washington publisher and politician Peter Force that included "245 bound volumes of newspapers printed prior to 1800 besides about 700 volumes, bound and unbound, of journals printed from 1800 to the present time."[22] Force compiled these materials to produce his book, *Documentary History of the American Revolution*.[23] This acquisition placed the LOC as second only to the American Antiquarian Society in its holdings of early American newspapers.

The American Antiquarian Society (AAS) was established by Isaiah Thomas (1749–1831), a leading printer, newspaper editor, book publisher, and bookseller. Starting at the age of seven, he served an apprenticeship in Boston as a typesetter before becoming a journeyman printer working in various locales from the West Indies to Nova Scotia.[24] In 1770, he set up a newspaper in Boston, the *Massachusetts Spy*. Shortly before the battle of Lexington in April 1775, Thomas moved his press and types to Worcester to escape the advancing British troops. He operated his publishing enterprises from Worcester for most of the rest of his life, retiring in 1802 to begin work on *The History of Printing in America*. The *History* was issued in 1810 after Thomas had spent years scouring the country for books, newspapers, and pamphlets that comprised the corpus of printing in the country to that point in time.

In 1812, Thomas donated his entire library of 7,000 books, 382 titles of newspaper files in 551 bound volumes, and more than $20,000 to found the AAS. He continued to collect and document early works printed in the United States until his death in 1831. In 1847, the AAS issued a second, revised edition of *The History of Printing in America*, based on Thomas's own 1815 changes and corrections, along with new scholarship to bring the work up to date. The work stands to this day as the definitive authority on this period of U.S. publishing.

Records in the Thomas collection at the AAS provide an insight into his efforts to collect newspapers. A document titled "List of Newspapers, that I have files of, printed in the United States, 1800 Isaiah Thomas"[25] details back files of 236 titles from seventeen states. Some of the newspapers in the list date to 1803, so it is likely that is the accurate date for this document. An article in the AAS's 1836 *Transactions* describes Thomas's process: "During the long period in which he contemplated the preparation of [the *History*], and while engaged in its progress, he was continually laying aside for preservation, every book, pamphlet, and file of newspapers, that came in his way, which might aid him in this undertaking, or prove of future use to the historians of his country."[26]

One way Thomas acquired newspaper back files appears to have been through purchasing office files of newspapers from the Revolutionary period and before.[27] Because newspapers did not yet have their own news libraries, in whose care such office files would be entrusted in later decades, many publishers would have welcomed the opportunity to sell these back files to Thomas after he explained his purpose: to record their history and preserve them for posterity.

Entries from the Thomas diaries indicate he was purchasing newspaper back files as he came across them. A diary entry for September 17, 1808, reads: "Dined with Mr. E. T. Andrews. Bought 3 Vols old papers of Ed Draper. Gave 4 dols for them."[28] The Draper family had published the *Boston News-Letter* for four decades until the paper's demise in 1776; we might presume that is the title of "old papers" Thomas purchased.

Other evidence of the efforts that Thomas made to collect newspapers surfaces in his correspondence to fellow collectors and publishers. One letter dated February 8, 1809, to collector William Bentley in Salem, Massachusetts, says: "I find my task [collecting newspapers] more arduous than I suspected. I have no fountain to go to for information, all the material appears to be in 'hidden places' but I hope to discover those that are most essential."[29] Another letter from Thomas to a fellow printer/publisher in Philadelphia, Mathew Carey, dated March 20, 1809, reads in part:

> I am *now* in great want of files of ancient Philadelphia Newspapers. I should be glad to purchase files of any newspapers, though incomplete (if complete files cannot be had) printed in Philadelphia, New York or in Williamsburgh. Will you permit me to request you to endeavor to procure me some of those papers printed before 1770? Perhaps by advertising they might be obtained—by that means I purchased a number in Boston. If they cannot be had by purchase, it may be that I can be favored with loans; in this case I should be willing to give ample security for their safe and punctual return at any time agreed upon.[30]

It is clear that Thomas was asking his fellow printers and publishers to help him find, borrow, and purchase (if necessary) the back files of all the newspapers that had been printed in the United States up until that time.

Another method Thomas used was to place an advertisement in his own *Massachusetts Spy* with a plea for newspaper publishers to send him copies of their papers. This ad ran in the May 16, May 23, June 6, and June 13, 1810, editions:

> To Printers of Newspapers.
>
> There will Speedily be issued from the press a "History of Printing in America," etc. which among other things will contain an account of all the Newspapers printed in British America, previous to the commencement of the Revolution in 1775; and the author wishes to add a List of all the Newspapers printed in the United States, as well as in the British, French and Spanish dominions—on this continent and in the West Indies, on the first day of January 1810.
>
> With a view to enable him to complete this list he requests the printers of Newspapers will do him the favor to forward one or two of their papers, addressed to 'I. T. printer, Worcester, Mass.' And in order, that this intelligence may become generally known, he begs they will give this advertisement one or two insertions in their respective papers, which will be considered as an additional obligation . . . Worcester, Mass.[31]

The ad that Thomas posted in the *Spy* was reprinted in other newspapers around the country and some publishers and others who saw the ad responded as he had requested.

Finally, after the AAS was established, Thomas remained deeply involved, and the volume titled *Donations to the American Antiquarian Society with the Names of Its Benefactors*, dated March 1813 to October 15, 1829, organized in chronological order and mostly in Thomas's script, records many gifts of newspapers, including those from his own personal collection.[32] Many of the newspaper files donated by Thomas himself came in the years 1814 to 1829, so it is clear he was still collecting newspaper files almost up until his death in 1831. Indeed, the last two entries in this volume, dated October 15, 1829, read: "Newspapers for many years past, viz. supposed to be worth $50 not bound by Isaiah Thomas" and "Memorandum: Files of several newspapers for 15 or 20 years, published in Boston (a wagonload)—belonging to Thomas & Andrews and to Ebenezer T. Andrews—were presented to the Society several years ago, but I believe were never recorded. They are now (unbound) in the Society library, and I believe they may be valued, at least $100."[33]

Isaiah Thomas's efforts to collect and preserve the record of printing in the United States before the Revolution stands as one of the major accomplishments of publishing history. Even so, archivists believe that all of

☞ To Printers of Newspapers.

There will Speedily be issued from the press, a "History of Printing in America," *&c. which among other things will contain an account of all the Newspapers printed in British America, previous to the commencement of the Revolution in* 1775; *and the author wishes to add a* LIST *of all the Newspapers printed in the United States, as well as in the British, French and Spanish dominions—on this continent and in the West Indies, on the first day of January* 1810.

With a view to enable him to complete this list he requests the printers of Newspapers will do him the favor to forward one or two of their papers, addressed to "I. T. printer, Worcester, Mass." *And in order, that this intelligence may become generally known, he begs they will give this advertisement one or two insertions in their respective papers, which will be considered as an additional obligation. If such publishers of Newspapers, or other gentlemen, as have newspapers printed in British or Spanish America, on the 1st of January, will do him the favor to forward one of each kind, as above, they will render him a very acceptable service.—It is intended to insert in the History of Printing, abovementioned, the titles of the papers, the names of the printers, the towns and States in which they are printed, and the periods of their publication, as daily, weekly, &c.*

Publishers of Magazines and periodical works, other than Newspapers, are also requested to favor the author with the titles of such publications, the names of the publishers, and an account of the periods when, and the places where, they are printed.

Worcester, Mass. May 16, 1810.

Advertisement placed by Thomas in May 16, 1810, *Massachusetts Spy* requesting newspaper copies. *Courtesy American Antiquarian Society* the newspaper collections now in existence represent a mere 15 percent of the entire output of U.S. newspapers ever printed.[34]

News Libraries

> March 15, 1955
>
> Unless I am mistaken, our morgue is uninsurable because it is irreplaceable.
>
> —Orville E. Dryfoos, *New York Times* editor to Frances A. Cox, *New York Times* vice president and financial officer[35]

There were no systematic news libraries (that is, a library established inside the news organization with the goal of storing the paper's daily output and serving the information needs of journalists, ad salespeople, and business staff) until 1845, when the *New York Herald* started to build a library of books. The *Herald* didn't start saving news clippings from the paper itself until 1860. The *Herald* also started an index to the news content that they continued until 1919.[36] The *Boston Herald* started its library in 1876, and the *Boston Globe* followed suit in 1887. The *San Francisco Chronicle* started clipping its newspaper in 1879; it was the first to use nine-by-four-inch envelopes placed in upright tin document boxes to store clips. News librarians used the envelope system for the next hundred years.[37]

Newspaper staff organized clip files alphabetically for retrieval by other newspaper staff members who needed to see what the paper had published on a specific topic or about a particular person in previous issues. In many newspapers, older clip files were regularly weeded out or discarded altogether as storage space grew scarce. Users would remove envelopes of clippings from the library and forget to return them. Clips would get torn, worn from folding and refolding, and the newsprint would yellow over time. Preservation of the news content for historical purposes was not the reason for creating and maintaining the clip files in news libraries, although some clip files donated by newspapers have ended up in public libraries or other memory institutions.

A *New York Herald* staffer, Gustav V. Lindner, wrote a book entitled *Newspaper Library Manual* in 1912. Lindner devotes just three sentences to the need for maintaining a "set of bound files for permanent record . . . kept in places where they are easily accessible for reference."[38] A 1933 manual on newspaper reference methods intended for newspaper librarians included passing reference to the care and preservation of the news library's collections. "The bound files of the newspaper itself are a priceless collection. Newspapers almost always bind the principal edition, day by day; some newspapers bind all editions."[39]

Jersey Journal clip files in crowded drawers. *Courtesy Timothy Herrick/Timhrklit.com*

News libraries also were on the forefront of microfilm development as a method of saving newspapers, discussed later in this chapter. The AP, after recognizing that its ten-year discard policy had resulted in the loss of all AP coverage of World War I, decided in the 1940s to microfilm nearly all of the World War II copy generated by the news service. However, consistent with the archival policies of the day, once filmed, the original materials were tossed.[40]

Reporters and editors eventually recognized the value of news library files to their work. When the Saigon AP bureau was about to close, correspondent Peter Arnett saved all of the dispatches from his time covering the Vietnam War rather than discarding them as he was instructed to do. He shipped the dispatches from Vietnam to his home in New Zealand in 1972. Arnett's collection has now made its way back into the AP corporate archive in New York.[41]

Academic Libraries

Beyond news organizations' libraries, libraries of various other sorts have played a role in collecting and preserving newspapers. But once again, the early history is one of fits and starts. Harvard College, established in Cambridge, Massachusetts, in 1636 as an institution for the training of clergy, also housed the first printing press in the colonies in 1638. The Harvard Library was established that same year with a bequest of four hundred books from founder John Harvard. The first printed catalog of the library appeared in 1723, but that catalog does not indicate that any newspapers were in the collection.[42]

By 1790, a category called "Libri Periodici" in the catalog included one newspaper title: 1768 and 1769 issues of the *Boston Chronicle* (a Loyalist newspaper published from 1767 to 1770). Even for a newspaper with a short publishing history it was difficult to preserve a full run of editions. Under the category "Miscellanea," eight volumes of the 1722 weekly *Independent Whig* (published in London to oppose the High Church Party) and four volumes of the same title from 1753 were listed.[43] No doubt these titles reflect that the vast majority of the collection up to that time was built from serendipitous gifts.

The library accelerated its acquisition of newspapers throughout the nineteenth century, and by 1934, the catalog category for "Periodicals, Learned Societies, and Other Serial Publications" described the library's policy as follows: "In history, continuous effort has been made to acquire original source material. . . . This same demand for original sources has led to emphasizing the importance of contemporary periodicals and news sheets. . . . The Ebeling collection of American newspapers of the late eighteenth and early nineteenth centuries contains many unique items."[44] Other early academic libraries had no newspapers in their collections.

Academic libraries expanded their view of newspaper collections once their value as historical sources was recognized during the late Victorian era. Books based on newspaper sources were published in the 1870s and 1880s.[45] An entire session of the 1908 annual meeting of the American Historical Association, the scholarly organization for academics in the history field, was devoted to a discussion of the use of the newspaper by historians.[46] In a May 1909 article in *The Atlantic Monthly*, the distinguished historian James Ford Rhodes argued that the newspaper should hold an honorable place in the study of the past. "The duty of the historian is, not to decide if the newspapers are as good as they ought to be, but to measure their influence on the present, and to recognize their importance as an ample and contemporary record of the past,"[47] he wrote.

Public Libraries

Public libraries as we understand them today were not established until the mid-nineteenth century. The first of these libraries, supported by tax dollars generated from their local communities, opened in Petersborough, New Hampshire, in 1833. The Boston Public Library—a more widely recognized "first" for this type of library—opened in 1848. The American Library Association was created in 1876 by a group of public library leaders to help member librarians do their work more effectively. The ALA became one of the primary forces urging preservation of library materials of all sorts, including newspapers.

Public libraries throughout the country were intended to meet the information needs of their communities. They naturally collected local and regional newspapers, and their librarians joined the growing movement to professionalize library staffs and standardize collection and preservation practices. Today some of the most complete collections of regional newspapers are found in public libraries.

Public libraries were at the forefront in developing solutions to the storage and preservation issues surrounding newspapers. While a community's public library served as the local memory institution, newspaper collections were a mixed blessing. When a local newspaper merged or shut down, the clip files, bound volumes, and related institutional materials might make their way into the public library but posed serious archival challenges. We discuss this in more detail shortly.

The Library of Congress

The first congressional library was established in 1801, but the collections were lost to fires several times over the ensuing decades, with the loss of both the book and newspaper holdings. By the time Ainsworth Rand Spofford, a former newspaper publisher, was appointed Librarian of Congress in 1864, the newspaper collection had been somewhat rebuilt through purchases and gifts. But the former newspaperman was unsatisfied with the collection and argued successfully in 1865 that Congress should appropriate the "sum of $1,500 for the purchase of the files of leading American newspapers."[48]

The Copyright Act of 1870 codified copyright laws and identified the LOC as the repository of materials to be copyrighted. Newspapers began to deposit issues in the LOC to gain copyright protection. This was an additional source of newspaper titles in the collection. It was not until May 1874, however, that the LOC established an *official* newspaper collection policy. Spofford, the former newsman–turned–Librarian of Congress, was again instrumental in persuading Congress to authorize the LOC to subscribe to "a number of newspapers daily and weekly, at least two from each State, of different politics, to be kept filed in the LOC as a matter for reference."[49] By July 1874, the LOC subscribed to more than one hundred dailies.[50]

Spofford began arguing on behalf of a new building, in large part due to the growing newspaper back files in the LOC. In his report to Congress in 1875, Spofford said: "The most copious and most valuable material for history to be found in this country is imbedded in the newspapers of the country. . . . The present librarian is making diligent efforts not only to secure and preserve current files of the leading newspapers from every State and Territory, but, as far as possible, to complete such files by carrying them back to the beginnings of our history."[51]

It took another twenty years, but by 1897 a new library building was opened, and by 1901 the number of newspaper titles received by the LOC had increased to more than four hundred. Of the cataloged papers, only about a quarter were being bound.[52] Most U.S. newspapers were sent to the LOC without cost; exchanges with other libraries, gifts, and purchases also helped the collection grow.[53]

The LOC continued to expand its newspaper collections in the first half of the twentieth century. Clarence Brigham's 1947 bibliography and list of library holdings for U.S. papers published between 1690 and 1820 identified 2,120 newspaper titles, of which the American Antiquarian Society possessed 1,496. The LOC had the second largest collection, with 936 titles. Unfortunately, 194 titles known to have been published during that time period couldn't be found anywhere.[54]

Historical Societies

Other institutions that collected newspapers were local or state historical societies. Typically, historical societies were concerned with preserving records of specific locales, topics, groups of people, or types of material rather than amassing a collection that was national in scope. The first in the United States was the Massachusetts Historical Society, established in 1791. By the mid-nineteenth century, historical associations had been established in most states east of the Mississippi, and local historical societies flourished.[55]

The Massachusetts Historical Society and the State Historical Society of Wisconsin, established in 1846, were more broad in scope than many others. Both collected newspapers from a wide geographical area and made a point to bind and preserve their titles. A description of the State Historical Society of Wisconsin newspaper collection in 1891 stated that in addition to subscribing to all of Wisconsin's newspapers, the library held five thousand bound newspaper volumes from *outside* the state, and that the collection was especially strong from 1750 forward.[56] The Massachusetts Historical Society was an early competitor with the American Antiquarian Society for the most complete collection of eighteenth- and early-nineteenth-century newspapers, but the two institutions eventually agreed to cooperate, with the American Antiquarian Society becoming the primary source for the originals of newspaper titles prior to the 1870s.[57]

Sometimes, archival treasures are found in the unlikeliest places. The one known surviving dispatch from the AP, written in cursive and datelined Little Rock, January 20, 1882, is in the papers of William Henry Smith at the Indiana Historical Society.[58] At that time, Smith was the manager of the Western Associated Press, before its merger with the AP in New York the following year. The dispatch was telegraphed to subscribers; it was published on page 2 of the *Cleveland Leader* the following day. Smith purchased the *Indianapolis News* in 1883. Smith's son took over the newspaper after his father's death and donated all of his father's papers to the Indiana Historical Society in 1922. The fact that the AP archivist in New York found this earliest artifact of the AP's work in a state historical society in the middle of the country is a testament to the scattered nature of news history preservation.

This discussion of the various institutions, organizations, and individuals that collected newspapers provides insights into why newspaper transmissions were saved, and why in so many other cases, they were lost to posterity. For every news format that has been collected, there are myriad issues that influence what is preserved and what is gone forever.

NEWSPAPER PRESERVATION CHALLENGES

> Newspaper files are a quarry from which the scholars of the future will cut the blocks wherewith to carve the statues of history.
>
> —*New York Times*, 1895[59]

Paper Quality

Early colonial newspapers survive, if they were kept at all, because the type of paper on which they were printed and the quality of the ink were instrumental in their preservation. Typical papermaking processes of the day involved recycling rags made from hemp, linen, or cotton to produce a sheet of "rag paper" that was both durable and absorbent. The printers' inks of the day produced a rich, dark imprint that was stable over time. In addition to owning printing presses, printers also had bindery equipment, primarily used for bookbinding. But if a printer was so inclined, he could keep some additional copies of the newspapers he was printing and bind them into collections. Bindings were hand sewn using durable linen thread.

Rag paper was in high demand, however, and many newspapers were forced to suspend publication due to shortages, especially during times of war, upheaval, or financial distress.[60] By the end of the U.S. Civil War, paper manufacturers started experimenting with wood pulp as a replacement for the raw material of scarce rags. Newspapers began converting from rag paper to wood pulp in 1868. By 1885 most papers had switched.[61]

Although wood pulp paper was more available and less expensive, it had chemical properties that made it a poor choice for preservation. The process of reducing wood to paper pulp fails to remove all of the wood lignin, which leads to acid hydrolysis of the paper, causing brittle and weakened pages. The curator of the newspaper collection at the Newseum, a museum dedicated to the history of the press and the First Amendment in Washington, D.C., said that the very worst newsprint in the collection is that from the 1880s.[62] Wood pulp paper from before the *1980s* also tends to be acidic from alum-rosin sizing, which was added to the paper to reduce absorbency and minimize ink bleeding. When exposed to moisture, the sizing generates sulfuric acid, which also discolors and weakens newsprint. Acids also form in paper from exposure to pollutants, and exposure to light further damages the paper fibers.[63] The petroleum-based ink used in newsprint from this time period also was vulnerable to light, which caused it to fade, and to handling by readers, which caused it to rub off, smudge, and smear.

Another newsman–turned–Librarian of Congress, John Russell Young, recognized in 1897, the first year of his appointment, that wood pulp newspapers were already deteriorating. He asked publishers to print some rag paper issues for copyright deposit purposes. An article in a 1902 edition of the *New York Times* raises the issue again. "The suggestion has been made that a few copies of all newspapers that are to be preserved be run off on substantial linen paper. Newspapers that were once printed on paper of that kind, and those in the library which were printed before the

Revolutionary war are in excellent condition, while files only about twenty years old are already showing the effects of time."[64]

By the early twentieth century, scholars and the public had recognized the value of newspapers as historical resources,[65] but issues facing those who sought to preserve and maintain access to newspapers from previous eras mounted. "Newspaper Files Decaying" declared a headline in 1910. The article began, "Where are the files of yester-year? is beginning to be the plaint of librarians of institutions were [sic] newspapers are kept. Those dating from about 1880 onward are literally disintegrating on librarians' hands, in spite of all they can do to preserve them, and within a few years these valuable sources of history will have to be swept away."[66] Another *Times* headline from that same year asked "Will Future Generations Lose Historical Records of To-Day?" again outlining the problem of wood pulp paper deterioration.[67]

The New York Public Library (NYPL) was established in 1895. The new main building was opened in 1911, when the newspaper collection consisted of the substantial files that had been amassed during the previous century by several private libraries that had merged to form the NYPL. Around the same time, a newspaper binding and preservation program was launched by chief reference librarian Harry Miller Lydenberg, who became concerned about the extent of newspaper deterioration. Lydenberg had been experimenting with preservation methods, testing more than one hundred over a number of years. He described the process in the August 12, 1921, issue of the *New York Times*:

> About 1914 we started our experiments. As a starter we exposed to the sun and air for 150 hours a piece of ordinary news print, a second sheet covered with silk and a third covered with transparent tissue paper. Then we applied the tests of the United States Bureau of Standards for pliability and binding and other tests for strength. The sheet covered with the tissue paper stood the tests better than the others. . . . Meantime, we tried many other methods, chiefly with varnishes and liquid preservatives—and we are still trying to find something that will be under the cost of $40 or so required for treating each month's volume of a newspaper file. We tried a liquid celluloid, shellac and glycerine, shellac, turpentine and paraffin, carbon tetrachloride and paraffin, several special paper preservatives, a flexible varnish with linseed oil, and many other methods.
>
> The best of all the methods was to face each newspaper page on both sides with transparent tissue, and . . . we learned that the best tissue for our purpose was a hand-beaten fibre product from Japan. . . . The best paste to use was a rice paste.[68]

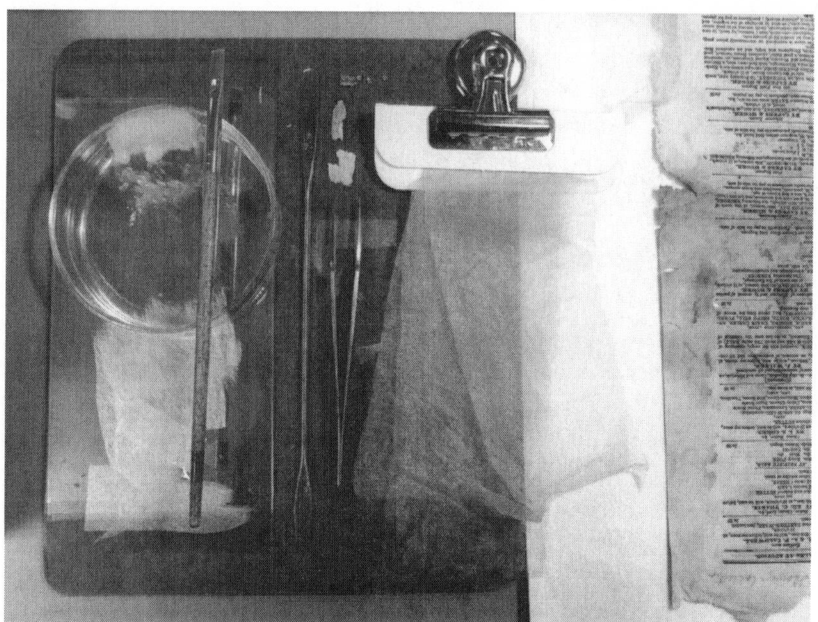

Rice paper and wheat paste used to restore 1828 issue of the *Charleston Courier*. *Courtesy David M. Rubenstein Rare Book & Manuscript Library, Duke University*

The article closes with this quote from Lydenberg: "How the future will improve the process or whether another will be developed, I cannot say. Who knows that we will not some day soon be printing our records on thin strips of imperishable metal that will endure for all time."

By the 1920s, news librarians had organized themselves into the Newspaper Group of the Special Libraries Association and were starting to pay attention to newspaper preservation issues. In 1925, Maurice Symonds, librarian of the *New York Daily News*, published an article in *Special Libraries* describing the rice paper method being used by the NYPL to stabilize its newspaper collections. Symonds called on his news library colleagues to adopt the preservation method and announced that the staff at the NYPL was willing to provide assistance in applying the technique.[69]

The NYPL's Lydenberg and the trustees asked five of the New York City newspaper publishers to each put up $10,000 per year to pay for the work of stabilizing newspapers using the rice paper method, which they did. Laminate strengthening of the newspapers continued for the next fifteen years. But by the early 1930s it was clear that although deterioration of wood pulp newspapers had been delayed, news pages were again disintegrating.

The *New York Times* started printing a rag edition in 1927 as had been suggested by the Librarian of Congress thirty years earlier. Some dozen papers followed suit, but the practice was discontinued during the paper shortage of World War II.[70] In 1933, the *Times* also led the field by issuing a sample copy of a "miniature edition" to supplement the rag-paper edition. The sample was shown to librarians at the American Library Association's convention that year in Chicago and was touted as a way to save between three-fourths and five-sixths of the space to shelve standard-size newspaper volumes. The miniature edition would also help preservation efforts, since the rag volume would "wear at least four times as long as its predecessor."[71] Tight library budgets doomed the idea, however.[72]

All of these developments indicate the interest that surrounded preservation methods for newspapers. However, current access to historical newspaper collections, such as it is, relies in great part on a technology that started to be widely adopted in the 1930s: micro-photographic reproduction of news pages.

Quality of Microfilm

Storing and preserving loose sheets and bound volumes of newspapers has vexed librarians, archivists, and collectors for centuries. At a conference of the American Council of Learned Societies in December 1931, Dr. Solon J. Buck of the University of Pittsburgh said that "wood pulp paper serves the historian badly" and suggested that "cameras capable of reducing facsimiles of newspaper pages to small size requiring little space in archives might solve the problem."[73]

Once the Eastman Kodak company perfected the process of photographing news pages for reproduction on microfilm in 1933, many thought that newspaper storage and preservation problems had been solved for good.[74] Libraries, historical societies, news organizations, and archives rushed to take advantage of the new process. Among the institutions to embrace microfilming was the NYPL. Librarian Keyes Metcalf sent tattered files of newspapers to the Recordak Company in the early 1930s for reproduction on 35-millimeter film. Pleased with the outcome, in May 1934 the library set up its own microfilming operation.

News organizations also embraced the microfilming solution. The *New York Herald-Tribune*, whose news librarian had worked with Eastman Kodak to refine the micro-reproduction process, was once again at the forefront, filming its files starting in 1935. Within three years, eight other newspapers had joined the ranks of news organizations microfilming their files.[75] Other microfilm companies entered the field, including Micro Photo, a division of the Bell and Howell Company, which made newspaper microfilming the cornerstone of its business starting in 1946.

The LOC threw its full support behind the conversion of newspaper back files to microfilm in 1941, when it launched a cooperative filming operation with the *Washington Star* and the District of Columbia Public Library.[76] This is also when a fateful decision was made regarding the way the filming was to be done. As a way to improve the image that was captured and to eliminate the "gutter" that resulted from trying to photograph a page while it was still in its binding, the LOC staff decided to cut the pages out of the binding before filming. Once the pages were guillotined, it was impossible to re-bind them. In many cases the original sheets were discarded, meaning that the print documents as original artifacts were lost.[77]

However, a growing crisis was percolating in the miles of microfilm cabinets that contained the millions of newspaper pages that had been filmed. Even though Recordak had been warning about microfilm deterioration as early as 1965,[78] no one attended to the problem until thousands of reels of microfilm had been lost to "vinegar syndrome" and other forms of deterioration. Unbeknownst to well-intended microfilm advocates, the cellulose acetate film stock that replaced highly flammable nitrate film in the 1930s was prone to its own problems. Cellulose acetate creates acetic acid as it deteriorates, subjecting the microfilm to buckling, shrinkage, embrittlement, and bubbling. The distinctive odor that is emitted as cellulose acetate decomposes led to the process being dubbed "vinegar syndrome." News librarians, archivists, and historians can describe the sickening feeling of opening a microfilm storage cabinet only to recognize the telltale smell and to discover that the contents have disintegrated into an unusable lump of goo.

By the late 1970s, the magnitude of the problem was obvious. But even then, many institutions didn't abandon their practice of microfilming newspaper pages on cellulose acetate stock, discarding the originals, and storing the rolls of film for posterity. It was not until 1983 that the Research Libraries Group Cooperative Preservation Microfilming Project mandated the use of polyester-based stock for all microfilm used by the participants in the project.[79] In the meantime, tens of millions of newspaper pages had been converted to microfilm, and most of the originals had been thrown away.[80]

Acetate film displaying late-stage vinegar syndrome damage. *Courtesy Christian Kurz/film archivist*

Polyester-based microfilm stock presumably lasts for hundreds of years, but that theory remains to be tested. In 1991, a University of Florida librarian who checked the condition of master negatives for the microfilm newspaper collection discovered that three-quarters of the cellulose acetate film in the sample had deteriorated, and every bit of the more recent polyester-based film in the sample displayed damage from mold. That microfilm collection includes the only back files of many Florida newspapers, the print copies of which had been filmed and discarded.[81] Nevertheless, information vendors such as NewsBank/Readex and ProQuest are still microfilming newspapers, and libraries and archives are still collecting and storing titles on microfilm. In many cases, a library will subscribe to the print edition of the newspaper and discard it when the microfilm arrives.

Microfilm readers themselves have improved dramatically since their early days. Reader/scanners are now capable of producing a digital image from a section of microfilm. However, microfilm users can eloquently describe the dilapidated and nearly unusable readers they find in many archival collections. As one firm put it, "Many of the original companies no longer support, maintain, or have the parts to fix these old reader printers. Or, if they do, the cost is too high."[82] Library and archive budgets are under pressure, so the need to maintain reader/printers or purchase new ones competes with other pressing priorities. And the popularity of digital databases has made microfilm the source of last resort for many researchers.

A NEWSPAPER HISTORIAN'S VIEW

David Copeland is the A. J. Fletcher Professor and professor of communications at Elon University in North Carolina. A historian and former journalist, Copeland focuses on the evolution of journalism and is the author of twelve books and dozens of book chapters and journal articles on the subject.[83] His work with colonial and early American newspapers has relied on archival collections of both printed newspapers and microfilm of historical titles. The time periods he has examined include the French and Indian Wars (1754–1763), the War of 1812, the antebellum period (the period following the War of 1812 to the Civil War), the press during the Civil War, and many other specific historical moments in press history. *Colonial American Newspapers*, a book that was based on his PhD dissertation, is an analysis of 7,400 newspaper issues published between 1690 and 1775.

Copeland knows through his research that many eighteenth- and nineteenth-century newspapers are fairly well documented in collections and that the publications a scholar needs are available in hard copy or on microfilm in major archives such as those at the American Antiquarian Society, the LOC, state historical societies, or university libraries. But as we have noted, early American collections are more or less dependent on individuals who contributed their personal archives, leading to the establishment of library collections. Copeland acknowledges that unless someone can travel to one of the repositories that still has newspapers in hard copy, researchers and hobbyists will most likely refer to microfilm.

Copeland says that some important titles from the South didn't survive the heat and humidity or the fortunes of war, but for the most part, the important newspapers are accessible. That said, his greatest concern is that a large proportion of the microfilmed newspaper collections he has used include poorly photographed pages that are difficult to decipher.[84] Of course, microfilm back files, even when in good condition, are black and white only and don't include a lot of the material that actually appeared in print (advertising supplements, inserts, special sections). In many instances the microfilm of historically important newspapers has been scanned and is now available digitally. However, a digital scan is only as good—or as bad—as the microfilm images from which it was generated. And the number of pages that have been digitally scanned remains miniscule compared to the millions of pages captured on microfilm and stored in collections around the country.

For historians seeking the smaller regional or local titles, it is still a challenge to determine whether an archive of that newspaper is available and where it might be found. It becomes a treasure hunt for the searcher. Even the more celebrated titles may still pose challenges if the content or the issue was unusual in any way. Copeland told a story about his search for a special edition of James Gordon Bennett's *New York Herald* that consisted of an accounting of all the nasty things Bennett's rivals and critics had said about him along with Bennett's rebuttals. Copeland knew about the special edition because he had seen other materials that referred to it, but despite his best efforts, he could not locate the actual edition itself. He believes that it was not archived because it was a one-off publication on a Saturday and not part of the regular production of editions throughout the day and the week.[85]

In 2004, Duke University Libraries acquired a collection of five thousand bound volumes of rare and historically important nineteenth- and twentieth-century U.S. newspapers that had been rescued by Nicholson Baker, author of the book *Double Fold* and harsh critic of microfilming.[86] Baker purchased the volumes with his personal funds after learning that the British Library was going to auction off its collection of bound American newspapers in favor of microfilm. Copeland was aware of Baker's collection at Duke and thought it was a timely example of an individual ensuring that irreplaceable historical artifacts survived. However, it also served as an example for Copeland of the serendipitous occurrences that result from material being available to historians.[87]

Copeland fears that historians of the future will face huge challenges in their attempts to document how the public got its news from our current time period. He believes that future historians will have a much more limited view and will have to rely on a much smaller sample of news content and a much narrower selection of voices because so much of what is being generated at this point in time is disappearing. Although newspapers are still microfilming their print editions and memory institutions are still collecting them, the digital content that newspaper organizations generate every day is all but lost for archival purposes. And as the public continues to get more of its news from digital sources, information in print newspaper pages provides a much less telling record of how the public overall is informed about the issues of the day. Copeland put it succinctly: "Historians in 2050 will always have to include an 'exceptions' list of why the conclusions they have drawn might be wrong because they don't have the full picture."[88]

NOTES

1. Clarence S. Brigham, *History and Bibliography of American Newspapers, 1690–1820*, 2 vols. (Worcester, MA: American Antiquarian Society, 1947; Hamden, CT: Archon Books, 1962), xvii.

2. Jeremy P. Meyer, "Rocky Mountain News Lives on at the Denver Public Library," *Denver Post*, March 22, 2013.

3. Associated Press, "Come Hell and High Water," *St. Louis Post Dispatch*, April 22, 1997.

4. David A. Copeland, *Colonial American Newspapers: Character and Content* (Newark, DE: University of Delaware Press, 1997), 17.

5. Copeland, *Colonial American Newspapers*, 279.

6. Richard D. Brown, "Afterword: From Cohesion to Competition," in *Printing and Society in Early America*, ed. William L. Joyce et al. (Worchester, MA: American Antiquarian Society, 1983), 300–309.

7. Nathan O. Hatch, "Elias Smith and the Rise of Religious Journalism in the Early Republic," in *Printing and Society in Early America*, 250–77.

8. S. N. D. North, *History and Present Condition of the Newspaper and Periodical Press of the United States with a Catalogue of the Publications of the Census Year* (Washington, DC: GPO, 1884), 38.

9. Shannon E. Martin and Kathleen A. Hansen, *Newspapers of Record in a Digital Age: From Hot Type to Hot Link* (Westport, CT: Greenwood Publishing Group, 1998), 24.

10. Reporters of the Associated Press, *Breaking News: How the Associated Press Has Covered War, Peace, and Everything Else* (New York: Princeton Architectural Press, 2007).

11. Martin and Hansen, *Newspapers of Record*, 29.

12. "Biographical Sketch," Joseph B. Felt (1789–1869) Papers, 1710–1868, MssColl 462, Phillips Library at the Peabody Essex Museum, Salem, MA, p. 2.

13. Francesca Pitaro (processing archivist, Associated Press Corporate Archives), interview with authors, April 26, 2016; Valerie Komor, "From the Stylus to Digital Text: Preserving AP's Historic News Copy," *AP World*, no. 2 (2015): 18.

14. John Y. Cole, *For Congress and the Nation: A Chronological History of the Library of Congress* (Washington, DC: Library of Congress, 1979), 4.

15. Library of Congress, *The 1812 Catalogue of the Library of Congress: A Facsimile* (Washington, DC: GPO, 1982), 93.

16. Clyde S. Edwards, "American Eighteenth-Century Newspapers," *Library of Congress Quarterly Journal of Current Acquisitions* 8, no.1 (1950): 40–43.

17. S. Branson Marley, "Newspapers and the Library of Congress," *The Quarterly Journal of the Library of Congress* 32, no. 3 (1975): 207–37.

18. "Asks Southerners to Save Records," *New York Times*, September 7, 1924.

19. Teri Hayt (executive editor, *The Repository*), interview with authors, November 11, 2014.

20. David Kaser, *A Book for a Sixpence: The Circulating Library in America*, chapbook no. 14 (Philadelphia: Beta Phi Mu, 1980); David Kaser, *Coffee House to Stock Exchange: A Natural History of the Reading Room* (Philadelphia: Gaylord, 1976); Louis B. Wright, *The Cultural Life of the American Colonies* (New York: Harper Brothers, 1957).

21. Massachusetts Historical Society, The Annotated Newspapers of Harbottle Dorr, "About the Collection," www.masshist.org/dorr/about.

22. Marley, "Newspapers and the Library of Congress," 210.

23. "Peter Force Library: Special Collections," Library of Congress, Manuscript Reading Room, www.loc.gov/rr/mss/coll/084.html.

24. Clifford Kenyon Shipton, *Isaiah Thomas: Printer, Patriot and Philanthropist, 1749–1831* (Rochester, NY: Leo Hart, 1948), 3–16.

25. Isaiah Thomas Papers, Collection T, box 13, folder 5, American Antiquarian Society, Worchester, MA.

26. Samuel M. Burnside, Esq., "Memoir of Isaiah Thomas, LL.D., Founder and First President of the American Antiquarian Society," *Archaeologia Americana: Transactions and Collections of the American Antiquarian Society* II (1836): xxvii.

27. Carol McKinley, "The New England Legacy of Isaiah Thomas," *AB Bookman's Weekly*, November 10, 1986, 1860.

28. Charles L. Nichols, "Isaiah Thomas Diaries for 1782–1804, and 1808," in *Proceedings of the American Antiquarian Society* 26 (1916): 75.

29. Isaiah Thomas to William Bentley, February 8, 1809, Isaiah Thomas Papers, Collection T, box 6, American Antiquarian Society.

30. Isaiah Thomas to Matthew Carey, March 20, 1809, Isaiah Thomas Papers, Collection T, box 6, American Antiquarian Society.

31. *Massachusetts Spy*, May 16 and May 23, 1810, p. 3, in both editions; June 6 and June 13, 1810, p. 4, in both editions.

32. Isaiah Thomas Papers, Collection T, folio 17.1, American Antiquarian Society.

33. Isaiah Thomas Papers, Collection T, folio 17.1.

34. Thomas Knoles (Marcus A. McCorison Librarian, American Antiquarian Society), interview with Hansen, February 3, 2016.

35. New York Times Company records, "Arthur Hays Sulzberger Papers: Morgue, 1947–1955," New York Times Corporate Archives, MssCol 17782, box 208, file 11, Manuscript and Archives Division, New York Public Library.

36. Barbara P. Semonche, *News Media Libraries: A Management Handbook*. (Westport, CT: Greenwood, 1993), 5.

37. Semonche, *News Media Libraries*, 6.

38. Gustav V. Lindner, *Newspaper Library Manual* (New York: Gustav V. Lindner, 1912), 22.

39. Robert William Desmond, *Newspaper Reference Methods* (Minneapolis: University of Minnesota Press, 1933), 135.

40. Komor, "From the Stylus to Digital Text," 18.

41. Pitaro interview.

42. W. H. Bond and Hugh Amory, eds. *The Printed Catalogues of the Harvard College Library, 1723–1790* (Boston: Colonial Society of Massachusetts, 1996).

43. Bond and Amory, *The Printed Catalogues of the Harvard College Library.*

44. Alfred Claghorn Potter, *The Library of Harvard University: Descriptive and Historical Notes*, 4th ed. (Cambridge, MA: Harvard University Press, 1934), 121.

45. Frederic Hudson, *Journalism in the United States, from 1690 to 1872* (New York: Harper & Bros., 1873); John Bach McMaster, *A History of the People of the United States* (New York: D. Appleton & Company, 1883).

46. Lucy Maynard Salmon, *The Newspaper and the Historian* (New York: Oxford University Press, 1923).

47. James Ford Rhodes, "Newspapers As Historical Sources," *The Atlantic Monthly*, May 1909, 657.

48. Marley, "Newspapers and the Library of Congress," 210.

49. Marley, "Newspapers and the Library of Congress," 211.

50. Marley, "Newspapers and the Library of Congress," 211.

51. Marley, "Newspapers and the Library of Congress," 211.

52. Marley, "Newspapers and the Library of Congress," 213.

53. Marley, "Newspapers and the Library of Congress," 216.

54. T. F. Mills, "Preserving Yesterday's News for Today's Historian: A Brief History of Newspaper Preservation, Bibliography, and Indexing," *Journal of Library History* 16, no. 3 (1981): 473.

55. Sara Lawrence, "History of Historical Societies in the U.S," Public History Resource Center, January 23, 2003, www.publichistory.org/features/Historical SocietyHistory.html.

56. Reuben G. Thwaites, "The Library of the State Historical Society of Wisconsin," *Library Journal* 16, no. 7 (1891): 205.

57. Knoles interview.

58. Komor, "From the Stylus to Digital Text," 18.

59. "Newspaper Files," *New York Times*, August 9, 1895.

60. Roger Mellen, "The Press, Paper Shortages, and Revolution in Early America," *Media History* 21, no. 1 (2015): 23–41; A. J. Valente, *Rag Paper Manufacture in the United States, 1801–1900: A History, with Directories of Mills and Owners* (Jefferson, NC: McFarland, 2010).

61. Mills, "Preserving Yesterday's News," 467.

62. Carrie Cristofferson (curator of collections, Newseum), interview with authors, May 25, 2016.

63. "The Deterioration and Preservation of Paper: Some Essential Facts—Collections Care—Resources," Library of Congress, www.loc.gov/preservation/care/deterioratebrochure.html.

64. "Preservation of Newspapers," *New York Times*, November 9, 1902.

65. Rhodes, "Newspapers As Historical Sources."

66. "Newspaper Files Decaying," *New York Times*, March 6, 1910.

67. "Will Future Generations Lose Historical Records of To-Day?" *New York Times*, July 24, 1910.

68. "Times Files Saved by a New Method," *New York Times*, August 12, 1921.

69. Maurice Symonds, "Preservation of Old Newspapers," *Special Libraries* 16, no. 8 (1925): 317–18.

70. Mills, "Preserving Yesterday's News," 467.

71. "Miniature Paper Shown," *New York Times*, October 17, 1933.

72. Edward N. Jenks, "Micro-Editions of Newspapers: A Survey of Developments (Illustrated)," *Journalism Quarterly* 27, no. 4 (1950): 391–98.

73. "Crumbling of Newspaper Files Declared Loss to Historians," *New York Times*, December 29, 1931.

74. Microfilm comes on a roll, like other types of film. Microfiche, introduced in the 1960s, reproduces the images on a four-by-six-inch transparent, flat, rectangular card able to store many pages on each card. Both formats have been used for newspapers.

75. Mills, "Preserving Yesterday's News," 468.

76. Mills, "Preserving Yesterday's News," 469.

77. Nicholson Baker, *Double Fold: Libraries and the Assault on Paper* (New York: Random House, 2001), 25–26; Marley, "Newspapers and the Library of Congress," 223.

78. V. B. Phillips, "Customer Memorandum on Preservation of Microfilm Records Issued by Recordak," *National Micro-News* 75 (1965): 215.

79. Thomas A. Bourke, "The Curse of Acetate: Or, a Base Conundrum Confronted," *Microform Review* 23, no. 1 (1994): 15–17.

80. Nicholson, *Double Fold*; Randy Silverman, "Retaining Hardcopy Paper Still Important in Digital Age," *Newspaper Research Journal* 36, no. 3 (2015): 363–72.

81. Erich J. Kesse, "Condition Survey of Master Microfilm Negatives, University of Florida Libraries," *Abbey Newsletter* 15, no. 3 (May 1991).

82. "Is Your Microfilm or Microfiche Reader Printer Broken?" *Generation Imaging*, http://generationimaging.com/2013/07/is-your-microfilm-or-microfiche-reader-printer-broken/.

83. "David Copeland," www.elon.edu/e-web/faculty/faculty-scholars/david_copeland.xhtml.

84. David A. Copeland, interview with Hansen, February 24, 2016.

85. Copeland interview.

86. "Unusual Collection of American Newspapers Comes to the Duke Libraries," Duke University Libraries, 2004, http://library.duke.edu/magazine-archive/issue15/notes.html.

87. Copeland interview.

88. Copeland interview.

3

VISUAL NEWS

> Too many photographs have vanished through the years. Old files . . . should be properly cared for in an archive, for the visual information they contain is more vital to the interpretation of history than volumes of words.
>
> —Emma H. Little, "The Father of News Photography: George Grantham Bain," 1940[1]

THE RISE OF VISUAL NEWS

By the time of the Civil War, the Hoe steam-powered press and other newsprint production technology improvements allowed news publishers an output of 20,000 newspapers per hour.[2] But there was little innovation in news design. Visually, news pages continued to be dense, text-only columns with little differentiation in type size.

Samuel F. B. Morse and Alfred Vail's improvements to telegraphy made possible more immediate reporting of the day's news, but those

In 1999 the University of Kentucky's Audio-Visual Archive was offered the Lexington *Herald-Leader*'s extensive clip and photo negatives collection. The collection included 1.8 million negatives and transparencies from the late 1930s through the 1990s. The newspaper's corporate owners had told the news librarians to stop recording and filing the negatives, which the owners said were unimportant. The librarians were supposed to throw all the old negatives in the trash. John C. Wyatt, the *Herald-Leader*'s chief photographer, rescued them from the trash heap.[3]

improvements were still just used for the delivery of words. Organizations such as the Associated Press (AP), established in 1846, were viable because the telegraph enabled the rapid dissemination of news. The steep rise in the number of newspapers in the United States helped make news a "salable commodity."[4] But the visual age of news media was not ushered in until the technology for printing images became readily available.

Graphics and Illustrations

Two publications launched in the mid-1800s, *Harper's Monthly* in 1850 (which switched to weekly in 1857) and *Leslie's Illustrated News* in 1852, were the first in the United States to leverage graphics as a sales point for their publications. Both employed artists who were sent out to sketch news events, battles, or slices of contemporary life. Master engravers then transferred the illustrations to woodcuts, which were inked and impressed on the printed page.

The illustrated newspaper brought "the genius of the pencil and the pen promptly to illustrate the recorded event."[5] Describing an example of the power of illustration to augment the written word, an article in *Leslie's Illustrated News* in August 1856 states: "On Saturday last a conflagration of unusual interest occurred in Brooklyn; not only is the event noticed in our paper with prepared description from the pen, but one of our most accomplished artists was early at the scene, and has made it permanent as a graphic picture."[6]

During the Civil War, images were not only used to depict people and scenes. Maps showing the progression of battles supplemented reporting in newspapers. In a *New York Herald* article published alongside a map of the skirmish at Chicamacomico, North Carolina, in 1861, the power of the visual is well described: "We have heretofore given a graphic description of the unsuccessful attack . . . but the map which we publish today will give our readers a clearer understanding of the position of the respective combatants than the most minute word picture could possible [sic] afford."[7]

The popularity of graphic reproduction of news events was such that, by 1891, more than 1,000 artists were working for news organizations, generating more than 10,000 drawings a week.[8]

The use of infographics evolved over the century after their first use. Maps of military actions, charts with election results, editorial cartoons—all of these became part of the mix of news storytelling. The *Chicago Tribune* used a map of Russian troop movements on its September 4, 1919, front page. A map on the front page of the November 1, 1920, *New York Times* displayed Warren G. Harding's 1920 presidential election votes across the country.[9]

During the ensuing decades maps and charts became a staple for news event illustration, and by the 1980s, informational graphics were a fixture in newspapers. A 1987 study of 114 dailies found that "graphic devices consumed 27 percent of total newspaper front page space."[10] A 1988 study found that the average newspaper used at least four informational graphics per issue.[11] After *USA Today* launched in April 1994, its colorful, graphic-rich presentation style, heavy use of illustrations, and stories told in chart form became the norm in American newspapers.

Photography

Experimentation with photographic image technology took place concurrently with the growth of illustrated news publications. Civil War photographer Mathew Brady and his troupe of photographers had demonstrated the power of the photographic image by chronicling the Civil War. By the 1870s, photography in book publishing became more frequent through the use of photogravure. However, the photogravure process (transferring a photographic negative onto a metal plate and then etching the image) required the image to be printed separately from the text, making it unfeasible to incorporate with a newspaper's full-page composition.

On March 4, 1873, twenty-three years after the launch of *Harper's Monthly* and the gradual refinement of photography, the first pictorial daily newspaper, the *Daily Graphic*, was published. The newspaper used photographs as the inspiration for the engravings that illustrated the news. Samuel L. Clemens, also known as Mark Twain, talking about the *Daily Graphic*, summed up the growing appetite for illustrated news: "I don't care much about reading (unless it be some tranquilizing tract or other), but I do like to look at pictures, and the illustrated weeklies do not come to me as often as I need them."[12]

By 1880, the technology was sufficiently advanced for photographs themselves to be published in newsprint. Stephen H. Horgan, the *Daily Graphic*'s art editor and engraver, took a photograph of the Shantytown area in New York City, and on March 4, 1880, for the first time, a legible halftone photo was published in a newspaper.[13]

The *New York Herald* in 1899 experimented with a machine called the "telediagraph," which, according to a description on the Dead Media Project website, "used telegraphy to transmit pictures, drawings, autographs, and designs that had been etched with a stylus on tinfoil using a non-conducting ink made from shellac mixed with alcohol. The image was received on carbon paper wrapped between two sheets of blank paper."[14]

The *Herald* tested the new device by asking publishers of the *Chicago Times Herald*, the *St. Louis Republic*, the *Boston Herald*, and the *Philadelphia Inquirer* to set up machines in their offices as a demonstration.[15]

An article in *Pearson's Magazine* described the transmission: "On this historical day the offices in these widely remote cities were connected with the office in New York, and when all was ready, received simultaneously and over the same wire, an accurate picture of the first gun fired at Manila. Then other pictures were sent back by telegraph, over the single circuit, from these cities to New York; with which remarkable achievement the invention carried itself beyond the stage of experiment to open up a new field in journalistic enterprise."[16]

The new market for news photography and the availability of technology to more easily transmit images led to the growth in photo agencies. By 1929, the radio, already being used for transmitting sounds, started to transmit images. And on January 1, 1935, the AP began a wire photo service to send their photographers' images to member newsrooms using the telephone lines being laid across the country. The first AP wire image, an aerial photo of the site of an airplane crash in New York, was transmitted to forty-seven newspapers in twenty-five states.[17]

Between the first wire transmission of news photographs and the dawn of the digital photography era, advances in photojournalism largely were in the realm of the cameras used to shoot the photos. Smaller, lighter cameras and faster lenses helped photojournalists create the iconic images that captured and illustrated the news.

The AP transmitted its first color wire photos in 1939—each transmission taking three times longer than a black-and-white photo. But color photography was not an instant hit in newsrooms. In 1979, forty years after the first wire photo transmission, only 12 percent of North American newspapers printed elements of their news pages in color. Part of the delay was the need for expanded printing facilities. Large newspapers, such as the *New York Times* and the *Philadelphia Inquirer* each invested $300 million to upgrade their presses to provide daily color on the printed page. By 1993, due to advertiser demand and a desire to attract younger readers, 97 percent of America's newspapers were colorized.[18]

WHY VISUAL NEWS WAS LOST

The images, illustrations, and photographs used in newspapers since the start of illustrated news are preserved in the pages of the publications that have been saved over the years. But they are only representations of the original images and serve as a reference; they are not sufficient for reuse or reproduction. The original engravings, glass negatives, photo negatives and prints, maps, and drawings that gave rise to the use of visuals in newsprint have had a precarious path to preservation.

Engravings

Until 1860 the process of making a new engraving required obliterating the old. The boxwood into which the engraver cut the illustration was expensive and therefore was reused by sanding the material down to create a new, fresh surface. The following description by historian David Omar Stowell of the engraving process shows a further complication to preserving original woodcuts:

> After the art superintendent chose a sketch to be worked up into an engraving, a staff artist drew a new version on paper, rendered in outlines. The drawing was then rubbed down in reverse upon the whitewashed surface of a block of Turkish boxwood, itself composed of smaller sections of wood secured together by a system of nuts and bolts. Draughtsmen applied further detail in washes and pencil (sometimes dividing up the block among artists with particular skills for rendering figures, architecture, landscapes, machinery, etc.), and then the composite block went to the engraving department where it was unbolted and distributed to a team of engravers. The engravers laboriously carved out the design on their individual pieces, after which the constituent blocks were rebolted together and a supervising engraver insured that the incised lines met across the sections. The engraved block was then sent to the composing room where it was locked into place with handset type to create a *Frank Leslie's* page to be made into an electrotyped copper plate.[19]

Although pieces of these blocks might be found, preservation of the multiple components of a woodblock engraving was rare.

As the creation of news graphics and illustrations moved from wood to metal to paper to computer program, the original map, chart, or drawing was rarely saved. Maps were generated as a template over which new information would be placed. Charts and graphs, too, were replicated, and the originals might be stashed under the news designer's desk until his files were tossed.

Wood engraving block titled "Rows in the Army—Mutiny of Part of General Spunola's Empire Brigade at East New York," used to print image in *New York Illustrated News*, September 13, 1862. *Courtesy Graphic Arts Collection, National Museum of American History, Smithsonian Institution*

Photographs

Photographs were first used in news publications as the source of the image for the artistic staff whose engravings were published in the newspaper. The development of the halftone process that turned a photographic image into different sizes and densities of dots inaugurated the actual publication of photos themselves in the newsprint product. These halftones would be imprinted on metal and affixed to a block of wood, which would then join the letter sorts in the typesetting form.

A 1902 edition of *The British Printer* contains a description of the best method for preserving halftone blocks after printing: "clean well with benzo and then cover with a greasy substance such as solidified oil or a preparation known as DMV. They should be stored in a cabinet of flat shallow drawers and not placed on the top of each other. Copper blocks are to be preferred as the metal is tougher than zinc and not so sensitive to chemical influence. It wears and finer results are obtained both in the block making and in printing."[20] Given that copper was valuable and easily recycled for use in other products, most copper halftone blocks ended up being melted down.

THE IMAGE CAPTURE

Each of the methods for capturing images for use in newspapers had their own specific preservation challenges or, as described by the Northeast Document Conservation Center, "unique deterioration characteristics."[21] Glass negatives, used from the 1870s until the early 1900s, had a narrow range of light and temperature tolerance and would fade under less-than-ideal conditions. Cellulose nitrate film, the medium of choice for photography by the early 1900s, was highly flammable. Cellulose acetate film, which replaced nitrate in the 1940s, suffered from vinegar syndrome. Color film negatives faded or discolored. Yet the quality of the negative was essential for reproduction in the newspaper.

Tom Flynn, a former library worker–turned–reporter at the *Rochester Times-Union*, explained in an oral history the way news photos were processed and archived.

> The photograph was shot by a camera, a negative was generated. The image was then etched onto a metal plate, and these were all cut to the size of the displays that were needed for the newspaper. . . . We

> routinely filed all of those metal cuts, so that when we needed [a] photo, the newsroom would call the library, and we would find [the cut] and deliver it to the composing room. . . . This meant every day . . . going to the so-called "hell box," which was just a large metal box in the composing room. When the pages were stripped after the editions were complete, all the type was re-melted, recycled. All the engravings or half-tones were thrown into a box. The name hell box had something to do with the fact it was next to the area where they melted all the lead. . . . I reclaimed these metal cuts and sent them to the library.[22]

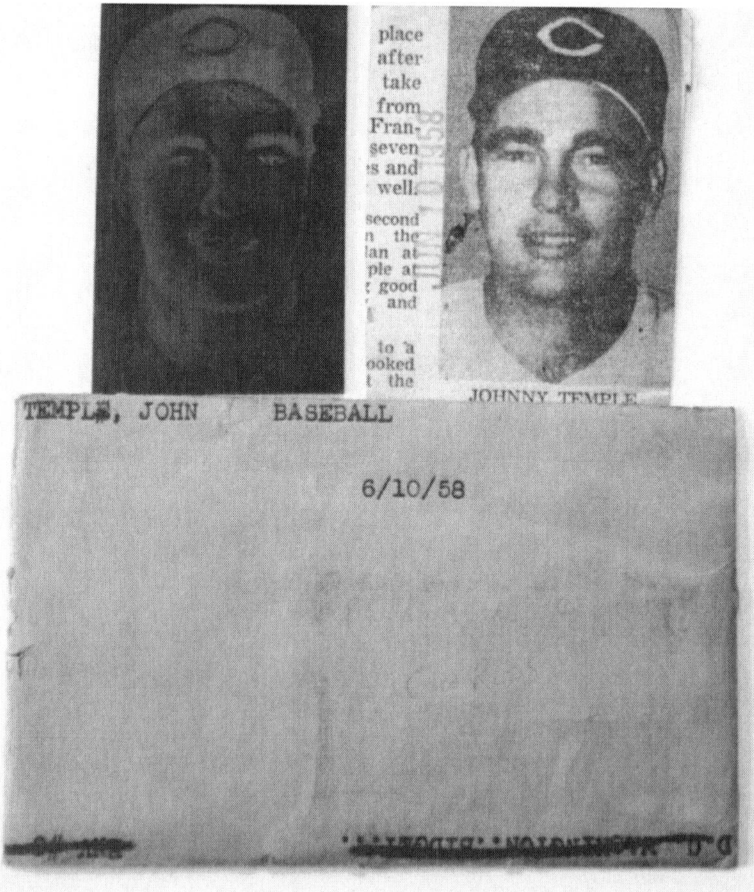

Newspaper metal cut used to print photo, newsprint photo clip, and photo morgue envelope. *Hansen photo/personal collection*

MATERIAL ISSUES

Both the material used to capture images and to make prints created challenges for news photograph preservation. The images that appeared in newspapers made their way to the library (or, as it was often referred to, the photo morgue) as metal cuts, and as either albumen prints (prior to the 1930s) or gelatin silver prints. Environmentally, the photo morgues were not designed for archival preservation. This would affect the quality of the images over the years.

Prints were especially vulnerable. Air pollutants and warm and humid storage environments all threatened the preservation of prints. A further issue was that resin-coated prints' surfaces could stick to one another under extreme heat.[23]

The fact that prints were reused in news production resulted in image quality loss as well. This description of the Ransom Center's *New York Journal-American* Photographic Morgue collection details the issues: "The prints in the collection formed the original working files for the editors and photographers of the *Journal-American*. They were subjected to all the traditional uses of a very active and long-term photo morgue and subsequently show signs of rough handling, bending, creasing, tearing, marking, rapid chemical processing, deterioration, and the advanced wear-and-tear of possible multiple uses."[24]

IMAGE USEFULNESS

For news organizations, archiving decisions were rarely based on potential future interest in the images. Instead, decisions were pragmatic. In a 1929 article in *Special Libraries*, J. Sheldon Cartwright, an appraisal engineer, wrote about how to assess the value of news library assets. He sets out the challenge of using an economic argument for preserving photos: "A Photo, in an emergency, or in an event of world wide importance, as a matter of value, at the moment would be worth hundreds of dollars, . . . but in forty-eight hours, the value would be negligible, and it might be a long time before they were again used." His conclusion, one that many news decision makers apparently took to heart, was: "Frankly a lot of the material which collects in a library, including photos, may never be used, and really would the 'Dear Public' suffer a bit of harm if it never did see them?"[25]

IMAGE ARCHIVE POLICIES

In addition to the problem of bottom-line cost justification for preserving photographs, there were few internal newsroom policies regarding what images should be archived and for how long. Space restrictions, legal issues, desires to keep files manageable, and, ultimately, lack of clear guidelines resulted in more elimination of news photographs than any other causes.

Some news libraries kept photos used in the publication as well as unpublished images photojournalists may have taken on the scene or during a photoshoot. Add to this a steady stream of wire photos the newsroom might receive and the problem becomes clear. One of the first mentions of a systematic method of filing and indexing pictures is in Gustaf V. Lindner's 1912 *Newspaper Library Manual*. In it he warns,

> Material in the portrait and picture section is bound to accumulate steadily, and no weeding-out process can be applied to any great extent. The acquisition of a photograph, or illustration, of more recent date does not warrant the discarding of an older one of the same person or subject, for it might happen that a picture of a certain date or period may be wanted instead of the latest one available. It is . . . safer to provide ample space for increasing portrait and picture collections rather than attempt some regular weeding method which might seriously impair their value.[26]

However, managing a constantly growing number of resources coupled with finite space to store them introduced a major enemy of archiving for preservation: weeding the collection. Consideration about the need for, and danger of, weeding the photo collection is well stated in Robert William Desmond's 1933 *Newspaper Reference Methods*, in which he discusses one of the important roles of the news library: preserving valuable material.

According to Desmond, "A reference library may save a great deal of money for a newspaper by preserving cuts and photographs from loss or destruction. . . . One photo-service executive admits that the financial success of his enterprise is based upon the carelessness of newspapers that lose or discard the photographs they have bought and later are forced to buy duplicates."[27] But he goes on to admit the need for culling the collections: "An overcrowded condition frequently brings about the necessity of reorganization. A thorough reorganization may result in the discard of from 40 to 60 per cent of the materials on file. No less than seven tons of metal cuts were removed from one library at the time of reorganizing. Some of these cuts should never have been saved in the first place; others were over ten years old and therefore out of date. Extreme caution should be used, however, in discarding photographs and clippings."[28]

A November 10, 1969, memorandum by John Rothman, the *New York Times*'s director of corporate archives, reveals some of these issues that affected news photo retention:

> On the issue of saving "forever" all photos ever published in *The Times* . . . let's institute the following rules:
>
> a. All photos, whether or not they have been published in *The Times*, should be kept as long as we consider them to have potential value for our users. We will try to develop criteria by which to assess "potential value" on a category-by-category basis, with the advice of our principal users.
> b. All pictures that have been published in *The Times* and are later judged to have no further value may be discarded.
> c. 7 years after the last publication date if they show people in circumstances or activities that may be grounds for libel action.
> d. 3 months after the last publication date if they show no persons at all, or show persons in circumstances or activities that would preclude the possibility of libel action.[29]

This kind of convoluted and, frankly, subjective determination of a photo's long-term worth further confounded image preservation.

SPACE ISSUES

Space requirements were one of the biggest factors with image storage. As real estate costs rose, newsroom staff contracted and printing facilities were moved off-site. Many newspaper buildings were sold, and their library collections were downsized. The launch of digital darkrooms eased the issue of physical photograph storage, but the decades of accumulated images stored in files and cabinets continued to be a challenge.

In what seemed too good a deal to be true during the economic recession of 2009, entrepreneur John Rogers of Little Rock, Arkansas, approached several dozen newspapers with this offer: he would buy their print photo collections from them and then provide free access to those photos after his company, Rogers Photo Archive, digitized them. Cash- and space-strapped newspapers jumped at the offer, sometimes neglecting even to draw up a written agreement.[30] With a stated goal "to digitize the photo archive of every American newspaper," Rogers's business model was described this way: "After the digital copies have been returned to the original owners, Rogers makes his money via several revenue streams, including licensing images of celebrities, politicians and sports icons, selling 'stock photo' rights, and selling original prints online. The Rogers Archive is, for example, the biggest seller on eBay right now, with over two million photos currently for sale in their eBay store. Rogers said eBay alone brings in $120,000 a week."[31]

Rogers explained how this idea came about in an article for the *Arkansas Times*: "I took every penny I had, borrowed the rest, and I bought the *Detroit News* [photos for $1 million], I went from having 3 million images to having 4.5 million images. I never dreamed I could go into an institution and buy their photos." The catch, however, was that the *Detroit News* still needed its photo archives to operate. Part of the deal was for Rogers to digitize them and return a digital copy to the Detroit newsroom within one year. The timetable was ambitious. "It was one thing to digitize 3 million of my images over seven years," he said. "It was another to do a million and a half images and they want them done in 12 months."[32]

Logistics aside, the *Detroit News* turned out to be profitable for Rogers, who quickly recouped his money through sales of the newspaper's historic prints (including one catalogue auction that he said grossed more than $400,000) and a ramped-up eBay sales presence. "We basically created the market of people buying news photos," he said. "There was always a market for original art photography, something that sells in a gallery for thousands, but there was no market for an individual who wasn't a photo buyer."[33]

News of Rogers's offer to trade physical photos for digital scans attracted more newspapers looking for space and cash. The McClatchy Company newspaper chain contracted with Rogers to scan the photo archives of all of its newspapers—somewhere between ten and twelve million images. In the McClatchy deal, Rogers Archives wouldn't own the negatives, but it would have an exclusive agreement to license content from McClatchy's photos.

Rogers presented himself as a savior of vital resources neglected by their creators. "Our nation's history is not preserved," he said. "The U.S. newspapers were there to document our history. . . . But in terms of long-term preservation, they've done a very poor job. . . . We're doing it the right way."[34]

He was doing it the right way, right up until the FBI raided his Arkansas warehouse. By the summer of 2015, one year after many newspapers across the country began shipping their collections to Rogers Photo, those newspapers were suing him in an effort to have their files returned. The *El Paso Times* was one of twenty newspapers that filed lawsuits. The suit states Rogers "failed and refused" to create and deliver the digital archive in exchange for the physical archive, and a promised website to "develop, market and maintain" the materials for the newspaper was never created.[35]

The *Salt Lake Tribune* had entrusted its collections to Rogers with the promise that its negatives and prints would be scanned and that a searchable digital database would be delivered. It took a year of negotiations for the collection to be recovered from a Rogers subcontractor and returned to the newspaper. Even so, a large number of negatives remained under control of a court-appointed receiver and were not returned. A lawsuit against Rogers filed by Digital First Media corporation (parent company for fifty-six newspapers) described the deal to deliver digitized images for free to the newspapers that sent him their files as "a ploy." The suit contended Rogers intended to "personally plunder and deplete" the newspaper archives for his own gain.[36]

DISASTERS

Fires and floods frequently caused wholesale news photo destruction. George Grantham Bain began a news photo agency at the turn of the twentieth century. In the book *Bain's New York*, author Michael Carlebach described Bain's importance in the history of early photojournalism. "His friends dubbed him the 'Father of News Photography,' not because of his photographic skills but rather as one of the first Americans to recognize that news photographs would ultimately transform the business of journalism."[37] In 1898, he established George Bain News Service and signed contracts to supply news photos to the growing number of newspapers in New York City. Success seemed assured, because "the demand for illustrations for periodical publications is now so imperative that almost every possible device is exercised by the publishers of them to secure original prints."[38]

By late 1907 Bain had more than one hundred newspaper clients. He also had moved to a large facility in the supposedly fireproof Parker Building, along with his collection of more than one million prints and negatives of New York City scenes.[39] But on January 10, 1908, a fire that started on a floor below Bain's offices had, within hours, killed three firefighters and destroyed Bain's entire inventory of images. By luck, one of his photographers sheepishly admitted the day after the fire that he had, against office policy, taken home a stack of prints. These became the foundation of the resurrected news service.[40] The fire was "a disaster for posterity: since Bain's was the only news picture firm in business at that time, irreplaceable photographs were lost forever, some of them surviving only as published illustrations in yellowed and crumbling newspapers."[41]

Sometimes photo collection disasters are narrowly averted. In October 2015 a water pipe burst in the storage area where the *New York Times* kept its historical photos, news clippings, reference books, and other overflow material from its library. It was sheer coincidence that a news assistant was sent to the basement photo morgue to retrieve an image of a former British cabinet minister who had died. The assistant walked in and discovered a river of water. He ran over to the rear wall of the morgue, where most of the card catalog sits, and saw what he said looked like a waterfall. Of the six million prints and contact sheets and ten million negatives, at least 90 percent were saved from ruin.[42]

Most importantly, the card catalog was not swamped. According to *New York Times* picture editor, Niko Koppel, "What makes the card catalog irreplaceable is that it has never been digitized. Hundreds of thousands of people and subjects are keyed by index numbers to the photo files. . . . Those getting even a little wet would have left them smudged, smeared and stuck together. They are our blueprints to the morgue. Without them, the material is lost."[43]

Beyond material degradation, disasters, collection weeding, wholesale tossing, and the occasional scam, there is another major reason that preservation of photographs is a challenge: organizational mission. There is a tension between preserving what has been created amid the pressure of creating new material. Quoted in a blog about the *New York Times* photo archive, Peter Galassi, curator at the Museum of Modern Art, expressed this pressure well: "I think we can agree that the first responsibility of [a newspaper] is not to its picture morgue but to today's news, and it is no secret that the old structures of newsgathering are under stress. The more attention and resources we devote to the past, the less remains for the present."[44] Without organizational consensus about the potential value of yesterday's images for tomorrow, little attention will be focused on preservation today.

HOW VISUAL NEWS WAS PRESERVED

Illustrations

The original illustrations and engravings used in newspapers are, for the most part, lost. The only record is what was inked onto the newsprint. The existence of collections of any size are usually the result of some individual collector's interest or the curatorial powers of a major library.

The Cabinet of American Illustration is a good example of collaboration between a collector and a library. William Patten, art editor for *Harper's Magazine* during the 1880s and 1890s, learned in 1932 about a gift given to the Library of Congress (LOC) by the widow of Alexander W. Drake. Drake had been art editor of *Century* magazine and had a collection of 498 wood engraving and proof prints signed by the artists that were used in the magazine.[45] Patten approached the LOC with the idea that, by adding to the original Drake gift, "a collection might be formed at the Library of Congress of original drawings for illustrations made in the 'Golden Age' at the end of the nineteenth century."[46]

As the art editor for one of America's most prestigious magazines, Patten knew most of the illustrators of that era. He reached out to the illustrators, or to their heirs, asking about any available original drawings. His efforts resulted in the creation of the Cabinet of American Illustration, a collection of more than 4,000 original drawings created between 1880 and 1910. Although most were illustrations used in magazines, some were used in early pictorial newspapers. With some pride, the 1932 Report from the Librarian of Congress stated, "There is thus every prospect that the Library of Congress will shortly possess a Cabinet of American Illustration unique in the world, which should not only serve as a historical record of a great American art but should provide invaluable material for study and inspiration to illustrators of later times."[47]

Sometimes the complete collection of a news illustrator has been preserved. The LOC's Herblock collection contains 14,300 finished drawings and 50,000 rough sketches created by editorial cartoonist Herbert L. Block between 1930 and 2001. The LOC also houses the Art Wood collection, which includes work by more than 2,800 artists and features a number of political cartoonists and news caricaturists. The collection of original drawings was started by award-winning cartoonist James Arthur Wood Jr. when he was twelve years old. Throughout the next sixty years Wood gathered by gift or purchase selections of a wide range of cartoonists and illustrators. In 1995 he opened the National Gallery of Caricature and Cartoon Art in Washington, D.C., but it closed after only two years. Wood turned to the LOC to ensure that his lovingly compiled collection would be preserved.[48]

Photographs

Although Mathew Brady's pioneering photographs of Civil War scenes were not reproduced in news publications, the story of how the glass negatives and prints he created were haphazardly preserved is a telling tale of early photojournalism archiving and noble preservation efforts.

During the course of the war, Brady and his studio employees generated more than 7,000 photographs on two sets of negatives. After the war, the U.S. government paid him $25,000 for one set, most of them glass plate negatives. Brady's personal set of negatives came into the possession of E. & H. T. Anthony & Company to settle a bill for photographic supplies.[49]

As related in Francis Miller's *Photographic History of the Civil War in Ten Volumes*, Anthony's set of glass plate negatives "were kicked about from pillar to post" for ten years, ending up in an "old garret." In the late 1890s a Civil War veteran, John C. Taylor, negotiated with Anthony to purchase the negatives and prints. Many of the negatives both in the Anthony collection and in the government's collections were broken, lost, or destroyed by fire.[50]

The fragility of images was described in 1882 by a chemist named Albert Bierstadt: "The breakableness of the glass and the fugitive character of photograph [sic] chemicals will in short time obliterate all traces of the scenes these represent. Unless they are reproduced in some permanent form they will soon be lost."[51]

As John C. Taylor described in an interview: "The Government collection had for nine years remained comparatively neglected but through ordinary breakage, lax supervision, and disregard of orders, nearly three hundred of their negatives were broken or lost. To assist them in securing the prints for Government Records I loaned my seven thousand negatives to the Navy Department and shipped them to Washington where they were placed in a fire-proof warehouse. I did all that was possible to facilitate the important work."[52]

A passage in a 1907 book about saving and securing Brady's historic images foreshadowed the sometimes conflicting battle between preservation and access: "The Government, as the years passed, became impressed with the value of this wonderful record, but has now officially stated with positive finality: 'It is evident that these invaluable negatives are rapidly disappearing and in order to insure their preservation it is ordered that hereafter negatives shall not be loaned to private parties for exploitation or to subserve private interest in any manner.'"[53]

Taylor wanted these images of the war to be more widely available and viewed, so he sold his collection to Edward Bailey Eaton, who set out to find as many Brady photographs as possible. His quest was aided by *The Review of Reviews*, a national publication, which requested "that persons throughout the country come forward with Brady photos in their possession."[54] The wide variety of places and people that had Brady photographs is described in *The Photographic History of the Civil War in Ten Volumes*:

> From all sorts of sources, from the Atlantic to the Pacific, from Maine to the Gulf, these hidden treasures have been drawn. Historical societies, Government and State bureaus, librarians, private collectors, military and patriotic organizations, old soldiers and their families have recollected, upon earnest insistence, that they did have such things or once knew of them. Singly and in groups they have come from walls, out of archives, safes, old garrets, often seeing the light of day for the first time in a generation, to join together once more in a pictorial army which daily grew more irresistible as the new arrivals augmented, supplemented, and explained. The superb result is here spread forth and illuminated for posterity.[55]

This example of early valiant efforts to save a unique collection of images shows the importance of preservationists in private and public sectors who saw the value of ongoing access to historic images. It also points to the challenges in archiving images: physical deterioration based on the process used to create the image, costs in converting images in one form to create a publishable form, and simple mishaps and mismanagement.

If one small collection dealt with all these issues, imagine the challenges faced as the growing number of news organizations began to shoot, develop, and use photos and to design graphics for use in creating illustrated news.

NEWS ORGANIZATIONS

Newspaper libraries were established to make the daily output of the news product readily available for reuse by news organizations. News libraries were not originally founded with a sense of responsibility for preserving the news for posterity.

Because of the nature of the various media used to shoot and print images, photographic preservation presents challenges unlike the preservation of newsprint. A news organization's photo collection might "consist of albumen, silver gelatin, and color prints; glass, nitrate, and cellulose acetate; and polyester negatives, slides, and other transparencies."[56] The storage units and individual files used to organize color prints, for example, would not be effective for slides.

New York Daily News librarian Maurice Symonds described in a 1926 *Special Libraries* article how the *Daily News* was kept well supplied with photographs:

> In the course of a week, photographs coming to us through this channel [wire photo services], used and unused, number approximately five hundred. But much depends upon our own staff photographers for things locally. . . . Over fifty assignments are covered each day, and several shots are taken of each subject covered. Photographs used and unused, from this source number one thousand a week. Publicity seekers, the mails, the stage and film world also help build up our department. Our city editor constantly sends in photographs of criminals, and missing persons. Editors from the various departments send in batches of photographs to be filed for future use. Counting all in all and from every angle, our weekly total amounts to two thousand photographs.[57]

As for preservation, Symonds had this advice: "The only way to keep a good working picture file is to guard it, keep in touch with it daily . . . insert only photos which have immediate or future use. . . . General weeding or discarding should not be considered until picture files are more than ten years in use."[58]

For some staff photographers, the news organization's photo collection policy was not entirely satisfactory. A survey of National Press Photographers Association members in the early 2000s elicited the following comment: "I also keep a personal archive of 100 percent of my work because of a belief to delete nothing; you never know what will be relevant in 10 years."[59] In some cases, particularly with prominent photojournalists, it is their personal archives that become valuable additions to photographic image collections in libraries and other memory institutions.

LOCAL LIBRARIES AND HISTORICAL SOCIETIES

Where do the resources produced by a newsroom go when the newspaper is shut down or the space available for archiving shrinks? In the early days of newspapers, one local newspaper might have been taken over by another, and their resources in turn were merged. In those early days, little was preserved beyond bound editions of the newspaper. But as newspapers developed archives and photo collections, local memory institutions often were the grateful (and sometimes overwhelmed) recipients of the clips and photos.

The LOC maintains a list detailing where photo archives from regional newspapers have been sent.[60] Photos from ten of California's now-defunct publications reside in a mix of local public libraries, historical societies, museums, and three different state universities. Dispersion adds to the challenge of discovering which institutions have acquired and are preserving historic news photo collections.

For example, after the Los Angeles *Examiner* (founded in 1903) and the Los Angeles *Herald-Express* (founded in 1871) merged to become the afternoon Los Angeles *Herald-Examiner* in 1962, the old *Examiner*'s photo collection of 1.4 million prints and negatives was donated to the University of Southern California. About 24,000 of the prints and negatives have been digitized.[61]

Twenty-seven years later, in 1989, the *Herald-Examiner* folded. Its 2.2 million news photos were given to the Los Angeles Public Library. As of mid-2016, about 26,000 of the images have been made available online.[62] Although it is very important that local memory institutions stepped up to preserve these invaluable local photo collections, the scattering of the archives and the constraints of budgets to make the them widely available present challenges for researchers.

LIBRARY OF CONGRESS

For newspapers, it was mandatory for copyright registration to send a copy of the paper to the LOC. Not so, however, for individual photographs. Therefore, the news photo collections available at the LOC are limited. The George Grantham Bain Collection of 39,744 glass negatives and about 1,600 photographic prints ended up there, as did the photo archives of *Look* magazine and *U.S. News and World Report*.

The only collection of a newspaper's photo archives in the LOC is the *New York World-Telegram & Sun*. The collection's description provides an excellent idea of the scope and state of organization of a typical news photography archive.

> The collection includes an estimated 1 million photographs that the *New York World-Telegram & Sun* newspaper assembled between the 1890s and 1967 (chiefly 1920 to 1967), the year in which the newspaper closed. No original negatives are included in the collection. The collection is divided into two parts: 1) a biographical file which contains portraits and other images related to specific people (750,000 photographs in 300,000

folders), and 2) a subject/geographical file which contains images related to topical subjects and places (250,000 photographs in 50,000 folders). This newspaper photo morgue is typical of the files that newspapers maintain of images that either were published or were believed to have some future publication potential. Such files were periodically weeded by newspaper staff members. Much of the photography used by newspapers is "quick copy," and many images have been cropped, retouched, or highlighted for publication. Some images were taken by the newspaper's staff photographers while others came from wire press services, studios, or amateur photographers. The *New York World-Telegram & Sun* newspaper itself is not indexed, but it has been microfilmed and is available for use in the Newspaper and Current Periodical Reading Room of the Library (LM 133). The clipping file is no longer extant.[63]

COMMERCIAL ENTERPRISES

Although the photo collections of some newspapers that are still being published have been donated to memory institutions, libraries, and universities (usually for some tax deduction), other newspapers facing space crunches and looking for additional revenue streams have sought partnerships with commercial enterprises.

The *New York Daily News*, established in 1919, was one of the first tabloid newspapers, starting a trend of combining columns of text with large photographic images. The *Daily News* partnered with Getty Images, a stock photo agency with an archive of eighty million still images. It is one of the success stories in news photography access. The New York Daily News Pix website[64] provides access to 100,000 images dating back to the publication's launch.

Getty Images also is the distributor of editorial photography from nearly one hundred organizations such as CBS, McClatchy, the *Christian Science Monitor*, and the *Washington Post*. In 2016 Corbis Images, owned by Bill Gates, was sold to the Visual China Group, which then contracted with Getty to provide photo seekers access to Corbis's collection. Although this type of aggregation may provide "one-stop shopping" for photos, it also portends the potential for monopoly pricing and the danger of losing millions of images if this company falls on hard economic times.

The AP's photo archive highlights challenges for news photography producers to generate revenue from their vast databases of resources. According to a Center for Research Libraries report, "Despite its history and ubiquity . . . AP's own news archives do not comprise an uninterrupted historic record. . . . There is historic AP material in a lot of places, but most of it isn't readily accessible."[65] As Chuck Zoeller, AP's special projects manager, explained in an interview, part of the challenge is the existence of two collections of images: analog and digital. Every digital picture transmitted on the wire is permanently saved, but the analog images were continually culled over the decades and fewer than 10 percent have been scanned. Even the storied AP does not have a complete archive.[66]

VISUAL NEWS PRESERVATION CHALLENGES

When the University of Kentucky's Audio-Visual Archive agreed to accept the *Lexington Herald-Leader*'s nearly discarded photo negatives, they were faced with doubling the size of their collection—and a slew of issues the university librarians tried to resolve. After finding little in the literature about how memory institutions managed the challenge of such large collections, the Audio-Visual Archive librarians surveyed other libraries to learn their approaches to the organization, description, maintenance, and preservation of photo morgues.[67]

Of the twenty-four libraries and memory institutions surveyed in 2001 by the university's librarians, 68 percent received collections during the 1970s and 1980s, a time when a number of evening papers shut down, and two- and three-paper towns became one-paper towns. This also was the time frame for the switch to the digital darkroom, when many news organizations were purging their physical photography archives. Some of the libraries had no record of the provenance of their collection's acquisition, and of those that did, there was an equal split between those who had been approached by the news organization about taking the collection and those who had themselves solicited the donation.

The survey identified two major challenges for those libraries that receive huge image collections: providing paths into the collection through enhanced organization and description and providing a preservation environment for the wide variety of materials that might be part of the archive depending on the number of years the collection represents.

Individually describing hundreds of thousands of items in a collection places tremendous burdens on library staffs. University of Kentucky librarian Jennifer Hain Teper explained the labor-intensive process: "Information produced for each series of photographs should include the location, date, and subject of each. This information should be searchable at the very least by a traditional finding aid or inventory but ideally by a tool, such as a database, which allows for nonlinear searches by date, subject, or location. This is especially important if the collection is maintained in the original order produced by the newspaper, which may not easily serve researchers' purposes."[68] Most of the surveyed institutions said this collection description process was "ongoing." Those reporting they had completed the process said it took anywhere from four to twenty-nine years.

Preserving different types of photographs and photographic methods depends on the years during which the photos were produced. The range of a collection might include items representing any of the following:

1851–1920: glass negatives
1860–1940: carbon prints
1880–1920: cyanotype prints
1885–1920: collodion prints
1880–1930: platinum prints
1885–1920: albumen prints
1885–2000s: silver gelatin prints
1890s–1940s: cellulose nitrate sheet film negatives
1920s–late 1950s: cellulose acetate film negatives
1939–2000s: color film negatives
1955–2000s: polyester film negatives

There are multiple challenges for institutions charged with preserving a collection containing so many different formats. Teper describes the many stages of attention these resources require if they are to be safely archived.

> By comparison, rehousing and basic cleaning and stabilization activities for these collections often requires as much or more staff time and much more money for supplies than does the description. In an ideal rehousing project, each item should be inspected for dirt, fingerprints, and physical damage before it is rehoused. When soiled items are found, as is common with the most frequently used photographic negatives and prints, steps should be taken to clean the image before further rehousing or any digitization can proceed. While basic cleaning of negatives and slides can be accomplished in-house using a soft brush, any use of solvents or cleaning of heavily soiled images must be undertaken by a professional. Additional preservation steps that may be taken would include the identification, separation, and reformatting of severely deteriorated acetate and nitrate negatives. If proper storage conditions cannot be met, the original acetate and nitrate negatives may be disposed of, in some cases requiring costly hazardous waste disposal.[69]

Despite these challenges, the effort was well worth it to those who responded to the survey. When asked, "what level of use do these collections receive?" respondents said they were the "most used collection," in "constant use," and "very heavy."[70] It is clear that preserving and making local news images available to the public is a valuable and appreciated part of a community library's mission but one that comes with a high price tag.

PHOTO ARCHIVE USERS

The LOC Prints and Photographs Division has digitally scanned and described hundreds of thousands of images from its collections of fourteen million items.[71] Photojournalism and related graphic arts counterparts are a special strength of the Prints and Photographs Division. With digital scanning, large numbers of people can view the images without handling fragile originals. For example, the glass and film negatives from the George Grantham Bain Collection are kept in cool storage while the scans help users locate photos they may need. Working with the scanning contractor, the LOC recorded the original captions from the Bain Collection, even though those captions were very brief and didn't provide much of the documentation that would be ideal.

To remedy the lack of identifying information, the LOC mounted 1,500 scanned journalistic photos from the Bain Collection on the social networking and photo sharing site Flickr in 2008.[72] The LOC also mounted 1,615 photos from the Farm Security Administration and Office of War Information that were shot during the Great Depression and World War II (1939–1944). The purpose was to ask the public to help identify and tag the photos—a type of crowdsourcing applied to photos. All of the photos were more than fifty years old, so there were no copyright issues with posting the scanned photos. Within twenty-four hours of the project's launch, all of the images had been viewed at least once, and more than 500 photos had received comments. The public added 4,000 unique descriptors to the images in that first day of accessibility.

The Bain Collection photos were tagged by women's suffrage historians who recognized well-known suffragettes; baseball images were tagged by sport historians who could identify baseball players, locations, and activities. Volunteers spotted typos in the Bain Collection captions, provided links to extensive background information on some of the subjects in the photos, and helped fill in documentation gaps.

One example, a portrait from the Bain Collection simply captioned "Corp. S. R. Drew" was enhanced by information from Flickr users. They explained that the photo was of "Sidney Rankin Drew (September 19, 1891–May 19, 1918), American actor and film director. He was flying in the British Aviation Corps and was shot down behind the German lines, *New York Tribune*, June 14, 1918, page 3, col. 1"[73] with links to a Wikipedia article and the *New York Tribune* article from the LOC's "Chronicling America" collection of digitized historical newspapers. Incorporating information supplied by the public obviously required further verification research on the part of the LOC staff, but the Flickr site was monitored by librarians who fact-checked the tags.

An assessment of the program conducted by the LOC in October 2008, ten months after the Flickr experiment was launched, showed that there had been 10.4 million views of the photos. Further, 67,176 tags were added by 2,518 unique Flickr accounts. "This project significantly increased the reach of library content and demonstrated the many kinds of creative interactions that are possible when people can access collections within their own Web communities. The contribution of additional information to thousands of photographs was invaluable."[74]

The successful program led to this conclusion from the LOC staffers involved in creating and monitoring the Flickr site:

> As the novelty of our account has worn off, we now find these historical photos used for a variety of creative purposes—a photo of two World War II nurses illustrates a blog post on giving blood; a half-built skyscraper announces a trip to New York City; a picture of a two-story high stack of paper outside a 1940s paper mill adds a humorous take on a judicial order regarding access to data. Creating a new life for these wonderful old photos has been a direct result of providing these pictures in a venue that makes it easy to share and integrate, mix past and present, and we hope, contribute to a better informed public.[75]

NOTES

1. Emma H. Little, "The Father of News Photography: George Grantham Bain," *Picturescope*, autumn 1972, 125–32.
2. David W. Bulla, *Journalism in the Civil War Era* (New York: Peter Lang, 2010), 90.
3. Ron Garrison, "Wyatt Collection," Kentucky Photo Archive, www.kyphoto archive.com/wyatt-collection/.
4. Robert Luther Thompson, *Wiring a Continent: The History of the Telegraph Industry in the United States, 1832–1866* (Princeton, NJ: Princeton University Press, 1947).
5. "How Illustrated Newspapers Are Made," *Leslie's Illustrated News*, August 2, 1856, 124.
6. "How Illustrated Newspapers Are Made," 124.
7. "The Affair at Chicamacomico," *New York Herald*, October 13, 1861.
8. John Stewart Knox, "Multimodal Discourse on Online Newspaper Home Pages: A Social-Semiotic Perspective" (PhD diss., University of Sydney, 2009), 59.
9. Eric K. Meyer, *Designing Infographics* (El Paso, TX: Hayden Books, 1997), 19.

10. Keith Kenney and Stephen Lacy, "Economic Forces behind Newspapers' Increasing Use of Color and Graphics," *Newspaper Research Journal* 8, no. 3 (1987): 33–41.

11. Edward J. Smith and Donna J. Hajash, "Informational Graphics in 30 Daily Newspapers," *Journalism Quarterly* 65, no. 3 (1988): 714–18.

12. Thompson, *Wiring a Continent.*

13. Thompson, *Wiring a Continent.*

14. Marcus L. Rowland, "Telediagraph," Dead Media Project, www.deadmedia.org/notes/27/279.html.

15. "Pictures Successfully Sent by Telegraph at Last," *San Francisco Call*, May 7, 1899, 19.

16. Charles Emerson Cook, "Pictures by Telegraph," *Pearson's Magazine*, April 1900, 346.

17. Mia Tramz, "Celebrating 80 Years of Associated Press' Wirephoto," *Time*, January 1, 2015.

18. William Glaberson, "The Media Business; Newspapers' Adoption of Color Nearly Complete," *New York Times*, May 31, 1993.

19. David Omar Stowell, *The Great Strikes of 1887* (Champaign: University of Illinois Press, 2008), 21.

20. T. Oldham, "City and Guilds of London Examination in Typography," *The British Printer* (London: Raithby, Lawrence & Co., 1902), 140.

21. "Care of Photographs," Northeast Document Conservation Center, www.nedcc.org/free-resources/preservation-leaflets/5.-photographs/5.3-care-of-photographs.

22. Bonnie Brennan, *For the Record: An Oral History of Rochester, New York, Newsworkers* (New York: Fordham University Press, 2001), 24.

23. "Preservation Self-Assessment Program (PSAP): Photographic Prints," https://psap.library.illinois.edu/format-id-guide/photoprint.

24. "Finding Aid for *New York Journal-American* Photographic Morgue," University of Texas, Austin, Harry Ransom Center, http://norman.hrc.utexas.edu/fasearch/pdf/00509.pdf.

25. J. Sheldon Cartwright, "Value and Depreciation of Photos, Newspaper Clippings and Cuts, from the Appraiser's Standpoint," *Special Libraries* 20, no. 9 (1929): 328–29.

26. Gustav V. Lindner, *Newspaper Library Manual* (New York: Gustav V. Lindner, 1912), 15.

27. Robert William Desmond, *Newspaper Reference Methods* (Minneapolis: University of Minnesota Press, 1933), 12.

28. Desmond, *Newspaper Reference Methods*, 12.

29. Memorandum on News Photo Retention by John Rothman, November 10, 1969, *New York Times* company records, "John Rothman Papers, 1959–1990," *New York Times* Corporate Archives, MssCol 22562, box 1, file 2, Manuscript and Archives Division, New York Public Library.

30. Brian Lambert, "More Trouble for John Rogers, the Man Who Bought the Photo Archives of the *Pioneer Press* and *Star Tribune*," *MinnPost*, June 17, 2015, www.minnpost.com/media/2015/06/more-trouble-john-rogers-man-who-bought-photo-archives-pioneer-press-and-star-tribune.

31. David Koon, "John Rogers Owns More Photos than Anyone, Anywhere," *Arkansas Times*, October 10, 2012.

32. Koon, "John Rogers."

33. Koon, "John Rogers."

34. Koon, "John Rogers."

35. Danielle Kloap, "Rogers Photo Archives Sued by 20 Newspapers," *Arkansas Democrat Gazette*, June 8, 2015.

36. Tony Semerand, "Salt Lake Tribune Gets Back Its Historic Photos, but the Picture Still Isn't Perfect," *Salt Lake Tribune*, May 18, 2016.

37. Michael Carlebach, *Bain's New York* (Mineola, NY: Dover Publications, 2011), vii.

38. Walter Sprange, "Copyright and Reproduction," *The Photographic Times*, January 1897, 80.

39. Carlebach, *Bain's New York*, xxii.

40. Carlebach, *Bain's New York*, xxii.

41. Little, "The Father of News Photography," 130.

42. "The Lively Morgue," *New York Times*, www.nytimes.com/interactive/multimedia/lively-morgue-tumblr.html?_r=0.

43. David W. Dunlap, "Flooding Threatens the Times's Picture Archive," *New York Times*, October 12, 2015.

44. Jessica Bennett, "Inside the New York Times' Photo Morgue, A Possible New Life for Print," May 7, 2012, www.wnyc.org/story/206643-wnyc-tumblr/.

45. Library of Congress, "Report of the Librarian of Congress" (Washington, DC: Library of Congress, 1932), 175. https://memory.loc.gov/service/gdc/scd0002/0007/00072432472/00072432472.pdf.

46. Library of Congress, "Report of the Librarian of Congress."

47. Library of Congress, "Report of the Librarian of Congress."

48. Library of Congress, "Wood Collection of Cartoon and Caricature Drawings," 2010, www.loc.gov/pictures/item/2009632516.

49. Donald W. Smith, "West Hartford Man Owns Rare Camera Record of Civil War Brady's 7,000 Glass Negatives Originally Discovered in Attic," *Hartford Courant*, February 11, 1934.

50. Francis Trevelyan Miller and Robert S. Lanier, eds., *The Photographic History of the Civil War in Ten Volumes* (New York: The Review of Reviews Company, 1912), 52.

51. Miller and Lanier, *The Photographic History*, 52.

52. Edward Bailey Eaton, Mathew B. Brady, and Alexander Gardner, *Original Photographs Taken on the Battlefields: During the Civil War of the United States* (Boston: E. B. Eaton, 1907), 9.

53. Eaton, Brady, and Gardner, *Original Photographs Taken on the Battlefields*, 9.

54. "Edward Bailey Eaton Obituary," *Hartford Courant*, December 29, 1940.

55. Miller and Lanier, *The Photographic History*, 52.

56. Jennifer Hain Teper, "Newspaper Photo Morgues—a Survey of Institutional Holdings and Practices," *Library Collections, Acquisitions, and Technical Services* 28, no. 1 (2004): 108.

57. Maurice Symonds, "Building a Photo Morgue," *Special Libraries* 17, no. 9 (1926): 367–68.

58. Symonds, "Building a Photo Morgue," 367–68.

59. Lucinda Davenport, Quint Randle, and Howard Bossen, "Now You See It; Now You Don't: The Problems with Newspaper Digital Photo Archives," *Visual Communication Quarterly* 14, no. 4 (2007): 218–30.

60. Library of Congress, "Newspaper Photo Morgues," www.loc.gov/rr/print/resource/newsmorgues.html.

61. "Los Angeles Examiner Photographs Collection, 1920–1961," http://digital library.usc.edu/cdm/landingpage/collection/p15799coll44.

62. Scott Harrison, "Los Angeles Herald Examiner Photograph Collection," Framework Blog of the Los Angeles Times, May 12, 2013, http://framework.la times.com/2013/05/12/los-angeles-herald-examiner-photograph-collection/#/0; Christina Rice, senior librarian, Los Angeles Public Library Photo Collection, e-mail message to Paul, May 5, 2016.

63. Library of Congress, "*New York World Telegram & Sun* Newspaper Photograph Collection (Prints and Photographs Reading Room)," www.loc.gov/rr/print/coll/130_nyw.html.

64. Daily News Pix, www.nydailynewspix.com.

65. Victoria McCargar, "Repository Profile: The Associated Press," 2011, www.crl.edu/sites/default/files/attachments/pages/AP_Profile.pdf.

66. Chuck Zoeller (special projects manager, associated press), interview with authors, April 26, 2016.

67. Teper, "Newspaper Photo Morgues."

68. Teper, "Newspaper Photo Morgues," 114.

69. Teper, "Newspaper Photo Morgues," 115.

70. Teper, "Newspaper Photo Morgues," 118.

71. Barbara Orbach Natanson, "Worth a Billion Words? Library of Congress Pictures Online," Journal of American History 94, no. 1 (2007): 101.

72. Brian Braiker, "Crowd-Sourcing a Library of Congress Photo Archive," *Newsweek*, January 23, 2008.

73. Flickr, www.flickr.com/photos/library_of_congress/28172950885/in/photo list-JVxJLv.

74. Michelle Springer, Beth Dulabahn, Phil Michel, Barbara Natanson, David Reser, David Woodward, and Helena Zinkham, "For the Common Good: The Library of Congress Flickr Pilot Project," October 30, 2008, www.loc.gov/rr/print/flickr_report_final.pdf, iv.

75. Springer, Dulabahn, Michel, Natanson, Reser, Woodward, and Zinkham, "For the Common Good," 16.

4

NEWSREELS

> Motion pictures are only 50 or 60 years old, yet much of the early, historically important material has already been permanently lost. We know more about the original documents of William Shakespeare than we do about many important events concerning motion pictures which have occurred during our own lifetime.
>
> —"Report of the Special Committee Investigating the Possibility of Establishing a National Film Archive on the U.C.L.A. Campus," ca. mid-1970s[1]

Dawson City was a small hunting and fishing village in the Yukon Territory until gold was discovered in 1896. By 1898 the population had swelled to 40,000 and the town eventually became the last stop on the silent film circuit. There was no attempt to return the films after that stop. By the late 1920s, 500,000 feet of nitrate film had accumulated in the basement of the town's Carnegie library building. In order to deal with the growing stash of nitrate, town leaders decided to fill in a swimming pool with the film cans, cover them with dirt, and create a hockey rink facility. Fifty years later, in 1978, a bulldozer working on a parking lot dug up the 538 film cans that had been buried in the swimming pool. The earliest was from 1908, and most were from 1913 to 1921, the height of the silent film era. Many reels were thought to have been lost forever, only to be recovered during this accidental excavation.[2]

In 1978, 12.6 million feet of footage from the *Universal Newsreel* collection (almost half of the total) went up in flames when the nitrate film spontaneously ignited in its vaults at the National Archives and Records Administration building in Suitland, Maryland, injuring fourteen firefighters, three civilians, and a police officer. The material lost in the fire covered content from 1929 to 1951 and included scenes from the Great Depression, the bombing of Pearl Harbor, and other World War II footage.[3]

THE NEWSREEL INDUSTRY

By the 1970s, it was clear that a huge proportion of the moving image legacy of the United States had already disappeared. Although the report that opens this chapter was referring primarily to entertainment films, the same could be said of newsreels, the influential new medium of news delivery at the turn of the twentieth century.

Raymond Fielding, a UCLA faculty member, documented the history of the newsreel in his definitive 1972 work, *The American Newsreel, 1911–1967*.[4] The form of news presentation most people recognize as a newsreel grew out of a number of earlier manifestations of news on film. Several innovators in the United States and Europe were experimenting with what they called news "actualities" in the 1890s. These silent film images of boxing matches, a horse race, waves breaking over a pier, and related short snippets of real life were making their way into nickelodeons and theaters.

The newsreel that we recognize today was introduced in the United States in 1911 by the American studio of the French company Pathé. By that time, the market for actualities had fallen off and was replaced by an appetite for a more coherent form of storytelling. *Pathé's Weekly* was advertised as "a film issued every Tuesday, made up of short scenes of great international events of universal interest from all over the world. An illustrated magazine on a film. The news of the world in pictures."[5] During the first year, prints of the newsreel were released to ninety-five theaters.[6]

Once it was clear that there was an audience for this new form of storytelling, competitors to Pathé entered the field. Vitagraph, Kinogram, Selig, and many smaller outfits started generating content, separately or in partnerships that came and went. By 1918 four of the five major players in the United States who would survive in the industry were established: Pathé, Hearst, Universal, and Fox. Paramount introduced a successful newsreel in 1927.[7] By the mid-1920s, ten-minute-long silent newsreels were being distributed to 85 or 90 percent of the 18,000 theaters in the Unites States. These reels were seen by more than forty million people each week. Theater owners paid one or more of the newsreel companies to get their exhibition prints, which were passed from first-run to second-run theaters over several days or weeks before being returned to the newsreel company.[8]

Films with sound had been around since 1895.[9] However, it was not until the Fox Movietone Corporation, the sound division of the Fox newsreel company, was founded in 1926 that sound on film was exploited commercially for newsreels.[10] The first all-sound newsreel of Fox's *Movietone News* debuted at the Roxy Theater in New York City on October 28, 1927.[11] The early sound newsreels presented raw sounds as they were captured by the recording system: voices, airplane engines, and crowd noises. But soon newsreel editors added narration and music to enhance storytelling and to create smooth transitions between sequences.[12]

Newsreel companies based their weekly or twice-weekly "issues" on the newsworthiness of footage that was captured each week by their cameramen. In many ways, newsreel content mirrored that of newspapers. Domestic and international public affairs, sports, fashion, human interest stories, and the arts were typically covered. Many U.S. and foreign newsreel firms had reciprocity agreements that allowed them to buy, sell, and exchange duplicate negatives of each other's weekly content.[13] Every newsreel company built up huge stock-shot libraries containing old newsreel footage. Sound clips were also stored in stock libraries.

As newsreel production values and picture and sound editing techniques improved, however, there was heightened concern about fakery, which had dogged the industry from the very beginning. A prominent film critic of the day complained in *American Mercury* magazine in 1933, "As history, as bottled samples of what is happening now, to be handed down to our great grandchildren, the newsreels are more often than not trivial, lazy, and misleading. . . . They have largely abandoned the service of history and set up shop as entertainers."[14]

In addition to weekly newsreels that covered a variety of topics, a number of specialty newsreels also were produced. In 1942, the weekly *All-American Newsreel* debuted for African American audiences and reached four million people in its first year, running in 365 of the nation's 451 African American theaters. This newsreel became a major source of news on "negro affairs" in the nation's five largest cities. According to an Office of War Information report, 85 percent of the African American community said they got their news from the *All-American Newsreel*.[15]

Newsreels were on their way out as the nascent television industry started its phenomenal growth. At first newsreel companies ignored their new competitor, but by 1950 many newsreel theaters had closed their doors.[16] By the time newsreel producers started allying themselves with the television industry, it was clear that the newsreel as a stand-alone form was dead. *Warner Pathé News* ceased operation in 1956; Paramount stopped newsreel production in 1957; Fox *Movietone News* ended in 1963; and Hearst *Metrotone News* discontinued its U.S. production in November 1967. *Universal Newsreel* was the last to go in December 1967.[17] As newsreel companies shut their doors, some of them sold their extensive film libraries to television networks or to other film companies. The *Universal Newsreel* ended up in the public domain after being deposited in the National Archives in 1970. Where much of the rest of the miles of newsreel footage ended up is a mystery.

WHY NEWSREELS WERE LOST

As was true for early photographs and entertainment films, newsreels were produced on 35-millimeter cellulose nitrate film stock, which is highly flammable. Nitrate film continued to be used until the introduction of cellulose triacetate–based film in 1949.[18] Even though safety (acetate-based) film had been available since the 1910s, newsreel companies used nitrate film because it was less expensive and more durable when run through projectors multiple times.[19] Much of the film from the first half of the twentieth century is lost, the victim of deterioration, disaster, or neglect. Nitrate film crumbled into powder or dust, or it spontaneously ignited in its canisters unless it was stored under the proper conditions. When ignited, nitrate film burns twenty times as fast as wood and can continue to burn under water.[20]

The Suitland fire mentioned at the start of this chapter demonstrates some of the dangers of nitrate film fires. The librarian at Fox's *Movietone News*, Bert Holst, reported in 1946 that the "film morgue" contained "42 million feet of negative scenes shot all over the world" and "a sound library containing every conceivable sound or a good facsimile of any sound."[21] Holst mentioned the danger of fire and deterioration but described the morgue's vaults as being "properly aired" to guard against these problems. He did not mention the disastrous 1937 New Jersey film storage facility fire that caused one death and two injuries and destroyed more than 75 percent of Fox's feature films from before 1930.[22] Once the

Stacks of deteriorating nitrate film and cans. *Courtesy National Archives, photo no. 64-NTA-61-NA-1-656*

problems with nitrate were understood, production companies started to transfer nitrate to acetate-based safety film. They then buried the film cans (in landfills or at sea) or salvaged the silver from the nitrate film as a way to avoid future fires.

However, just as with acetate-based microfilm used for newsprint, the safety theatrical film that replaced nitrate midcentury was equally prone to deterioration. Despite well-intentioned efforts to transfer the volatile nitrate negatives to safety film, acetate film stock suffers from vinegar syndrome, mold, color fading, and other forms of physical damage. Studies indicate that acetate safety film deteriorates within forty to fifty years unless properly stored.[23]

Aside from physical deterioration, another factor in the loss of newsreel film was the fact that the studios simply didn't see any reason to archive it. In a 1993 statement before the National Film Preservation Board of the Library of Congress, film preservationist Robert A. Harris said, "Most of the early films did not survive because of wholesale junking by the studios. There was no thought of ever saving these films. They simply needed vault space and the materials were expensive to house."[24]

Newsreel companies kept stock footage libraries of both images and sound for their own use and for exchange or sale to others. However, most

Acetate film with damage from vinegar syndrome. *CC BY 4.0: © 1993–2016 by Reto Krome*

companies did not archive each week's newsreel as it was exhibited in theaters. The week's issue was cut up into component pieces and logged into the stock footage library as individual snippets. Theater owners received their distribution copies each week, then passed them along to the second-run theaters, and eventually the distribution copies were returned to the newsreel company, where they were likely recycled to recover their silver content or destroyed to prevent piracy.

HOW NEWSREELS WERE PRESERVED

By 1981, the University of California, Los Angeles Film and Television Archive became the permanent home to the extensive Hearst Metrotone News Collection of newsreels consisting of more than twenty-seven million feet (5,000 hours) of footage documenting the fabric of life in the twentieth century.[25] Other archives of newsreels were established long after miles of footage and thousands of hours of content had been lost. Nevertheless, this form of news production played a significant role in creating an audience for news with moving images and, later, with sound. A variety of players have been involved in newsreel archiving efforts.

Individual Collectors and Hobbyists

As was true for newspapers and photographs, individual collectors and hobbyists played an important role in archiving newsreels. George Post was a projectionist at art theaters in San Francisco after emigrating from Russia after World War I. Post collected more than 15,000 newsreel stories about the history of San Francisco from before the 1906 earthquake until 1934. Post also collected many silent entertainment films because he didn't like the "talkies." When the American Film Institute purchased Post's collection in 1970, the archive comprised one of the best records of the history of a specific urban location and its development over time.[26]

Actor George (Andre) Beranger started collecting 28-millimeter films in the late 1910s. He had newsreels from American Biograph and Pathé Frères in his possession, along with many entertainment titles. His collection was eventually purchased by the Academy of Motion Picture Arts and Sciences in 1942.[27]

Businessman John E. Allen had one of the largest private film collections in the United States.[28] As a young man, Allen worked as the film editor for a traveling film exhibitor that offered B-run and older films to small communities without a theater. Allen's job was to edit the films to take out references that dated the performances. As compensation, he was allowed to keep the film he edited out. With this clipped material, he started his film collection. In 1936, Allen incorporated a film-based business in Rochester, New York, and continued to distribute and exhibit films while expanding his personal collection.[29]

In the 1950s, Allen moved the business to New Jersey where he started an archive and a small film preservation laboratory and continued his prodigious collecting. At that time, Allen also sold or transferred a large amount of film and paper documentation to the George Eastman House, where he knew film curator James Card was building a film collection.[30] Allen collected, purchased, and traded in any type of film content, and the bulk of his business was focused on silent features, related paper documentation, and supplemental materials. However, his real passion was for news actualities; Janice Allen remembers her father displaying an original negative of a piece of actuality film from the 1910s and saying, "You can't get any closer to this moment."[31]

Janice Allen also remembers a spectacular fire at their huge storage building that destroyed a major portion of the Allen nitrate collection in 1960. The only part of the collection that survived was what was in the vault at their home. It is clear that Allen rebuilt the collection because at the time of his death in 1976, the archive consisted of 25 million feet of 35-millimeter and 16-millimeter films. The business offered stock footage sales and did film preservation work for the Museum of Modern Art, the George Eastman House, and other archives.[32] The company moved again to northeast Pennsylvania in the late 1980s, with John E. Allen, Inc., maintaining the archive and Cinema Services and Cinema Arts running the film lab.[33]

In 2007, ninety-eight wooden pallets of nitrate film, including many newsreels, were shipped in semitrailer trucks from a former coat factory building in Taylor, Pennsylvania, where the Allen company had been storing them, to the Library of Congress nitrate film vaults, then on the Wright-Patterson Air Force Base in Dayton, Ohio. Due to the less-than-optimal storage conditions in Taylor, many reels were in poor shape and the crew handling the film had to work in hazmat suits to avoid exposure to the dusty nitrate. Shortly thereafter, the Library's National Audio-Visual Conservation Center Packard Campus in Culpeper, Virginia, opened and the reels were moved again, this time to a state-of-the-art facility for preservation and restoration.[34] The gift was described at the time thusly:

> ***John E. Allen, Inc., Collection.*** Donated to the Library in December 2006, the John E. Allen Collection was the most historically significant collection of nitrate film still held in private sector hands, containing many unique and best-surviving 35mm negatives and copies of American fiction and documentary films. Comprising 10,000 items and more than 10 million feet of film, it contains WWI- and WWII-era actualities, sound-era dramatic features, unique early silent films from New York area studios (e.g., Kalem, Solax, and Thanhouser), and "all-black newsreels" from the 1940s.[35]

Another major individual collector, Richard Prelinger, founded the Prelinger Archive in 1983 in New York City. The inventory of the items in the collection provides a record of many individual collectors whose materials ended up with Prelinger.[36] "In 2002, the film collection was acquired by the Library of Congress, Motion Picture, Broadcasting and Recorded Sound Division. Prelinger Archives remains in existence, holding approximately 11,000 digitized and videotape titles (all originally derived from film) and a large collection of home movies, amateur, and industrial films acquired since 2002."[37] The archive includes a number of newsreel items from the 1940s on.[38] A portion of the collection is accessible through the Internet Archive; Getty Images represents the collection for stock footage sales.

Newsreel Company Archives

Newsreel stock footage libraries responded to all manner of requests for content from both in-house and external sources. Fox *Movietone News* librarian Bert Holst said that in 1946 the newsreel film library supplied the industry with millions of feet of stock shots each year. "Practically every West Coast production company uses our facilities, that is when they do not conflict with our service to our parent company, Twentieth Century Fox Film Corporation and of course our own newsreel and short subject department," he said.[39]

From this description, it is clear that many entertainment film production houses used materials from the newsreel libraries of the day. The newsreel companies themselves saw their stock footage libraries as another source of revenue and maintained collections for that purpose rather than as a historical archive of what appeared in theaters.

Memory Institution Archives

The Library of Congress (LOC) started accepting moving-picture images for copyright deposit in 1894.[40] However, actual film was not deposited. Instead, the LOC accepted images on paper strips, which were entered into the collection as photographs. Between 1897 and 1917, approximately 5,000 paper prints of films were submitted for copyright, including many news actualities and early newsreels.[41] Mike Mashon, head of the moving image section of the LOC said about the Paper Print Collection, "its survival can be considered a minor miracle of foresight and serendipity."[42]

After passage of the Townsend Act of 1912, motion pictures were recognized as deserving of copyright protection, and film companies started depositing the film stock itself. However, the LOC had neither the facilities nor the staff to properly care for the highly flammable nitrate film, so the parties agreed that the LOC would register a copyright for a film and then return it to the movie company.[43] The LOC ended up with a strong collection of scripts and memorabilia for the period between 1912 and 1942 but not many actual films.[44]

The Museum of Modern Art (MOMA) in New York established a film library in 1935 and amassed a considerable collection of nitrate prints, which it cataloged and eventually converted to safety stock. When the MOMA's grant funding ran out in 1938, it looked for partners, which it found in the LOC and the Rockefeller Foundation. The result was that the LOC began accepting films for copyright again, with the agreement that MOMA would select and store them.[45]

In 1943, Librarian of Congress Archibald MacLeish initiated a project to restore and organize the collection of 5,000 paper prints, which, it was discovered, could be rephotographed frame by frame to make safety prints of projection quality.[46] The paper prints had been recovered in 1939 from an old vault under the main reading room of the library that hadn't been opened for thirty-five years.[47] A motion picture engineer with the National Archives was tasked with developing a process for restoring the prints without mutilating them.[48]

Anthony Slide's *Nitrate Won't Wait* includes a 1990 interview that he conducted with Howard Walls of the LOC. According to Slide, Walls said that in the 1940s, the library considered newsreels to be a major problem. "We wouldn't want to take all the newsreels, because they were substantially the same. So we thought it would be good to have *Fox Movietone* one year, *Paramount News* the next year, *Pathé* the next year, and so on. Each one would come around every five years."[49] As a result, there are no complete collections of the newsreels from each company at the LOC.

The George Eastman Museum opened in 1949 (as the George Eastman House) to "collect, preserve, study, and exhibit photographic and cinematic objects and related technology from the inception of each medium to the present."[50] The museum's original collections of still photographs were considered among the best in the world, and the museum accepted material from other archives, collections, and artists to add to its holdings. Founding film curator James Card helped establish the museum as a leader in the fields of cinema and film preservation. He had been a personal film collector and his holdings formed the basis of the core collection from the silent era of filmmaking (1895–1928) and the golden age of Hollywood (1920s–1940s) and included newsreels.[51]

By the 1950s, the LOC drew up rules for the descriptive cataloging of film, but concerns about the condition of the collection led to the library surplussing 6.83 tons of nitrate film to the General Services Administration, which sold it as scrap for its silver value.[52] The transition of the paper prints to safety film was completed in 1964 and resulted in the preservation of works by a number of the early newsreel producers, including Edison, Biograph, Vitagraph, Selig, and Pathé.[53]

The National Endowment for the Arts (NEA), established in 1965, included "media arts" in its area of interest. The NEA announced the formation of the American Film Institute in June 1967, with a mandate to cultivate incentives for the production of quality American films, develop appropriate training for filmmakers, and foster preservation of American film.[54] Within three years, a Film Archives Advisory Committee made up of members from the LOC, American Film Institute, the George Eastman House, and MOMA had established an Archival Film Program that worked with other film preservation institutions to advance those efforts.[55]

Films acquired by the American Film Institute became part of the LOC collection. As a result of the establishment of a secure plan for film preservation, private donors and other memory institutions started to clear out their storage facilities. Individuals and institutions such as RKO, Paramount, Warner Brothers, and the Guggenheim Museum unloaded their nitrate and historical films on the LOC.[56]

Academic Institutions

Just as they had neglected to collect newspapers in the early days, academic libraries were equally slow to recognize the appropriateness of film for their collections early on. As early as 1906, film industry publications suggested that academic institutions should play a role. "Perhaps the day will come when motion pictures will be treasured by governments in their museums as vital documents in their historical archives. Our great universities should commence to gather in and save for future students, films of national importance."[57] Needless to say, the call wasn't heeded.

Film studies programs weren't introduced into colleges and universities until the 1960s and early 1970s. Academic libraries collected books and other print materials about film as a subject of scholarly inquiry, but the task of collecting the films themselves, if they were available at all, was taken up by audio-visual centers on campus. It was not until film content started becoming available on laser disc (a precursor to CDs and DVDs) and videotape that academic libraries were able to add this form of material to their collections. When they did purchase films, academic libraries focused on documentaries or films with historical significance.[58]

NEWSREEL PRESERVATION CHALLENGES

Most archivists distinguish between preservation, conservation, and restoration. According to archivist Carolyn Clark Morrow, the differences are as follows:

> *Preservation*: action taken to anticipate, prevent, stop, or retard deterioration.
> *Conservation*: maintenance of each item in the collection in a usable condition.
> *Restoration*: the act of returning the deteriorated item to its original or near-original condition.[59]

For those working with newsreel footage, all three activities are important. Given the fragile nature of the nitrate and acetate film stock, however, the first and most pressing need is to slow physical deterioration, which is inevitable for all film. This requires that the film be stored under conditions of controlled temperature and humidity and that the film be continuously inspected for signs of damage. Ideal conditions call for temperatures ranging from 35 to 45 degrees Fahrenheit and relative humidity levels between 25 and 45 percent, depending on the type of film being preserved.[60] Even after producing a copy of an original film, archivists now also agree that keeping and continuing to preserve originals as historical artifacts is crucial. This means providing for long-term storage and committing to an ongoing inspection routine. Such storage facilities are expensive to build and maintain, as is the personnel required to oversee the stored material.

Conservation requires selectively reproducing fragile originals in newer, more stable formats in order to provide users with access. A study done in 1993 found that much of the early work in film conservation was of substandard quality and needed to be redone.[61] Technical guidelines have since been developed to help archivists do this type of copying properly, using less harmful chemicals and newer processes than were originally employed. Nevertheless, miles of footage, including newsreel stock, have not been conserved and remain inaccessible.

In the case of newsreels, restoration also poses serious problems. Because much of the surviving film stock consists of individual clips, many with the sound removed, it is a puzzle of mind-boggling proportions for archivists to reconstruct originals as they would have been theatrically exhibited. In many instances, it is a case of educated guesswork. And many scholars are more interested in viewing the outtakes—the content that was never used in the first place.[62] So how do archivists select which materials will be restored? Should they restore the sound to individual clips whether they were publicly exhibited or not? Should they restore the version of the newsreel that would have been exhibited in the theater? Should they re-create the logos, text titles, and related newsreel material that was discarded long ago and add that back to the restored version? The issues and problems are endless.[63]

Institutional Preservation Efforts

> Most moving image archives are accidental. Yes, the larger institutions were founded for that specific purpose, and there are specialized institutions that were born to preserve moving images. But most started collecting by accident and preserving out of necessity. And most archivists are latchkey children, working in isolation from the broader culture.
>
> —Rick Prelinger, "We Are the New Archivists: Artisans, Activists, Cinephiles, Citizens," 2010[64]

Once people recognized that it was important to preserve newsreels, a number of efforts began under the auspices of different organizations with a variety of intentions and budgets. In 1978, the film curator at the National Archives prepared a report for the American Film Institute about the crisis in newsreel preservation with recommendations for action.[65] One of the first steps was to identify where such collections might be found.

The National Film Preservation Board (NFPB) was established by the National Film Preservation Act of 1988 and "works to ensure the survival, conservation and increased public availability of America's film heritage."[66] Under the auspices of the LOC, the NFPB is probably best known for its selection of entertainment films each year for preservation, but the collection also includes a number of the early news actualities and early sound experiments done by newsreel companies. Research and experimentation on film preservation methods also is a key aspect of the NFPB.

Researchers conducted a study for the LOC in 1993 that examined the current state of American film preservation[67] and found that despite the work being done by the NFPB and the National Center for Film and Video Preservation at the American Film Institute, there was a film preservation crisis, in part because so many types of films (including newsreels) had been added to the list of materials that should be preserved. The LOC then worked with film industry representatives, technical experts, archivists, and scholars to prepare a report, *Redefining Film Preservation: A National Plan* in 1994.[68]

The National Film Preservation Foundation, a nonprofit organization charged with generating funds to implement the national plan, was authorized by Congress in 1996.[69] Long-neglected types of film, including newsreels, were incorporated into the plan, along with the philosophy that under proper storage conditions, even nitrate film could be archived and retained.[70] Now, once a film is selected by the NFPB, the LOC stores it under the best possible physical conditions in the Packard Campus of the National Audio-Visual Conservation Center in Culpeper, Virginia, a facility with the world's largest and most comprehensive collection of films, television programs, radio broadcasts, and sound recordings.

Professional groups and independent organizations concerned with film also finally started paying attention to newsreels. Fifty-five years after the International Federation of Film Archives was established in 1938, the group convened a symposium called "Newsreel Collections in Film Archives" in 1993.[71] As far as the symposium planners knew, this was the first time people from the newsreel field were brought together.[72] Specialists from around the world described their newsreel collections and discussed best practices for preserving, cataloging, and making accessible the material that had managed to survive.

The National Archives and Records Administration (NARA) also has a role in preserving newsreel content donated to the American public or generated by entities of the U.S. government. Today they describe their collections as follows: "The National Archives and Records Administration has amassed one of the largest and most historically rich documentary film collections in the world. As the official repository for permanently valuable federal records, it possesses over 360,000 reels of film dating from the 1890s to the end of the twentieth century. These films are part of 349 federal and donated motion picture collections within NARA."[73]

MOMA in New York continues to serve as a preservation repository for today's filmmakers. Individual state arts councils, historical societies, museums, and commercial entities also play a role. Members of the Association of Moving Image Archivists, the American Film Institute, and other professional associations continue to bring their archival expertise to preservation efforts. The National Endowment for the Arts and the National Endowment for the Humanities have provided funding for various preservation efforts over the years.

ARCHIVAL NEWSREEL COLLECTIONS

There are many conceivable uses for archival newsreel footage. In June 1979, William Murphy, a NARA archivist working with its newsreel collections, testified before the congressional subcommittee investigating the fire at the Suitland vaults. He said "since the Universal newsreel library was placed in the public domain in 1974, every major film and television organization in the United States has used it at one time or another, including a number of universities," indicating that in a mere four years there had been a rush to access the collection.[74] Film and television production houses referred to the collection as a source of information for set design, costuming, historical site images, and related artistic purposes.[75] Others used the collection for scholarly purposes, described by Murphy in a report prepared for the American Film Institute in 1978, just three months before the NARA fire.[76]

While savvy users recognized that newsreels sometimes included faked and staged content and reflected editorial decisions of news organizations with specific social, political, economic, and communication goals, newsreels nonetheless captured a point in time in a way that the entertainment films of the day did not. Thus, they have both documentary and artistic value. Historians long eschewed the use of news sources—and especially newsreels—as an unreliable—and in many cases academically unacceptable—form of evidence about historical topics, persons, and events.[77] It was not until film studies programs sprang up in the academy in the 1960s and 1970s that news on film was taken as a serious subject of academic study.

Two major collections in academic institutions hold a good part of the newsreel material that has survived. The University of California, Los Angeles (UCLA) Film and Television Archive is home to major portions of the Hearst newsreel legacy and the University of South Carolina (USC) Moving Image Research Collections houses Fox newsreel materials. Both acquired their collections through efforts of individuals who thought newsreel history was important and who worked with university bureaucracies to make it happen.

UCLA Film and Television Archive

> Five hundred years from now, people will look back on this century, the century that discovered film, and ask, "Why didn't they take better care?"
>
> —Robert Rosen, director of the UCLA Film Archive, 1994[78]

The archive was initially established in 1965 with a gift from the National Academy of Television Arts and Sciences Foundation of the then-largest collection of kinescopes, films, and TV ephemera in existence.[79] This ushered in the "buccaneer era" of the UCLA Archive, defined by grassroots preservation efforts taken on by a core group of UCLA faculty members and staff. Maintaining the collection was an extracurricular activity, and the buccaneers continued to add to the archive through personal efforts.[80] The UCLA group was painfully aware of previous film history losses, including the 20,000 DuMont Television Network kinescopes that now rest at the bottom of New York City's East River and the fifty-gallon steel drums full of nitrate prints that Hollywood studios routinely dumped in the Pacific fifteen miles off the Santa Monica coast.[81]

In 1971, archive staff rescued 700 studio nitrate prints of Paramount sound films made between 1928 and 1948 that were destined for disposal. As word of this rescue circulated, more studios, museums, and individual collectors started donating to the archive. By 1976, most of the buccaneers were ready to pass the torch, and film historian Robert Rosen became director of the UCLA Archive.[82] Preservationist Robert Gitt was hired in 1977, and the archive began its work in earnest to preserve and restore newsreel and film collections that were arriving by the truckload.[83]

When UCLA faculty member Raymond Fielding informed the archive staff that the Hearst Metrotone News Collection might be available, they wanted to seize the opportunity.[84] Senior newsreel preservationist Blaine Bartell described UCLA faculty and administrators' efforts to enlist the help of Catherine Hearst, then a regent of the university, who encouraged the Hearst family to deposit the collection at UCLA.[85] Their efforts paid off when the family donated the entire commercial run of its newsreel series in December 1981, along with the copyrights to the content.

The Hearst Metrotone News Collection consists of a variety of materials produced by Hearst between 1919 and 1967. The oldest materials are two silent newsreel titles called *International News* and *International Newsreel* produced by Hearst and distributed by Universal between 1919 and 1929. They represent only a fraction of the total footage that was released. In total, Hearst's Metrotone News Collection includes one hundred thousand feet of the one million feet that once existed. Between 1927 and 1929, Hearst also worked with MGM News, but fewer than 20,000 feet of Hearst's silent MGM News content survives today as part of the UCLA collection.[86]

Most of the UCLA collection is comprised of sound newsreels produced by Hearst in collaboration with MGM between 1929 and 1930 (about 10,000 feet) and the Hearst *Metrotone News/News of the Day* from

1929 to 1967 (27 million feet). However, almost none of the surviving content consists of the newsreels as they were theatrically released. The film donated to UCLA had been broken down into individual stories, and the opening and closing logos had been removed. Further adding to the problem, the film stock used for the titles that introduced each segment of the newsreel was more prone to deterioration than the stock used for the actual images, so those titles also had been removed by Hearst employees at some time in the past.[87]

After Hearst terminated its working relationship with Fox in 1934, Fox kept most of the original materials that had been jointly produced. Hearst's film library at that point consisted of the surviving silent film footage and a set of nitrate projection prints of Hearst *Metrotone News* kept on the MGM studio lot in California.[88] It was still in the hands of MGM in the 1970s when the studio decided it no longer wanted to store the nitrate film. Longtime Hearst film librarian Ted Troll and other Hearst employees in New York convinced King Features, then the Hearst subsidiary in charge of the newsreel collection, to transport these prints to New York rather than have them destroyed by MGM.[89]

The material saved from MGM and the Hearst newsreels produced after the partnership with Fox ended were reconstituted as the Hearst collection donated to UCLA in 1981. Although UCLA owns the rights to the materials in the collection, there are complicated issues involved in licensing materials to outside users. The archive has a media licensing department that helps producers get legal access to content in the collection for commercial uses. Potential licensees receive a screening copy of the content on videotape as part of a licensing agreement. Documentary filmmakers such as Ken Burns and entertainment filmmakers such as Martin Scorcese and Woody Allen have used newsreel clips from the collection for their work.[90] Archive preservationist Blaine Bartell also described a call from staff members from the California Department of Transportation who were hoping to find newsreel footage of California roads as they were being built so that they could do a better job of understanding how to repair or replace them.[91]

The UCLA Film and Television Archive does not actively seek to add to the newsreel collection; it has no acquisition budget and is self-funded through gifts, grants, donations, and licensing proceeds rather than through the university budget. To date, the UCLA Film and Television Archive has transferred more than 10,000 items from the collection to formats available for viewing.[92]

Digital reproduction and conservation efforts also are being considered, but the Film and Television Archive is still doing photochemical duplication in many cases. Otherwise, transfers are made to a digital tape format for viewing. Another factor that complicates digital reproduction relates to ownership and licensing issues for much of the collection. Thus the idea of eventually streaming digitally converted content from the archive remains an elusive goal. Limited funding and staffing also make digital conversion difficult and time consuming, and concerns about the backward compatibility and longevity of prospective digital formats means that the archive will always be cautious about digital conservation.[93] And many purists insist that nothing replaces the rich and nuanced images of the original nitrate film.

The Moving Image Research Collections

> The University is prepared to accept not only the estimated 50 million feet of acetate-based film, but the cellulose nitrate–based film as well. The University recognizes that such film will be lost forever if it is not properly maintained, and proposes to evaluate, catalogue, and convert to "safety" film, as indicated by value, the nitrate outtakes.
>
> —"The University of South Carolina and the Twentieth Century-Fox Movietonews [sic] Film Library," 1979[94]

The Moving Image Research Collections at the University of South Carolina (USC) in Columbia is home to the archive of Twentieth Century Fox Film Corporation's *Fox News* (silent) and *Movietone News* (with sound) newsreels. Once again, it was the efforts of several individuals who shepherded the collection to its USC home. Twentieth Century Fox had maintained the stock footage library for *Fox News* and *Movietone News* after Fox ceased production in 1963 and then opened its New York library to the industry for stock footage sales.

In the early 1970s, a USC faculty member and independent producer, Jim Jackson, began efforts to have the Fox library deposited at the university for educational purposes. Jackson was friends with broadcast legend Lowell Thomas, who had been the voice of *Movietone News* since 1935. The two men had worked with South Carolina Educational Television to successfully produce a PBS series, narrated by Thomas, built around newsreel footage from the Fox collection. The *Lowell Thomas Remembers* series impressed Fox executives, who admired the university's commitment to converting newsreel footage into educational productions and believed that USC was dedicated to newsreel preservation.[95]

The appraised value of the Fox collection in 1980 was $100 million.[96] The tax benefit of a donation of that size was an important factor for Twentieth Century Fox. In fact, both the Hearst Corporation and Twentieth Century Fox were applying to Congress for legislation[97] and to the Internal Revenue Service for rulings that would provide the best tax benefit for their film library donations to nonprofit institutions (in both cases, public universities).[98] At the time, the law prohibited charitable donations that exceeded 5 percent of corporate gross income in a single year. Both Hearst and Fox wanted donation caps raised to 30 percent to avoid dragging out their delivery of film to external institutions over many years.

The Fox film collections were extensive and were located across the world. At the height of the company's production in the late 1930s, newsreels were being produced in New York, London, Paris, Berlin, and Sydney, and they were released in fifty countries in forty-seven different languages. When the gift to USC was being considered in 1979, the storage locations of film collections included:

- a Fox facility at 54th Street in New York;
- Rank Film Laboratories in Britain;
- Fox Film Germany in Munich;
- Fox Movietone in France;
- Movietonews Australia;
- a Davenport, Iowa, library of film formerly stored on the Fox West Coast lot;
- *Movietone News* materials stored in Ogdensburg, New Jersey;
- materials that had been given to the National Archives and the Library of Congress; and
- materials given to the Library and Archives Canada.[99]

Each collection included silent and sound film, and in some instances a mix of both nitrate and acetate-based stock. The vaults (repurposed World War II–era concrete bunkers) in Ogdensburg stored nitrate only, but the conditions did not even minimally meet the standards for storing such volatile film.

Needless to say, the widespread geographic locations of the libraries and the varied nature and condition of the film stock were major topics of concern in negotiations between Fox and USC.

The tax implications of the proposed donations were eventually sorted out to the satisfaction of corporate executives negotiating the deal.[100] Twentieth Century Fox Film Corporation announced in January 1980

Movietone News nitrate film storage vaults in Ogdensburg, New Jersey. *Courtesy Moving Image Research Collections, University of South Carolina*

that it was making "one of the largest corporate gifts in American history" by donating to the University of South Carolina the "largest collection of newsfilm in the world."[101] The announcement included mention of a plan for USC to build a Fine Arts Center that would include facilities to house and maintain Fox's materials.

Two annual "deeds of gift" in 1980 and 1981 laid out a plan for Fox to convert the volatile nitrate film stock to safety stock and to convey all the copyrights for the newsreels to USC, a condition for the company to be able to claim tax benefits from the donation. In addition to the converted newsreel films themselves, the gift also included filing cabinets full of continuity sheets, film library index cards, and related paper documentation about the generation, use, and disposition of individual news image and sound clips through the decades. The shipments of gift materials started arriving on campus in March 1980.

But the deal started to unravel after Fox ownership changed hands and the new owner, oil man Marvin Davis, balked at the cost of converting nitrate film. He also bristled at the thought of losing rights to the *Fox*

News and *Movietone News* libraries. Additionally, the proposed Fine Arts Center at USC was a victim of state house legislative bickering and never received funding. As renegotiations over the already signed "deeds of gift" continued, USC agreed to accept nitrate film even though it meant storing the volatile reels in ammunition bunkers at the U.S. military's nearby Fort Jackson facility.[102]

By the time the "deeds of gift" expired, the university had accepted seven million feet of original nitrate stock and four million feet of safety film transfers that had been made by Fox. As for rights to the portions of the collection that still hadn't been transferred, Fox's Movietone News, Inc., stock footage sales division stayed open for business in New York.[103] In the mid-2000s, Fox negotiated a deal with the LOC to deposit the remainder of the collections to get them out of the New York offices. Fox retained the rights to all of the material deposited with the LOC, however, meaning that the collection there is of limited use to any except those who can pay the licensing fees.[104]

Nevertheless, the collection that was transferred to USC includes silent and sound moving-image records of invaluable importance. All the silent newsreel nitrate clips from the original *Fox News* library (1919–1930) and the related paper documentation is available. The collection also includes all of the outtakes and unused film (some on safety film, most on nitrate) from volumes 1 through 7 of Fox *Movietone News* with sound from 1928 to 1934 and the paper archive supporting that material. The collection also includes the Fox newsreels as they actually ran theatrically along with outtakes and unused film from volumes 25 and 26 of Fox *Movietone News* (September 1942–August 1944) on safety film, plus the paper archive relating to that content.[105]

The paper files are in filing cabinets and the acetate film canisters are housed in climate-controlled vaults in the Moving Image Research Collections (MIRC) building on the edge of the USC campus, along with work space for eight staff members. The nitrate reels are still at Fort Jackson. Curator Greg Wilsbacher described the access issues posed by military security measures at Fort Jackson. After the September 11 attacks in 2001, MIRC staff lost access to the nitrate vaults for several months as the fort tightened security. And after an undisclosed security threat was identified on the base in 2014, the MIRC once again lost access to the vaults. Since that time, any person stepping foot on the base must have Department of Defense security clearance, meaning that only two MIRC staff can now get access to the nitrate collection.[106]

The new security measures at the fort affected the annual Film Library Inspection Program. Once a year, in a three-day effort, staff and student volunteers would open every nitrate film canister in the vaults, inspect each reel, and turn it over in its canister. Any signs of deterioration or damage would be noted, and the canisters removed for further film inspection and repair. That type of inspection is now done by the nitrate film manager during his daily trips to the vaults. Wilsbacher estimated that it now takes two years for the nitrate film manager to visually inspect the entire collection.[107]

Despite these limitations, much of the Fox collection is accessible via streaming from the MIRC website. Film is transferred to digital formats as requested and as deemed appropriate by newsreel staff. Because the MIRC maintains the rights to its holdings, a staff member handles licensing for commercial users. The collection has been used by many media professionals, including Ken Burns, who used content for his documentary series on American baseball.[108]

As a result of the publicity surrounding Fox's gift to USC, a number of other collections were donated to the university. For example, an individual newsreel collector, C. E. Feltner, donated his entire collection of newsreels from a variety of producers. Another collection came from celebrated father and son newsreel cameramen from Chicago, Harry and William Birch. Harry was a news cameraman starting in 1915 and his son William followed him into the business, first as a cameraman with Fox *Movietone News* and eventually in television, where he established the NBC Network News Bureau in Chicago. Several local television stations also donated their archival film to USC.

AN ARTIST'S VIEW OF NEWSREEL ARCHIVES

Artist and documentarian Bill Morrison has used archival newsreel film for a variety of projects. For his 2002 film *Decasia*, Morrison sought out deteriorating silent film to create a meditation on the nature of decay, the passage of time, and the process of filmmaking itself. The images come from real films that are decaying, mostly nitrate stock from before 1929. Clouds, bubbles, scratches, and blobs move across the screen as the original images interact with them through Morrison's selection and editing. A boxer from a silent actuality film appears to battle a blob of decay as it moves toward him. The score by Michael Gordon adds out-of-tune pianos and an off-tempo orchestra to Morrison's artistry. *Decasia* was the first twenty-first-century production selected, in 2013, for preservation in the U.S. National Film Registry.

Morrison made an earlier film about the deteriorating Paper Print Collection in the LOC: his 1996 release, *The Film of Her.* Morrison was at the inaugural Orphan Film Symposium at the University of South Carolina in 1999 to present that film, and at that time he visited the Moving Image Research Collections to explore its holdings. He was looking specifically for newsfilm that displayed emulsion deterioration.[109] On that very first visit, Morrison found the bit of film with the boxer and the blob. That convinced him that the project *Decasia* was viable. Work proceeded from there.[110] Other footage came from the LOC, MOMA, the George Eastman House, and the Cinémathèque Suisse.

In an interview, Morrison explained that he likes the unrehearsed aspect of newsreel and news actuality film. Images of non-actors in natural settings, even if some of the content was faked or reproduced, are markedly dissimilar to the actors and images in scripted silent entertainment films of the same time period. Morrison said, "I'd like to think that anything is fair game, but I just prefer real people."[111]

Morrison described a new project, *Dawson City: Frozen in Time.* The Dawson City nitrate film discovery was described at the start of this chapter. After being unearthed from the permafrost, the nitrate films were repatriated to the Library and Archives Canada or to the LOC, depending on each newsreel's source. The libraries shared the cost of restoration and gave each other masters of the entire collection.

Morrison is making a documentary about the collection and about the beginnings of cinema reflected in that collection. "A newsreel is a time capsule. The swimming pool was a time capsule filled with little time capsules."[112] The value of newsreels from this early period, he says, is that there wasn't much "big corporate" oversight of the content. Stories could be told without some of the later editorial and political filters that emerged as the newsreels became big business. Early newsreels reflected how language operated in culture (a labor agitator one year might be described as a terrorist another), and they reflected the changing world events that were deemed newsworthy. Morrison supplements the newsreel content with what he finds in newspaper accounts from the same location and time period to flesh out the documentary.

When asked how well the newsreel collections are indexed for his purposes, Morrison said it varies. Some of the collections are well described; the South Carolina MIRC is where he usually starts because he says the films there have both "excellent descriptions and excellent deterioration" (if that is what he is looking for). If he used "Yukon" as a search term for the Dawson City project, however, it would turn up far too much material, so he has to start narrowing his searches. His search involves "serendipity, but I am setting the parameters. Then it becomes problem solving."[113] For example, if he wanted to represent what it might have looked like as horses were hauling the newsreel cans to the swimming pool, he would search for "hauling" and "horse." For an image of permanence, he would search for an image of "laying a cornerstone."

Morrison says his attitude is "very opportunistic" when looking for deteriorated film. He has a rare level of personal access to the film vaults at the Packard Campus of the National Audio-Visual Conservation Center collection in Culpeper. He has a production budget to scan the deteriorating film, and staff at the LOC Packard Campus keep an eye out for things that might interest him.

Ironically, for someone so involved with archival film, Morrison experienced his own archival disaster. Morrison's house was under twelve feet of water after Superstorm Sandy in 2012 and he lost a lot of film. Luckily, the negative masters were being stored in a lab in Pennsylvania, and he had the lab reprint the film. But that lab is now out of business and there aren't many labs that can still do black-and-white film printing. In fact, Rob Stone, the LOC moving image curator, said during a 2016 tour of the National Audio-Visual Conservation Center Packard Campus that the library's six film processors "will be the last lab standing" for this type of work in the near future.[114]

NOTES

1. "Report of the Special Committee Investigating the Possibility of Establishing a National Film Archive on the U.C.L.A. Campus," ca. mid-1970s, National Library of Television hanging file, UCLA Film and Television Archive, Los Angeles, California. The Online Archive of California has a copy, incorrectly dated 1958, in box 94, folder 4. Mark Quigley at the UCLA Film and Television Archive confirmed in an e-mail to Hansen, July 25, 2016, that the correct date is the mid-1970s.

2. Bill Morrison, "Director's Statement/Notes on *Dawson City: Frozen in Time*," 2014, www.picturepalacepictures.com/DAWSON_CITY__FROZEN_TIME.html.

3. Associated Press, "Flames Destroy Old Newsreels in Washington," *Los Angeles Times*, December 7, 1978; M. C. Hudson and Robert MacLauren, *Nitrate Film Testing for the National Archives: December 1978 Fire Investigation* (Indian Head, MD: Naval Ordnance Station, 1979); *National Archives and Records Service Film-Vault Fire at Suitland, Maryland: Hearings before a Subcommittee of the Committee on Government Operations, House of Representatives*, 96th Cong., 1st sess., June 19 and 21, 1979; "Sprinkler System Blamed in Suitland Blaze," *Washington Post*, December 12, 1978;

U.S. Congress, *National Archives Film-Vault Fire, Suitland, Maryland, December 7, 1978: Fifth Report* (Washington, DC: GPO, 1979).

4. Raymond Fielding, *The American Newsreel, 1911–1967* (Norman: University of Oklahoma Press, 1972).

5. Fielding, *The American Newsreel*, 72–73.

6. Fielding, *The American Newsreel*, 75.

7. Fielding, *The American Newsreel*, 108.

8. Fielding, *The American Newsreel*, 133.

9. Fielding, *The American Newsreel*, 159.

10. Fielding, *The American Newsreel*, 161.

11. Fielding, *The American Newsreel*, 163.

12. Fielding, *The American Newsreel*, 167.

13. Fielding, *The American Newsreel*, 199.

14. Robert Littell, "A Glance at the Newsreels," *American Mercury*, November 1933, 263.

15. "Negro Newsreel Seen by 4,000,000," *American Cinematographer*, November 1943, 408.

16. Fielding, *The American Newsreel*, 307.

17. Fielding, *The American Newsreel*, 309.

18. Anthony Slide, *Nitrate Won't Wait: A History of Film Preservation in the United States* (Jefferson, NC: McFarland, 1992), 1.

19. Henry Anderson, "Fire Safety in the Motion Picture Industry," *Quarterly of the National Fire Protection Association* 30, no. 1 (July 1936): 27.

20. Anderson, "Fire Safety in the Motion Picture Industry," 27.

21. Bert Holst, "The Newsreel—Its Production and Significance: The Film Library," *Journal of the Society of Motion Picture Engineers* 47, no. 5 (1946): 365.

22. James L. Neibaur, *The Fall of Buster Keaton: His Films for MGM, Educational Pictures, and Columbia* (Lanham, MD: Scarecrow Press, 2010).

23. James M. Reilly et al., *IPI Storage Guide for Acetate Film* (Rochester, NY: Image Permanence Institute, 1993).

24. "Robert A. Harris's Statement at the Film Preservation Study: Washington, D.C., Public Hearing, February 1993," www.widescreenmuseum.com/rah.htm.

25. UCLA Film & Television Archive, "About the Archive," www.cinema.ucla.edu/about-archive.

26. David Shepard, "The Search for Lost Films," *Film Comment* 7, no. 1 (1971): 62.

27. Slide, *Nitrate Won't Wait*, 51.

28. Slide, *Nitrate Won't Wait*, 52; Janice Allen (owner, Cinema Arts), interview with Hansen, April 5, 2016.

29. Allen interview.

30. Allen interview.

31. Allen interview.

32. Slide, *Nitrate Won't Wait*, 54.

33. Allen interview.

34. George Willeman (nitrate film vault manager, Library of Congress), e-mail message to Hansen, March 9, 2016.

35. Library of Congress, "Update for 2007 ALA Midwinter Meeting: June–December, 2006," www.loc.gov/ala/mw-2007-update.html.

36. Prelinger Archives, "FAQ: Licensing, Access, Collections," www.prelinger.com/prelarch.html.

37. Prelinger Archives, "Internet Archive," https://archive.org/details/prelinger&tab=about.

38. Prelinger Archives, "Internet Archive," https://archive.org/details/prelinger.

39. Holst, "The Newsreel," 366.

40. Doug Herrick, "Toward a National Film Collection: Motion Pictures at the Library of Congress," *Film Library Quarterly* 13, nos. 2–3 (1980): 6.

41. Herrick, "Toward a National Film Collection," 14.

42. Mike Mashon, "10th Orphan Film Symposium (April 6–9, 2016): Bill Morrison and the Paper Print Collection," Now See Hear! The National Audio-Visual Conservation Center Blog (Library of Congress), March 10, 2016, http://blogs.loc.gov/now-see-hear/2016/03/10th-orphan-film-symposium-april-6-9-2016-paper-prints/.

43. Herrick, "Toward a National Film Collection," 10.

44. Herrick, "Toward a National Film Collection," 10.

45. Slide, *Nitrate Won't Wait*, 21.

46. Herrick, "Toward a National Film Collection," 14.

47. Bill Morrison, *The Film of Her*, 12 min., 1996, 35mm, http://billmorrisonfilm.com/short-films/the-film-of-her/1; Slide, *Nitrate Won't Wait*, 38.

48. Carl Louis Gregory, "Resurrection of Early Motion Pictures," *Journal of the Society of Motion Picture Engineers* 42, no. 3 (1944): 159–69.

49. Slide, *Nitrate Won't Wait*, 25.

50. George Eastman Museum, "History of the George Eastman Museum," https://eastman.org/history-george-eastman-museum.

51. Slide, *Nitrate Won't Wait*, 56; George Eastman Museum, "Founding Curator: James Card," https://eastman.org/james-card.

52. Herrick, "Toward a National Film Collection," 17.

53. Herrick, "Toward a National Film Collection," 19; Slide, *Nitrate Won't Wait*, 38.

54. Sarah Ziebell Mann, "American Moving Image Preservation, 1967–1987," (MLIS thesis, University of Texas at Austin, 2000), 14.

55. Mann, "American Moving Image Preservation," 19.

56. Herrick, "Toward a National Film Collection," 22.

57. "History and Motion Pictures," *Views and Film Index*, December 1, 1906, 1.

58. Kristine R. Brancolini and Beverly L. Teach, "Film Studies Collections," in *Managing Performing Arts Collections in Academic and Public Libraries*, ed. Carolyn A. Sheehy (Westport, CT: Greenwood, 1994), 73–74.

59. Paraphrased in Wesley L. Boomgaarden, "Preservation Planning for the Small Special Library," *Special Libraries* 76, no. 3 (1985): 204.

60. Annette Melville and Scott Simmon, *Film Preservation 1993: A Study of the Current State of American Film Preservation* (Washington, DC: Library of Congress, 1993).

61. Melville and Simmon, *Redefining Film Preservation: A National Plan; Recommendations of the Librarian of Congress in Consultation with the National Film Preservation Board* (Washington, DC: Library of Congress, 1994).

62. Blaine Bartell (senior newsreel preservationist, UCLA Film and Television Archive), interview with Hansen, February 18, 2016.

63. Henning Schou, "Preservation of Newsreels," in *Newsreels in Film Archives: A Survey Based on the FIAF Newsreel Symposium*, ed. Roger Smither and Wolfgang Klaue (Trowbridge, Wiltshire, UK: Flicks Books, 1996), 92–95.

64. Rick Prelinger, "We Are the New Archivists: Artisans, Activists, Cinephiles, Citizens," (presentation, Reimagining the Archive, UCLA, Los Angeles, CA, November 13, 2010).

65. William T. Murphy, "Appendix 8.—American Film Institute-Sponsored Study of Preservation of Newsreels," in *National Archives and Records Service Filmvault Fire*, 409–37.

66. National Film Preservation Board, "About This Program," www.loc.gov/programs/national-film-preservation-board/about-this-program.

67. Melville and Simmons, *Film Preservation 1993*.

68. Melville and Simmons, *Redefining Film Preservation*.

69. "National Film Preservation Foundation: Why the NFPF Was Created," www.filmpreservation.org/about/why-the-nfpf-was-created.

70. Melville and Simmons, *Redefining Film Preservation*.

71. Smither and Klaue, *Newsreels in Film Archives*.

72. Smither and Klaue, *Newsreels in Film Archives*, viii.

73. Phillip W. Steward, "Frame after Frame: Taking a Look at the Motion Picture Collections in the National Archives," *Prologue Magazine*, summer 2010, www.archives.gov/publications/prologue/2010/summer/frame-film.html.

74. *National Archives and Records Service Filmvault Fire*, 85.

75. *National Archives and Records Service Filmvault Fire*, 169.

76. Murphy, "Appendix 8," 417–18.

77. Mia E. M. Treacey, *Reframing the Past: History, Film and Television* (New York: Routledge 2016), 36–50.

78. Adrian Maher, "Reeling in the Past: Preservation," *Los Angeles Times*, June 12, 1994.

79. *UCLA Film & Television Archive: 50 Years* (Los Angeles: Regents of the University of California, 2015), 13.

80. *UCLA Film & Television Archive*, 13.

81. *UCLA Film & Television Archive*, 14.

82. *UCLA Film & Television Archive*, 12, 14, 18.

83. *UCLA Film & Television Archive*, 22.

84. *UCLA Film & Television Archive*, 31.

85. Bartell interview.

86. "Hearst Metrotone News Collection," UCLA Film and Television Archive, www.cinema.ucla.edu/collections/hearst.

87. "Hearst Metrotone News Collection."

88. "Hearst Metrotone News Collection."

89. "Hearst Metrotone News Collection."

90. Bartell interview.

91. Bartell interview.

92. "Hearst Metrotone News Collection."

93. Bartell interview; Mark Quigley (director, UCLA Film and Television Archive, Research and Study Center), interview with Hansen, February 19, 2016; Dan Einstein (television archivist, UCLA Film and Television Archive), interview with Hansen, February 19, 2016.

94. Pamphlet, "The University of South Carolina and the Twentieth Century-Fox Movietonews Film Library," attached to letter from James B. Holderman, president, USC, to Dennis Stanfill, chairman and CEO, Twentieth Century Fox, December 3, 1979, Twentieth Century Fox Correspondence, Raymond Bennett papers, MSS collection at the University of South Carolina, Moving Image Research Collections, Columbia, SC.

95. Greg Wilsbacher, "The Fox Movietone News Donation: A Brief History," http://library.sc.edu/p/Collections/MIRC/FoxMovietoneNewsGift.

96. *Appraisal Report: Movietone News Film Library* (Milwaukee, WI: American Appraisal Company, March 10, 1980), Twentieth Century Fox correspondence.

97. A bill to encourage film corporations to donate certain historical film to educational organizations by increasing the limit on the charitable contribution deduction of such corporations, S. 3238 and H.R. 8137, 96th Cong. (1979–1980).

98. Raymond T. Bennett to commissioner of Internal Revenue, ca. 1979, "A Ruling Is Respectfully Requested," Twentieth Century Fox correspondence.

99. Memorandum by Jack Muth to all concerned, October 18, 1979, "Movietone Conversion Project," Twentieth Century Fox correspondence.

100. Memorandum by Jim Kelly to Richard Garzilli, Ray Bennett, and Robert E. Frisch, December 5, 1979, Twentieth Century Fox correspondence.

101. "Fox Donates Movietonews Footage to University of South Carolina," Twentieth Century Fox Film Corporation News, Los Angeles, January 3, 1980, Twentieth Century Fox correspondence.

102. Memorandum by Raymond T. Bennett, April 21, 1982, "Movietonews—N.Y. Meeting," Twentieth Century Fox correspondence.

103. Wilsbacher, "The Fox Movietone News Donation."

104. Greg Wilsbacher (curator, Moving Image Research Collections, University of South Carolina), interview with Hansen, March 28, 2016.

105. Wilsbacher, "The Fox Movietone News Donation."

106. Wilsbacher interview.

107. Wilsbacher interview.

108. Wilsbacher, "The Fox Movietone News Donation."

109. Dave Heaton, "Portrait of Decay: Bill Morrison on *Decasia*," *Erasing Clouds*, Issue 13, April 2, 2003, www.erasingclouds.com/02april.html.

110. Bill Morrison (filmmaker), interview with Hansen, April 8, 2016.

111. Morrison interview.

112. Morrison interview.

113. Morrison interview.

114. Hansen tour of Library of Congress National Audio-Visual Conservation Center, Packard Campus, Culpeper, VA, April 6, 2016.

5

RADIO NEWS

> Sound recordings have existed as one of the most salient features of America's cultural landscape for more than 130 years. As a nation, we have good reason to be proud of our historical record of creativity in the sound recording arts and sciences. However, our collective energy in creating and consuming sound recordings in all genres has not been matched by an equal level of interest, over the same period of time, in preserving them for posterity.
>
> —*The State of Recorded Sound Preservation in the United States*, 2010[1]

Researchers interested in local radio broadcasts are frequently frustrated; few local radio stations archived their programs. But scholars interested in Cincinnati, Ohio, radio history are in luck, thanks to Edwin B. Dooley. Dooley began working at WLW, the local radio and television station, as a broadcast engineer in the 1950s. During the next forty years he used a technique employed by many rescuers of tossed news, the dumpster dive. The collection of rescued airchecks, transcription discs, equipment, and other recordings numbered in the thousands when it was donated by Dooley's widow to the Library of American Broadcasting at the University of Maryland. In all, 1,471 cellulose acetate transcription records, 3,612 vinyl records, and 235 reel-to-reel tapes capturing local radio broadcasts from the past can be heard today.[2]

THE RADIO INDUSTRY

Between 1886, when Heinrich Hertz offered proof that electromagnetic waves could be transmitted and received wirelessly, and 1906, when Reginald Fessenden made the first long-range voice transmission from Brant Rock, Massachusetts, the building blocks of wireless voice transmission were created by a large cast of inventors and scientists.

Initially, the "wireless telegraph" was seen as a boon for ship-to-shore communication. The 1912 Titanic disaster and the mangled radio communication about its status helped add urgency to national legislation that was already being planned to regulate the use of radio waves. The Radio Act of 1912 established communications backup requirements for maritime operations, and it instituted the requirement that all radio operations be licensed by the government.

Radio was under the control of the U.S. government during World War I, but by 1918 the commercial enterprises that would come to dominate the market had established a tradition of private radio ownership. The Radio Corporation of America, General Electric, Westinghouse, Western Electric, International Radio Telegraph Company, and AT&T were busy dividing up broadcast patents and functions. By 1920 the path for American radio broadcasting was set.[3]

In 1920, *Detroit News* owner William Scripps also saw the market potential for radio transmission and radio's potential challenge to newspapers' virtual monopoly on news delivery. A young radio pioneer, Michael DeLisle Lyons, was hired by Scripps initially to fix the antenna for a radio broadcast facility they were building in a corner of the newspaper's newsroom. They were anxious to test news delivery via the airwaves.

The U.S. Department of Commerce and Labor regulated radio at that time. Scripps instructed Lyons to request permission to broadcast in Detroit. The new station began to experiment with broadcasting music on August 20, 1920, using the call letters 8MK (though the call letters changed to WWJ in 1922). After two weeks of practice, the radio project team felt ready to use this new medium to deliver election results for the local, state, and congressional primary.[4]

Readers of the September 1, 1920, *Detroit News* front page learned about the paper's move into a new news medium:

> The sending of the [primary] election returns by *The Detroit News*' radiophone Tuesday night was fraught with romance and must go down in the history of man's conquest of the elements as a gigantic step in his

> progress. In the four hours that the apparatus, set up in an out-of-the-way corner of The News Building, was hissing and whirring its message into space, few realized that a dream and a prediction had come true. The news of the world was being given forth through this invisible trumpet to the waiting crowds in the unseen market place.[5]

The broadcast, heard by people in roughly thirty Detroit-area households that had radio receivers, heralded the beginning of a new age of news.[6] Learning about news as it was unfolding was now possible, because radio provided an immediacy that even a "stop the presses" extra edition of a newspaper could not satisfy.

In Pittsburgh, Pennsylvania, a Westinghouse employee named Frank Conrad had been transmitting phonograph music and connecting with amateur radio operators since 1916. A few months after the first radio newscast in Detroit, Conrad was encouraged by Westinghouse executives to build a stronger wattage transmitter in order to create content for the growing number of Westinghouse radio purchasers. On the evening of November 2, 1920, KDKA transmitted news of the U.S. presidential election results.[7]

Because Detroit's WWJ radio was founded in a newsroom, the broadcast content was journalistically oriented. Alternatively, Westinghouse's KDKA broadcast sporting events, plays, and church services along with its news bulletins.[8] The appetite for radio transmission was whetted and within four years there were 600 radio stations nationwide.[9]

Equipment manufacturers and department stores were early investors in radio stations—the former to sell equipment, the latter to serve as publicity and promotion vehicles for their establishments.[10] According to a Commerce Department's report in 1922, "Among the 98 sending stations are 10 newspapers, a church, a YMCA, several large department stores, and two municipalities. Many manufacturers, radio sales and equipment shops, and five universities are also sending out amusement features in several forms so that today 'all who listen may hear'"[11] By December 1922, radio broadcasting operations were running in every state in the nation.

Public clamoring for the latest technology overwhelmed manufacturers, with customers standing in long lines to complete order forms for radios after the dealers' in-house supplies were exhausted. Between 1923 and 1930, 60 percent of American families purchased radios.[12]

A new federal regulatory structure responded to this increase in broadcasting business and the chaos caused by overlapping radio signals in many markets. The Federal Radio Act of 1927 replaced the 1912 version and established the Federal Radio Commission (which would subsequently be replaced by the Federal Communications Commission in 1934). The act included a provision that was used in the regulation of other public utilities: that radio must conduct its operation in the "public interest, convenience, and necessity."[13]

Except for occasional news flashes and some public affairs content such as political speeches or presidential addresses, most radio programs in the 1920s were live concerts, quiz shows, and radio plays. Early restrictions kept the stations from broadcasting very much news, and the little news content that was broadcast from this period hasn't survived. Part of the reason news programs were not a regular feature of the program offerings was an early, and reasonable, concern about the powerful newspaper industry.

The Press-Radio War

Newspapers, which had long had a monopoly on the distribution of daily news, eyed the potential radio news competition with caution. Newspapers feared this competing source for news distribution could threaten their bottom lines, both in terms of competition for advertising dollars and for subscribers who could now get news for free. Some newspapers launched radio stations and used short news flashes as a way to steer people to their newspapers.

The Radio Corporation of America (RCA), a major manufacturer and distributor of radio equipment, also was acquiring radio stations. Under the leadership of president David Sarnoff, RCA launched the National Broadcasting Company (NBC) in 1926. Nine years earlier, Sarnoff had predicted the day when "events of national importance can be simultaneously announced and received."[14] The Columbia Broadcasting System (CBS) went on the air in 1927. NBC's two networks ("Red" and "Blue") and CBS's network had both owned-and-operated stations and a large number of affiliated stations that subscribed to network programming.[15] With the success of these networks, concerns about radio news continued to grow.

NBC's first president, M. H. Aylesworth, was invited to give a speech at the 1928 annual Associated Press luncheon and tried to address this concern. After noting that newspapers owned or managed seventeen of the fifty-two stations in the new NBC chain, Aylesworth pointed out the complementary roles newsprint and radio news played: "Radio broadcasting appeals to the ear in the same way the printed page appeals to the eye. Both will increase literacy and together make a well-informed and happy people," Aylesworth said.[16]

Perhaps the radio audience was happy. Increasingly, however, the newspapers and wire services were not.

Journalist F. Parker Stockbridge summed up this growing anxiety in an article titled "Radio vs. the Press: Will the Newspaper Control Broadcasting?" at the end of December 1930. He wrote: "there has not been a gathering of newspaper men anywhere in which somebody has not called upon the assemblage to declare war on broadcasting. Here is a new medium of news publishing and of advertising. Worse, it is growing while the newspapers are slipping. On the face of it, here are all the elements of a war to the death."[17]

On one hand, there was a sense that radio broadcasting of news was inevitable. Edwin L. James, managing editor of the *New York Times*, instructed his reporters in a December 7, 1932, memo: "Radio has now become such a commonplace tool of our civilization that the mere fact that something is broadcast is no longer startling news. . . . This means that it is no longer necessary to put into headlines the fact that something was broadcast. What a man says over the radio should be emphasized rather than the circumstance was that he said it over the radio."[18]

On the other hand, although newspapers were resigned to news routinely being broadcast, a heated battle was brewing over the sources of that news.

Again, the *New York Times* managing editor James was pragmatic. In a June 28, 1933, memo James posited an approach that would help forge a more peaceful collaboration between legacy newspapers and radio news broadcasting outlets. Titled "Broadcasting of News," James laid out the following key points:

1. It will be admitted that broadcasting is with us to stay. . . .
2. There is a persistent demand from radio listeners for news broadcasts. . . .
3. The public demand for news broadcasts is such that the broadcasting companies are now considering seriously setting up machinery of considerable size for the gathering of news . . . to supply for the broadcasts the public demands.
4. It may therefore be assumed that . . . the broadcasting companies will broadcast news. In the nature of things, this material will, to a considerable degree, correspond in nature to material published in newspapers.[19]

He went on to propose the newspaper might "supply a broadcast summary of its contents at an hour corresponding to the time it appears on the street.

Such a broadcast would of course, refer radio listeners to the paper in question and advise that full details would be found in that paper."[20] Despite a sense of inevitability among some newspapermen that radio would become a competitor for news distribution, newspapers fired the first volleys in the Press-Radio War in 1933.

The news wire service agencies and their newspaper members banned the use of any wire copy by radio stations until newspapers hit the streets. Newspapers refused to publish the radio programming schedule, or they grudgingly agreed to publish it as paid advertising. The news wire services boycotted supplying radio stations with news copy. The boycott led CBS and NBC to begin developing their own news-gathering units. This further convinced newspapermen that radio upstarts would lead news consumers to bypass reading the newspaper.

In December 1933, under the auspices of the Publishers National Radio Committee, representatives of NBC, CBS, the National Association of Broadcasters, the United Press, the Associated Press, and International News met at the Biltmore Hotel in New York City. According to a confidential, not-for-publication report written by National Radio Committee chairman E. H. Harris, "After lengthy discussion of the situation with particular reference to news broadcasting, the committee feels that great progress has been made, not only toward a solution of this matter of controversy, but it is positive that a more cordial and harmonious relationship between the newspapers of the country and radio will result therefrom."[21]

The meeting's outcome was an agreement imposing limits on the amount of news copy the news wires could share and when that news could be aired. According to the so-called Biltmore Agreement, radio stations could air "selected bulletins of not more than thirty words" and "not earlier than 9:30 a.m. local station time . . . [or] prior to 9 p.m. local station time."[22] In addition, the agreement stipulated that CBS "withdraw from the news agency field" and disband the Columbia News Service Corporation it had established to generate its own news. NBC agreed not to enter the news collection field.[23]

Despite debate and protest about the Publishers National Radio Committee plan in the growing radio community, a key component of the agreement, the Press-Radio Bureau, launched on March 1, 1934. The Press-Radio Bureau served as the wire service for broadcasters with copy supplied by newspapers. Radio station subscribers received news items that could be used for two five-minute-long daily broadcasts. However, only the large radio networks signed the agreement. Many independent and affiliated local stations started up their own news services and ignored the rules.[24] Local radio stations purchased news from United Press and International News Service wire services as a way around the Press-Radio Bureau. With more stations flaunting the agreement over the next few years, the newspapers effectively lost the war against radio, and the Press-Radio Bureau finally disbanded in December 1938.[25] However, this early history helps explain why there is so little archival radio news from this time period.

The Golden Age

News broadcasts became more common after the Press-Radio War was over and as tensions in Europe and Asia mounted. The Associated Press started allowing radio stations to use its content on the air in 1939 and established a special radio wire by 1941.[26] By late 1939, CBS had fourteen journalists stationed in European capitals, with Edward R. Murrow in London, Eric Sevareid in Paris, and William L. Shirer in Berlin.[27] Along with their NBC counterparts, these journalists provided powerful news reporting, bringing the sounds and urgency of World War II into Americans' living rooms. Franklin D. Roosevelt's death in April 1945 and the end of the war in Europe that May ushered in an era of live radio reporting.

Regulatory action by the Federal Communications Commission forced RCA to sell the Blue network in 1945. The sale created the American Broadcasting Company (ABC), the third major radio network.[28] The fourth radio network, Mutual, lagged behind the competitors in audience size and advertising income; it never presented serious competition to NBC, CBS, or, eventually, ABC.[29]

With the growth of the television industry, radio found itself scrambling to distinguish its programming. On June 12, 1955, NBC's Pat Weaver introduced *Monitor*, its attempt to differentiate radio programming from what could be seen on television. Dennis Hart, author of *Monitor: The Last Great Radio Show*, described the program in a National Public Radio interview celebrating the fiftieth anniversary of the *Monito*r premiere. "It was a radical revolution in radio. Remember that by the 1950s, network radio was in the same pattern of programming that network television is today: half an hour or hour-long comedies, drama, variety, mystery. . . . What Weaver did was throw everything out. He came up with this radical idea that he would program a forty-hour continuous broadcast hosted by big-name TV people, and he would put everything into the broadcast. It would have news, sports, comedy, variety, live interviews, live comedy."[30] *Monitor*'s programming innovation is credited with the rise of all-news radio.

In 1967, President Lyndon Johnson signed the Public Broadcasting Act, which established the Corporation for Public Broadcasting (CPB). The new law was intended to encourage competition to commercial radio's hold on the marketplace and the CPB's charge was to focus on public-interest programming.[31] Support for noncommercial radio led to the founding on February 26, 1970, of National Public Radio, a network that provided nonprofit radio programming across the country, including long-form radio news, commentary, and documentaries. National Public Radio went on the air in 1971. Since then, its affiliate stations have built on the early excitement over news radio, using the medium's audio storytelling to its fullest potential.[32]

WHY RADIO NEWS WAS LOST

> Many important recordings have been lost or have become unplayable since the introduction of recorded sound in the late nineteenth century. Many others are at risk of becoming lost. It is unclear how large a universe of recordings will remain undocumented and allowed to deteriorate before additional resources are invested in their preservation.
>
> —*The State of Recorded Sound Preservation in the United States*, 2010.[33]

Why were the earliest examples of news broadcasting on the radio lost? The simple answer is that it is impossible to save something that was never recorded. Early radio news programming was entirely broadcast live.

Even though the voices of notable figures such as Thomas Edison and Calvin Coolidge were recorded, they were not allowed to be aired. In fact, when Thomas Edison died in 1931, NBC had someone re-read Edison's last speech rather than air the recording of it. Given this self-imposed edict, it is no wonder that incentive to record was nonexistent.[34]

Why the rules against airing recordings? There were several factors at play.

Although optical film was available for sound recording in the early 1920s, few stations availed themselves of the technology. According to Dr. Michael Biel, professor of radio and television at Morehead State University, "I have no evidence of any of [these recordings] being aired as 'repeats' except for WFAA playing on August 4, 1927 . . . the NBC broadcast of Lindbergh's arrival back in Washington, D.C., in June."[35] Once entertainment programming was syndicated, the use of recorded sound was more acceptable. However, news broadcasts, such as they were, continued to be broadcast live.

Another issue was sound quality of the recordings. Early recordings were "done on wax and thus had to be processed by electroplating and then making shellac pressings. Embossing on uncoated aluminum was available by 1930, but the sound quality was not sufficiently good to allow for use for rebroadcasting."[36] Not until the development of the lacquer-coated disc in 1934 was there a recording medium that made possible "high quality instantaneous recordings relatively inexpensively and available for immediate playback."[37] The Presto company became a major supplier of lacquer discs, and historical references to "presto discs" as a generic name for lacquer discs indicate the brand's dominance.

Even after radio developed the ability to record, network strictures on the use of recordings were tight. On January 4, 1935, radio stations broke the taboo on rebroadcasting a recording when they re-aired President Roosevelt's State of the Union Address. Since the address was given at 12:15 in the afternoon, it meant most working people would miss the live broadcast. With permission given by the White House to record the address, it was possible to re-air the speech that evening.[38] However, this first loosening on the policy to ban broadcasting recordings did not immediately affect the day-to-day practice of live-only broadcasting.

There were some early exceptions to this, such as the Hindenburg disaster on May 6, 1937.[39] The story of how the Hindenburg disaster came to be recorded is one of luck and timing. Media historian Helen York describes how the recording came to be:

> This historic broadcast has survived in recorded form today, but only because of a technical coincidence. Announcer Herbert Morrison and his audio engineer had been covering the arrival of the Hindenburg Airship as an experiment in recording news for delayed broadcast [on a Presto transcription disc]. Morrison's description began as a routine description of the docking operation, but became galvanized by emotion as the giant dirigible exploded before him. The sound of his voice cracking under the emotional stress of the moment conveys far more than any static reading of a transcript ever could. The important point to abstract from this narrative is that the preservation of this bit of history was an accident of technology. Had the event not been chosen for an experiment in recording no one would ever have heard Morrison's words and the explosion of the Hindenburg would have remained an image surrounded by silence.[40]

Reporter Herb Morrison (left) and sound engineer Charles Nehlson with the recording device tested during the Hindenburg tragedy. *NBC NewsWire/contributor/Getty Images*

At the network level there were a few means by which programming was recorded, but most was for entertainment programs, and it was intended to maximize the potential placement of advertisements. NBC used a variety of recording services: (1) studio recordings both from NBC's program department and ones produced by advertising agencies, (2) "live talent" programs recorded simultaneously with the broadcast, and (3) syndicated transcriptions. NBC's Electrical Transcription Service recordings on laminated discs were created for the purposes of "selling or leasing recorded programs to advertisers and their agencies, and directly to radio stations for broadcast purposes."[41]

These electronic transcription discs are the most likely format of recorded radio programming from the 1930s that are still available today, but they were also a fragile format. Unlike audiotape of later days, they could be recorded on only once, so they captured a single program that could be saved. Transcription discs were created by placing a laminate over an aluminum or glass disc. If improperly stored, the discs would delaminate or crack and chemical reactions caused the laminate to shrink and become brittle. The fragile nature of glass-based discs almost ensured their loss. Additionally, in as few as a half dozen plays, the grooves on which the sound was recorded wore down and the sound deteriorated. According to the Audio Archive, the future availability of past radio programming was reliant on "the most fragile formats and the most at risk of being lost due to deterioration, poor storage or mishandling."[42]

At the local radio broadcast level, there were further challenges to preserving news programming. Jim duBois, executive director of the Minnesota Broadcasters Association, outlined a variety of reasons local radio stations

Delamination of an instantaneous recording disc. *Hansen Photo/Recorded Sound Research Center/Library of Congress*

rarely preserved recordings: "Over the years things got tossed. [Stations] had a transcription library but some of them [the transcription discs] began disappearing because you could melt them down and get money for the aluminum that was under the substrate. Some just deteriorated; with each subsequent play the audio quality deteriorates, they became unplayable."[43]

No Copyright Imperative

Unlike printed publication copyright, which required publishers to deposit two copies to the Copyright Office, there was no imperative to send a copy of a broadcast to the Library of Congress (LOC). In the description of the LOC radio collection, under the category "weaknesses and exclusions," the impact of this on the collection is clear: "Because there was no U.S. copyright law covering sound recordings until 1972, the Library's initial collection was developed solely through gifts from individuals and corporations. Private collectors have donated thousands of recordings. However, because of this, the collection tends to reflect what has been given to it. It is very strong in certain areas, such as NBC and WOR [Mutual], but is deficient in others. . . . We have little local or contemporary radio."[44]

Broadcast News Libraries Didn't Archive

For newspapers, a key part of the organization's library mission was archiving past issues. These were valuable references and the extensive story clip files and photo archives were part of the raw material that helped create each day's publication.

Not so with radio stations. When Frances Sprague was hired to establish a general library for NBC radio in February 1930, the library was there to serve the reference needs of newscasters and to answer inquiries from the business office, engineers, researchers, or staff members, not to save all of NBC's programming.[45] There was no preservation mission for the broadcasts themselves.

Even after the large radio and television networks instituted more consistent archiving routines, they still failed to create comprehensive collections of their broadcasts. An undated CBS document from the late 1970s described the organization's various television and radio archiving efforts. According to the document, the CBS Audio Archive "gathers, organizes and makes available audiotape copies of CBS News radio broadcasts." The document also outlined CBS's retention of material: "All hourly newscasts are held in complete form . . . for one month and the cuts from the hourlies are saved for an additional six months. After that time, the most important stories from these newscasts are edited onto hour-long reels, known as X-reels, which are kept in the Archive's permanent collection. This collection dates from the mid-1960s."[46]

Equivalent to weeding images in a newspaper library, culling audio clips made it impossible to create a complete record of the news that was distributed over radio airwaves.

According to an article in *Atlantic* magazine, by the time archivists turned their attention and interest to preserving audio programming in the 1960s, "decades of historic audio had been lost, destroyed, or never recorded in the first place."[47] Added to the already reduced inventory of audio recordings available for preservation were challenges regarding the variety of formats on which sound was recorded. Wax cylinders, transcription discs made of aluminum or glass, shellac and acetate gramophone discs, magnetic wire recordings and reel-to-reel tape—each of these media presented its own archiving challenges.

HOW RADIO NEWS WAS PRESERVED

Radio news programming was sporadic and limited in many ways before the end of the Radio-Press Wars in the late 1930s. Radio's coverage of World War II demonstrated the medium's power and led to radio's "golden age" of news reporting. The reason we have any record of this golden age of radio news is in part due to the actions taken by the news organizations, libraries, archives, and related institutions at the time.

Radio Networks

As was true for newspaper, photojournalism, and newsreel creators, radio news producers themselves were not primarily concerned with preserving a record of their output. In the early days of the medium, recording options were limited and the quality of those recordings was poor. The cylinder recording machines could capture just a few minutes at a time, and spoken word programming was difficult to capture. As recording technology improved, it was entertainment programming that was captured on transcription discs, and later on audiotape, for distribution to affiliated stations and for rebroadcast in different time zones. It wasn't until networks started broadcasting from the various World War II theaters of action that the archival record of radio news began.

By an accident of history, a major collection of CBS network radio broadcasts from January 30, 1939, to October 22, 1962, was saved by

Seattle-based KIRO. The West Coast CBS affiliate wanted to "time shift" the live broadcasts from New York for its Pacific time zone audience. As described by University of Washington faculty member Milo Ryan in his 1963 guide to the collection,

> KIRO . . . had been experimenting with ways of improving instantaneous recordings and had found it possible to gain a usable quality of sound through them. As the reality of the war approached, KIRO decided to record the network programs of significant informational value, and to present them on a delayed basis to Pacific Northwest listeners at times when the citizenry might be available to listen to them. In addition, there was among management personnel a fairly lively sense of history, a realization that what was being broadcast mirrored a cataclysm and might even foretell what was to follow in ensuing years.[48]

Using sixteen-inch lacquer transcriptions discs that could not be recorded over, the station not only captured each program, but then made the unusual decision to keep the discs. Ryan explains, "As the shelves filled up [the discs] could be thrown away, dumped into the sea, hauled away to oblivion. Or, as in the case of KIRO, they could be preserved, provided a place could be found to store and cherish them."[49] Indeed, they did find a place at the station's transmitter building on Vashon Island, and when the station decided to give the collection to the University of Washington in 1957, it comprised the "best extant archive of CBS News during World War II."[50] The CBS Foundation, Inc., provided a grant to transfer the bulk of the programs to tape and to catalog the contents. The disc collection was moved to the National Archives and Records Administration in the early 2000s while the university maintains the tapes.

The CBS network also archived audio content as part of its internal news library. But the audio archive was abandoned in the early 1980s due to staff shortages, and the materials were sent to a warehouse in New Jersey. CBS News Archives manager Roy Carubia described the audio archive as "a mess" consisting of a mixture of glass and aluminum lacquer transcription discs and quarter-inch reel-to-reel audiotapes with no inventory and no way to identify and retrieve items.[51]

NBC maintained a transcription disc archive, part of which eventually made its way to the LOC and the University of Wisconsin. ABC and Mutual also maintained internal archives. Some ABC network content is held by the National Archives and Records Administration. Mutual network recordings from the 1930s to 1950s also are in the LOC.[52]

A 2010 report from the LOC about the state of recorded sound preservation in the United States included this observation about the radio networks:

> The exact intentions of radio networks in making recordings of their broadcasts, and how they singled out specific broadcasts for recording are not entirely known. The NBC Collection at the Library of Congress includes more than 150,000 lacquer discs . . . from the mid-1930s to the early 1970s. However, many popular and culturally significant programs aired by the network are not represented in the collection. . . . It is likely, but not confirmed, that the network recorded programs that its executives thought more significant, such as news broadcasts or programs it produced or owned, as opposed to those leased from sponsors or outside producers. Programs also may have been recorded and retained solely to protect against possible litigation. Compounding the issue of seemingly erratic runs of programs recorded, radio transcription collections in archives are often incomplete.[53]

One type of network broadcast that *was* recorded originated with live reporting from World War II battles. A cover story in the October 1944 *Radio Craft* magazine described a "combat recorder" using blank optical film as the recording medium. The Amertape Recordgraph Commando model captured more than five hours of sound on one fifty-foot roll of 35-millimeter film. Once recorded, the film needed no further processing for immediate playback.[54]

Some former radio reporters and engineers who were serving in the military got assigned to run the Recordgraph during battles to capture live sound. The recording made on the deck of an Allied warship during the D-day invasion of June 6, 1944, became the "most in demand of all invasion recordings yet to reach the air."[55] The recording captured the ship being attacked by Junker airplane bombers and the sound of an anti-aircraft gun bringing down one of the planes. Shouts of the cheering gunners are clearly audible. The film recording was sent to London and relayed by shortwave radio to the radio networks. All four major U.S. networks broadcast the recording simultaneously at 11:15 p.m., June 7, 1944, and rebroadcast it innumerable times in response to listener demand.

A 2015 posting on the online auction site eBay offered sixteen Recordgraph tapes of the D-day invasion for $450,000. The seller wrote: "I have owned all of this material, which is one of a kind in the world, for twenty years. I have been asked by the Library of Congress and the Imperial War Museum to part with it but it wasn't the right time. Now I'm moving and it's time for another collector to own this or for someone else to purchase it and donate it to the LOC. I am selling it." The owner of the tapes had found them in the attic of a home purchased from the estate of a deceased man who had run one of the Recordgraph machines during the war. There were no bids on the tapes.[56]

Cover of *Radio Craft* magazine depicting Amertape Recordgraph operators during D-Day invasion. *Courtesy AmericanRadioHistory.com*

Noncommercial radio stations, and networks in many cases, served as custodians for their own archives. National Public Radio entered the scene when audiotape was the recording medium of choice. Unlike cylinders or transcription discs from earlier time periods, tape could be used over and over. Nevertheless, NPR has programming from the network's launch in

1971 to mid-1999 on tape, with content since those years recorded onto digital recordable compact discs. Public radio affiliates WNYC in New York City and WGBH in Boston also have extensive archives. WNYC's goes back to 1927; WGBH's goes to back to 1951. Pacifica Radio Network started taping its programming in 1949. But as is the case with so many other noncommercial entities, these public radio networks and stations lack funding to maintain their archives at the level they would like.[57]

Local radio stations were unlikely to capture their day-to-day broadcasts, and, in any case, most stations offered just short newsbreaks on the hour and half hour. The all-news format for local stations became popular for those that could not or did not want to pay the royalty fees for playing music. But local all-news stations typically saw no reason to create an archive for preservation purposes. Local stations would create "logger tapes" that captured the day's broadcast, but they were for internal purposes, such as to document that an ad ran when scheduled or for possible legal problems that might arise. The logger tapes were poor quality and weren't intended to serve as an archive. And as is true for audiotape collections, the tapes were re-recorded and used over and over.

RADIO NEWS PRESERVATION CHALLENGES

> Commercial radio began in the early 1920s. Perhaps no other sound medium has conveyed to listeners so much of the nation's history. . . . Few, if any, other forms of sound recordings are held in as wide a variety of archives and collections, both professional and amateur. Yet support for broadcasting archives has been sporadic; American radio broadcasting has never been documented systematically, and few archives have provided formal support of radio broadcast recordings.
>
> —*The State of Recorded Sound Preservation in the United States*, 2010[58]

Radio preservation began to gain attention from the formal institutions of archival stewardship after the passage of the 2000 National Recording Preservation Act.[59] The law established the LOC National Recording Preservation Board (NRPB) and the National Recording Registry, both of which were intended to help the library "implement a comprehensive national sound recording preservation program."[60] The NRPB produced a National Recording Preservation Plan in 2012 that laid out a systematic blueprint for preserving recorded sound, similar to the plan published in 1994 to preserve the nation's film heritage. The plan called for a coordinated effort in four categories: (1) preservation infrastructure, (2) preservation strategies, (3) access challenges, and (4) long-term national strategies for preservation and access. The plan recognized that the nation's libraries, archives, and museums held some forty-six million sound recordings, and millions of additional recordings were in the hands of record companies, performing artists, broadcasters, and collectors.[61]

Broadcasters

The nation's commercial radio broadcasters continue to maintain internal news libraries that are primarily used for their day-to-day needs. With massive industry consolidation and budget cuts, however, the commercial stations' and networks' current attention to archival practices for radio is limited—if it exists at all. The 2012 National Recording Preservation Plan barely mentions private companies, and then mostly addresses music recording firms, not commercial radio broadcasters.[62] Although most of the network television broadcasters make archival news video available online, radio networks generally do not provide access to archived radio streams on their websites.

Noncommercial stations, however, have taken their archival role seriously with a commitment to create the American Archive of Public Broadcasting (AAPB), a collaboration between the LOC and the WGBH Educational Foundation. The initiative aims to preserve and make accessible historical public television and radio programs and to coordinate a national effort to save at-risk public media. The vast majority of the initial AAPB content consists of regional and local programs selected by more than one hundred public broadcasting stations and archives across the United States. To date, approximately 68,000 items comprising 40,000 hours of programming from the 1950s to the present have been digitized for long-term preservation. Much of it can be accessed through the American Archive website, http://americanarchive.org. However, as with many archiving efforts, due to funding or grant parameters, there is a limit to the scope of the initiative. For the AAPB, no broadcasts produced after 2013 have been collected.

The work of one public broadcasting radio station is illustrative of local efforts. Minnesota Public Radio (MPR) was founded in 1967. According to the MPR website, "There are few recordings from 1967 to 1971; reels of MPR daily news were saved regularly starting in 1972. For many years there was no comprehensive catalog or inventory of the archive, so its contents were mostly known [only] by the people who created it, listened to it, and dug through it."[63] MPR's archiving efforts depend on a long roster of public and private financial supporters who are providing the funds to properly inventory and digitize the station's history. Without this type of financial commitment, current and future archiving efforts for local content will continue to struggle.

That financial need is being addressed in part by the National Recording Preservation Foundation, "an independent, nonprofit charitable corporation established by the U.S. Congress for the purpose of supporting archives, libraries, cultural institutions and others committed to preserving America's radio, music and recorded sound heritage."[64]

Library of Congress

The LOC holds what is believed to be the largest broadcast archives in the United States. However, the collection includes fewer than fifty pre-1933 radio broadcast recordings and fewer than 1,000 made before 1936.[65] Technologies for recording before the 1930s was primitive. Live news broadcasts were very brief and the radio networks did not allow recorded sound to be rebroadcast, so there was little incentive to record live broadcasts.

The 1976 Copyright Act revisions established the American Television and Radio Archives (ATRA) and mandated that the LOC preserve television and radio programs "which are of present or potential public or cultural interest, historical significance, cognitive value, or otherwise worthy of preservation."[66] The major effect of the law was that the LOC was allowed to record broadcast content off the air without violating copyright. But since the provisions for ATRA did not include funding for capturing, cataloging, and archiving such recordings, very little was done.

Even so, in the decades following the passage of ATRA, the LOC acquired through purchase or gifts thousands of radio broadcasts. Major collections included NBC Radio, Voice of America, Armed Forces Radio and Television, and National Public Radio. The collections included every type of recording medium: wax cylinders, aluminum and glass lacquer discs, wire recordings, reel-to-reel tapes, tape cassettes, and digital formats.

One of the first activities of the National Recording Preservation Board after the passage of the National Recording Preservation Act of 2000 was to direct the Librarian of Congress to conduct a national study about the state of recorded sound preservation in the United States. The findings of that study, conducted by the LOC and the Council on Library and Information Resources, were published in 2010.

The report's findings concluded "major areas of America's recorded sound heritage have already been destroyed or remain inaccessible to the public."[67] Nevertheless, the LOC made substantial progress between signing of the 2000 law and the 2010 report. The LOC completely transformed its facilities for storing and preserving its recorded sound and audiovisual collections with the 2007 completion of the Packard Campus of the National Audio-Visual Conservation Center in Culpeper, Virginia, funded with a $200 million gift from the Packard Humanities Institute. As described by Librarian of Congress James Billington, "The Packard Campus has brought together in a single facility almost all of the Library's staff and resources at this critical time when our statutory responsibilities for national leadership in recorded sound and moving image preservation are expanding in order to implement the multiple mandates of the National Recording Preservation Act of 2000."[68]

Starting in 2002, the LOC has chosen twenty-five recordings from its collections for the National Recording Registry each year. The selections showcase the range and diversity of American recorded sound heritage in order to increase preservation awareness. Among the news-related content in the National Recording Registry are the following: Herb Morrison's description of the crash of the Hindenburg on May 6, 1937; president Franklin D. Roosevelt's "Fireside Chat" radio broadcasts from 1933 to 1944; General Dwight D. Eisenhower's June 6, 1944, address to the Allied nations; Dr. Martin Luther King's "I Have A Dream" speech on August 28, 1963; and remarks by Apollo 11 astronaut Neil Armstrong broadcast from the moon on July 21, 1969.[69]

The LOC continues its leadership role in coordinating current and ongoing radio preservation activities on behalf of a large number of public and private institutions, primarily academic libraries, historical societies, museums, and private collectors. As part of the National Recording Preservation Board's activities, the LOC convened the Radio Preservation Task Force in 2016 to examine the challenges to radio archival work. The Radio Preservation Task Force's work is discussed in more detail later in this chapter.

Current radio content is being collected by the LOC through radio web-streaming captures. Many talk radio programs and other types of public affairs programming are being archived.[70] The LOC has been deeply involved in strategies for digital media archiving as well, although they are not currently archiving podcasts or other types of born-digital radio sound.

University Libraries

Academic libraries exerted little effort at finding and preserving radio news broadcasts. A 2004 report conducted by the Council on Library and Information Resources on the state of audio collections in academic libraries found that almost all of the sixty-nine libraries surveyed reported holding significant or rare audio collections. However, the majority of those collections consisted of music rather than spoken word archives.[71] The 2004 report also identified one of the key impediments to the availability of recorded sound in academic libraries:

> Providing easy access to audio in its analog form has always been a challenge. Recorded sound depends on playback equipment for access, and the rapid development and obsolescence of recording formats and playback equipment have resulted in an unending progression of recorded sound that is stranded on superseded media. It takes significant resources—time, money, and technical and curatorial expertise—to transfer recorded-sound content from obsolete and decaying formats onto newer ones. Perhaps for this reason, audio has taken a backseat in the research and teaching resources that academic libraries routinely provide to their users, despite its undisputed value in archives and libraries.[72]

Many institutions have begun collaborating to avoid duplication of efforts. Syracuse University's Belfer Audio Archive has partnered with the Department of Special Collections at the University of California, Santa Barbara to ensure that the two institutions' substantial wax cylinder collections are digitized in a coordinated and nonduplicative manner.[73]

Nevertheless, academic audio archivists describe the problems they face in properly caring for these types of materials.[74] "No institution currently has sufficient resources to ensure preservation of even all the unique materials they hold."[75] Audio preservation is likely to be dependent on grant funding rather than on recurring, line-item library budget allocations. Further complicating the problem is the lack of visibility for these collections among library users. "If the collections are hidden from the view of users because they are undescribed or otherwise hard to find, demand for access will be low," meaning the arguments for more funding will be met with skepticism.[76]

The problems facing all academic institutions were summed up in a 2008–2009 case study of the collections at Indiana University in Bloomington. Mike Casey, associate director for recordings services at the university's Archives of Traditional Music, and a team of colleagues conducted a study to assess preservation challenges for audio and moving image holdings on campus. The census found that more than 569,000 audio and video recordings and motion pictures were held by eighty administrative units on campus; nearly 365,000 (more than 60 percent) were audio recordings. The audio collections were comprised of twenty-three different audio formats (not including born-digital content), each with its own hardware requirements for playback. Contrary to archival best practices, 95 percent of the collections were stored in room-temperature conditions. To its credit, Indiana University made a major commitment of funding and administrative support to preserve and properly catalog these collections based on the findings of the census.[77]

Historical Societies and Archives

As was true for so many other types of content, local and state historical societies and archives also were recipients of donations and gifts throughout the decades. One of the largest collections is at the State Historical Society of Wisconsin's Mass Communication History Collection (MCHC). Although the news collection primarily contains television broadcasts, it does include a variety of radio programs on discs. Unlike many such collections, the MCHC is well documented with finding guides and online catalogs. However, countless additional collections are squirreled away in historical societies around the country with little to no documentation.

Individual Collectors

Individual collectors are the true heroes for many types of news content preservation. Radio content is no exception. Whether it was radio station staff members who saved material from the dumpsters or individual radio listeners who regularly recorded their favorite station and became accidental archivists in the process, individuals are responsible for preserving much of the radio content we have today. The "Old Time Radio" or OTR movement made up of collectors and radio enthusiasts is credited with holding tens of thousands of tape recordings and vintage broadcasts.[78]

The first radio station in the United States programmed by and for African Americans, WDIA in Memphis, Tennessee, prepared a commemorative compact disc set in 2003 to honor its history. The airchecks and program excerpts on the discs came from tapes made by listeners who recorded their favorite programs, saved them, and then shared them with station staff producing the CD.[79]

There are hobbyist groups and associations that focus on specific content, such as bluegrass music or comedy serials of the 1930s, or on specific recording media such as wax cylinders or wire recordings. These groups trade, buy, and sell recordings of all sorts along with the equipment to play back their treasures. These OTR groups are a major resource for those formal institutions trying to preserve radio content. However, because of the twisted copyright status of recorded sound, many of these individual collectors are not interested in donating their collections to libraries, historical societies, or archives, because they know that copyright rules will make the recordings more difficult to access.

Another preservation issue with private collections is that so few individuals have the facilities and resources to properly care for their treasured cylinders, lacquer discs, reel-to-reel or cassette tapes, and digital media. And few have made arrangements for their collections' handling after their deaths.[80] As a result, many collections get broken up, widely dispersed, or simply discarded after their original stewards pass away.

The Internet Archive is trying to curate the OTR collections that still exist. The Old Time Radio section of the massive online archival site (https://archive.org/details/oldtimeradio) not only digitizes these prized individual collections, it also streams them and makes them accessible to anyone. A huge portion of the collection is comprised of entertainment radio, but there is a good sampling of classic news broadcasts and important event coverage is represented, as well.

A NETWORK OF PRESERVATION HEROES

The collections of radio newscasts in various large institutions consist mostly of the national networks' feeds. But what about local radio broadcasts? According to the LOC's report on preservation of recorded sound, the preservation of local commercial radio presents unique challenges. Among the challenges cited are frequently changing ownership and station consolidation, and the perception that there is no revenue potential for archival content.[81]

One of the initiatives arising from the LOC's 2012 National Recording Preservation Plan is the Radio Preservation Task Force. Established in

2014, it brings academics and archivists together with the common goal of preserving radio history. One of the goals of the task force is to identify audio collections nationwide. It seeks to "develop an online inventory of extant American radio archival collections, focusing on recorded sound holdings" and "to identify and save endangered collections."[82]

Major collections are fairly well documented. A good portion of national network radio entertainment programming has survived. If caches of local radio material exist, however, they are not documented. And Josh Shepperd, director of the Radio Preservation Task Force, estimates that 90 percent of all local and regional radio content that had existed is gone forever.[83]

To meet the ambitious goal of creating a national inventory of radio collections, the task force assembled a network of research associates and archive affiliates to identify where major collections of American radio recordings are housed. One of the research associates who stepped up is Professor Michael Stamm, a political and cultural historian in Michigan State University's Department of History.[84] Volunteers were assigned regions and asked to seek out places that held collections of local radio programming, whether large or small. Stamm described the importance of the work and the methods he and this network of seekers of local recorded sound have employed:

> The local stuff is what is most interesting to me in general. Radio is already the least well-preserved medium and what has been preserved is almost exclusively national network programming or serials like *Amos and Andy*—the stuff that was put on transcription discs and sent around the country for asynchronous broadcasting. It is the local voices that went out over the ether once and then they were never heard again. We're lucky if we have an hour of it.[85]

As a media historian he wishes he could reconstruct the everyday sound that would be heard on regional radio broadcasts. "We don't have the sound of regional voices, which was a huge part of radio into the 1950s. What I've heard of the various smaller and regional broadcasters is unique. It's a whole different thing to hear someone doing the news from Texas who is from Texas."[86] The task force project's initial idea was to compile as complete a national database as possible of the location of audio recordings, particularly those that are not digitized.

Stamm and a graduate student set out to find whatever audio recording stashes they could in Michigan. "It was basically just grunt work—a lot of cold calls, a lot of e-mailing. Some of it involved going to the university library and special collections websites, putting in the search term 'radio' and then wading through hundreds of resources," Stamm said.

He also found random troves by "cold e-mailing people involved in local historical societies. I'd write, 'Please don't throw away this e-mail—it isn't a phishing scam.' I'd try to develop a dialogue with people. In some cases I never heard back. In some cases people said, 'We have five things—here's a list, good luck.' And in other cases people said, 'Oh my goodness, we're so glad to hear from you. We have this amazing box of transcription recordings from the local radio but we don't have any equipment to listen to it!'" he said. His graduate student had luck connecting with a group of OTR enthusiasts in western Michigan, all of whom had "little stashes of print materials and audio recordings."

The delightful surprise for Stamm was that they found unique local recordings, ones not already noted as existing in large national collections. In all, Stamm found twenty-five Michigan collections of various sizes and content to help populate the project database.[87] Nationwide, the network of searchers has located 350 archives from around the country. By the time the project is finished, more than 1,000 are anticipated. When it comes time to digitize and make available these newly found caches of radio content, the focus will be on making radio programming from underrepresented groups and unique local broadcasts available online.[88]

In the hunt for recordings, Stamm also found material that will be the basis of a grant and, he hopes, a resource for media scholars. He said, "We found these two collections—about one hundred transcription discs of some western Michigan public affairs programming from the '50s and '60s. We also found this program produced by WKAR called *State Edition*. It was the fifteen-minute lead-in to NPR's *All Things Considered*. It was broadcast every day and we have seven or eight years of the complete recordings." The grant he is seeking would fund the digitization of the files, which would make content analysis and other research easier.

Stamm is also interested in linking this newly discovered collection of local news lead-ins to the related national radio news programs, such as those on National Public Radio. "We have the metadata and if we can get these [local news lead-ins] digitized we hope to dovetail this with what NPR is doing [with the AAPB]. If we do it right, you could link the metadata so you could find the national coverage of something and go to the Michigan coverage that was right before," he said.

Stamm and the other Radio Preservation Task Force's regional scouts will provide the foundation for a resource of tremendous benefit to media researchers and historians. But another beneficiary of Stamm's discoveries will be his students. "I'm teaching a class on the theory and practice of audio storytelling," he said. "Having access to the voices broadcast over the years and from a range of regions will be invaluable."[89]

NOTES

1. Council on Library and Information Resources and the Library of Congress, *The State of Recorded Sound Preservation in the United States: A National Legacy at Risk in the Digital Age*, (Washington, DC: National Recording Preservation Board of the Library of Congress, 2010).

2. Digital Collections, University Libraries, University of Maryland, "Edwin B. Dooley Collection," http://digital.lib.umd.edu/archivesum/actions.DisplayEADDoc.do?source=/MdU.ead.lab.0036.xml.

3. Christopher H. Sterling and John M. Kittross, *Stay Tuned: A History of American Broadcasting*, 3rd ed. (Mahwah, NJ: Lawrence Erlbaum Associates, 2002), 60–61.

4. John C. Abell, "News Radio Makes News," *Wired*, August 31, 2010.

5. Abell, "News Radio Makes News."

6. Detroit Historical Society, "WWJ," http://detroithistorical.org/learn/encyclopedia-of-detroit/wwj.

7. Wikipedia: The Free Encyclopedia, "KDKA (AM)," last modified May 20, 2016, https://en.wikipedia.org/wiki/KDKA_(AM)#The_beginning.

8. Edward Bliss Jr., *Now the News: The Story of Broadcast Journalism* (New York: Columbia University Press, 2013), 6.

9. "KDKA Begins to Broadcast," A Science Odyssey: People and Discoveries, www.pbs.org/wgbh/aso/databank/entries/dt20ra.html.

10. Victor Rawlings, "Radio in Department Stores," *Radio News*, December 1921, 485.

11. "Sources of Entertainment, News and Weather Reports," *Radio News*, June 1922, 1136.

12. Anna Robertson, Steve Garfinkel, and Elizabeth Eckstein, "Radio in the 1920s: Emergence of Radio in the 1920s and Its Cultural Significance," Third Annual Radio Show of 1924, last updated May 1, 2000, http://xroads.virginia.edu/~ug00/3on1/radioshow/1920radio.htm.

13. Radio Act of 1927, Pub. L. No. 69-632, 44 Stat. 1162, February 23, 1927.

14. "Our History," NBC Universal, www.nbcuniversal.com/our-history.

15. Sterling and Kittross, *Stay Tuned*, 122.

16. "Dr. Cadman Extols the Associated Press; An Aid to American Democracy, He Says—Aylesworth Links Radio and Newspaper," *New York Times*, April 24, 1928.

17. Michael Stamm, "Newspapers, Radio, and the Business of Media in the United States," *OAH Magazine of History* 24, no. 1 (2010): 25–28.

18. Memorandum by Edwin L. James to reporters, December 7, 1932, New York Times Company records, "Arthur Hays Sulzberger Papers: Radio, 1932–

1962," New York Times Corporate Archives, MssColl 17782, box 234, file 7–8, Manuscript and Archives Division, New York Public Library.

19. Memorandum by Edwin L. James, June 28, 1933, New York Times Company records, "Arthur Hays Sulzberger Papers: Radio, 1932–1962," New York Times Corporate Archives, MssColl 17782, box 234, file 7–8, Manuscript and Archives Division, New York Public Library.

20. Memorandum by Edwin L. James, June 28, 1933.

21. Confidential memo by E. H. Harris, 1933, National Broadcasting Company History Archives, file 315, Library of Congress, Motion Picture, Broadcasting and Recorded Sound Division.

22. Publishers National Radio Committee Report, December 11, 1933, New York Times Company Records, "Arthur Hays Sulzberger Papers: Radio, 1932–1962."

23. Publishers National Radio Committee Report.

24. Sterling and Kittross, *Stay Tuned*, 137.

25. Gwenyth L. Jackaway, *Media at War: Radio's Challenge to Newspapers, 1924–1939* (Westport, CT: Greenwood Publishing Group, 1995), 33.

26. Sterling and Kittross, *Stay Tuned*, 193.

27. Sterling and Kittross, *Stay Tuned*, 195.

28. Sterling and Kittross, *Stay Tuned*, 232.

29. Sterling and Kittross, *Stay Tuned*, 174.

30. "Recalling a Media Pioneer: NBC Radio's 'Monitor'," NPR.org, June 12, 2015, www.npr.org/templates/story/story.php?storyId=4700009.

31. "Overview and History," NPR.org, www.npr.org/about-npr/192827079/overview-and-history.

32. "Overview and History," NPR.org.

33. CLIR and the LOC, *The State of Recorded Sound Preservation*.

34. Michael Jay Biel, "The Making and Use of Recordings in Broadcasting before 1936," (PhD diss., Northwestern University, 1977), 811–12.

35. Michael Biel, "Time Shifting by the Networks," *Old Time Radio Digest* (listserv), June 17, 1997, www.durenberger.com/documents/NETTIME.pdf.

36. Biel, "Time Shifting by the Networks."

37. Biel, "Time Shifting by the Networks."

38. Biel, "The Making and Use of Recordings," 815.

39. Biel, "Time Shifting by the Networks."

40. Helen York, "Transmission and Transience: Durability of Media in the Electronic Age," *University of Bucharest Review* 11, no. 1 (2009): 146.

41. "Transcription Services," 1935, National Broadcasting Company History Archives, file 525.

42. "Learn about Electric Transcription Discs," The Audio Archive, www.theaudioarchive.com/TAA_Resources_Disc_Transcription.htm.

43. Jim duBois (executive director, Minnesota Broadcasters Association), interview with authors, May 5, 2016.

44. Library of Congress, "Radio—Acquisitions," www.loc.gov/acq/devpol/colloverviews/radio.html.

45. Frances Sprague, "A Library for Radio and Television," *Stechert-Hafner Book News*, April 1952, 115.

46. "Guide to the CBS News Archives," n.d., National Broadcasting Company History Archives, file 100.

47. Adrienne LaFrance, "Saving Historic Radio before It's Too Late," *The Atlantic*, March 24, 2016.

48. Milo Ryan, *History of Sound* (Seattle: University of Washington Press, 1963), x.

49. Ryan, *History of Sound.*

50. Feliks Banel, "KIRO Radio Accidentally Saves American History," Mynorthwest.com, March 2, 2016, http://mynorthwest.com/225429/kiro-radio-accidentally-saves-american-history/.

51. Roy Carubia (manager of archives, CBS News), interview with authors, April 22, 2016.

52. CLIR and the LOC, *The State of Recorded Sound Preservation*, 21.

53. CLIR and the LOC, *The State of Recorded Sound Preservation*, 22.

54. "Combat Recorder," *Radio Craft*, October 1944, 16.

55. "Dramatic Hicks Film Record in Demand by All Networks," *Broadcasting*, June 12, 1944, 11.

56. Posting on eBay, "D-Day Invasion Historical Recordgraph Amertape Recordings," last updated April 1, 2015, www.ebay.com/itm/D-DAY-INVASION-HISTORICAL-RECORDGRAPH-AMERTAPE-recordings-/221723707133.

57. CLIR and the LOC, *The State of Recorded Sound Preservation*, 25–26.

58. CLIR and the LOC, *The State of Recorded Sound Preservation*, 20.

59. National Recording Preservation Act of 2000, Pub. L. No. 106-474, 2000.

60. CLIR and the LOC, *The State of Recorded Sound Preservation*, vi.

61. CLIR and the LOC, *The State of Recorded Sound Preservation*, 1.

62. Council on Library and Information Resources and the Library of Congress, *National Recording Preservation Plan* (Washington, DC: Library of Congress, 2012), www.loc.gov/today/pr/2013/files/pub156.pdf.

63. "About the MPR Archive," http://archive.mprnews.org/about.

64. National Recording Preservation Foundation, "About the NRPF," http://recordingpreservation.org/about/.

65. CLIR and the LOC, *The State of Recorded Sound Preservation.*

66. Copyright Act of 1976, "American Television and Radio Archives Act," Pub. L. No 94-553, 1976.

67. CLIR and the LOC, *The State of Recorded Sound Preservation*, vii.

68. CLIR and the LOC, *The State of Recorded Sound Preservation.*

69. "Complete National Recording Registry Listing," 2016, www.loc.gov/programs/national-recording-preservation-board/recording-registry/complete-national-recording-registry-listing/.

70. Library of Congress Web Radio Recording Project, "2016 Schedule of Recording Programs," www.loc.gov/rr/record/webradioschedule2016.html.

71. Abby Smith, David Randal Allen, and Karen Allen, *Survey of the State of Audio Collections in Academic Libraries* (Washington, DC: Council on Library and Information Resources, 2004).

72. Smith, Allen, and Allen, *Survey of the State of Audio Collections in Academic Libraries*, 20.

73. Jeremy A. Smith, "Recent Efforts toward Collaborative Preservation of Recorded Sound," *Notes* 72, no. 3 (2016): 486.

74. CLIR and the LOC, *The State of Recorded Sound Preservation*, 11.

75. CLIR and the LOC, *The State of Recorded Sound Preservation*, 13.

76. CLIR and the LOC, *The State of Recorded Sound Preservation*, 15.

77. Mike Casey, "Why Media Preservation Can't Wait: The Gathering Storm," presentation at AMIA conference, Richmond, VA, November 8, 2013, www.avpreserve.com/wp-content/uploads/2013/11/casey_amia2013.pdf; Mike Casey, *Media Preservation Survey: A Report* (Bloomington: Indiana University, 2009).

78. CLIR and the LOC, *The State of Recorded Sound Preservation*, 30.

79. CLIR and the LOC, *The State of Recorded Sound Preservation*, 27–28; "Celebrating 65 Years of Goodwill & Good Times," WDIA-AM1070, http://mywdia.iheart.com/pages/history/about/.

80. "Survey Conducted by Kurt Nauck," Nauck's Vintage Records, no. 41 (n.d.): 118.

81. CLIR and the LOC, *The State of Recorded Sound Preservation*, 27.

82. Radio Preservation Task Force, "National Recording Preservation Plan," www.loc.gov/programs/national-recording-preservation-plan/about-this-program/radio-preservation-task-force/.

83. Josh Shepperd (professor, Catholic University of America, and director, RPTF), interview with authors, June 16, 2016.

84. "MSU History Department," http://history.msu.edu/people/faculty/michael-stamm/.

85. Michael Stamm (professor, Michigan State University), interview with authors, June 13, 2016.

86. Stamm interview.

87. Stamm interview.

88. Shepperd interview.

89. Stamm interview.

6

TELEVISION NEWS

Perry Wolf, a CBS News documentary producer, once said: "The name of the organization is CBS News. It's not the CBS Public Library," aptly alluding to the role of archives within the network news divisions.

—*Report on the Current State of American Television and Video Preservation*, 1997[1]

The DuMont television network produced more than 20,000 television episodes between 1946 and 1956. The episodes were initially broadcast live in black and white, and they were recorded on film kinescope for reruns and for West Coast rebroadcasts.

Testifying at a 1996 Library of Congress public hearing about television preservation, Edie Adams, an actress and the widow of early television legend Ernie Kovacs, said, "In the early '70s, the [last vestige of the DuMont] network was being bought by ABC, and the lawyers were in heavy negotiation as to who would be responsible for the library of the DuMont shows currently being stored at the facility, who would bear the expense of storing them in a temperature controlled facility, take care of the copyright renewal, et cetera.

One of the lawyers doing the bargaining said that he could 'take care of it' in a 'fair manner,' and he did take care of it. At 2 a.m., the next morning, he had three huge semis back up to the loading dock at ABC, filled them all with stored kinescopes and two-inch videotapes, drove them to a waiting barge in New Jersey, took them out on the water, made a right at the Statue of Liberty, and dumped them in the Upper New York Bay."[2]

THE TELEVISION INDUSTRY

The development of television technology in the United States goes back to the 1920s with inventors such as Philo T. Farnsworth and Vladimir Zworkin, who competed to create the machinery that would eventually make television possible. In 1928, an experimental station in Schenectady, New York, was broadcasting regularly scheduled content three days a week using the mechanical television standard, as opposed to the later electrical one, with accompanying audio supplied by radio.[3] By 1931, the Federal Radio Commission (precursor to the Federal Communications Commission) had issued twenty licenses for experimental television stations in U.S. communities east of the Mississippi River.[4]

But it was not until the New York World's Fair in April 1939 that electrical television as we understand it today was introduced to the American public. In part to promote RCA's nascent plans to sell television sets, the NBC (owned by RCA) telecast of the opening ceremonies of the World's Fair included the first-ever televised appearance by a sitting president, Franklin D. Roosevelt.[5] Fairgoers could watch the live coverage on four different types of RCA sets in the company's pavilion located nearby.[6] Not surprisingly, the telecast from the World's Fair was not captured for posterity.[7]

Radio legend Lowell Thomas simulcast his *Nightly News* program on NBC radio and television for a year starting in 1940, and by 1941, CBS was broadcasting two fifteen-minute, local TV newscasts each day in New York. Anchored by Richard Hubbell, the CBS programs consisted primarily of the anchor reading from a script with an occasional cutaway to a map or still photograph.[8] Obviously, the audiences for these early broadcasts were miniscule, since very few people had television receivers. Again, the broadcasts themselves were not recorded by the station.

World War II interrupted the development of television as the country turned its production facilities to military uses. The Federal Communications Commission set the standards for television transmission in 1941. The newsreel companies produced several programs for use by early television stations, but regular commercial network broadcast news programs didn't start using content specifically generated for television in the United States until 1948.

Broadcast Network Television News

Douglas Edwards was the first to anchor a regularly scheduled broadcast news report. *CBS Television News*, a fifteen-minute nightly newscast, debuted on May 3, 1948. Just five stations, linked by coaxial cable, belonged to the CBS network at the time. ABC aired its first regular newscast in August 1948, called *News and Views* with anchors H. R. Baukhage and Jim Gibbons. NBC's *Camel News Caravan* with John Cameron Swayze began in February 1949.[9] The DuMont network also offered news programs until the network's demise in 1956.

The 1960s saw the rise in status and prominence of the network news anchors, especially Walter Cronkite on CBS and Chet Huntley and David Brinkley on NBC. The evening network news programs expanded from fifteen to thirty minutes in 1963, starting with CBS in September of that year. Just two months later, President John F. Kennedy's assassination marked the point when live television news coverage became the national hearth around which a shocked populace gathered. The networks understood the potential future historical value of their coverage and captured their four days of nonstop news programming for posterity.

By the 1970s the format and structure of the national networks' evening news programs was well established. Television networks opened news bureaus around the country and around the world. When the Westar I satellite was launched in 1974 and made available to commercial enterprises, the networks rushed to take advantage of the new means of transmitting live signals without being bound to AT&T's monopoly on coaxial landlines and microwave relay towers.[10]

The 1980s saw the development of network formats for breaking news, the most acclaimed of which was ABC's *Nightline*. Launched as a Monday-to-Friday late-night news update in response to the November 1979 hostage crisis when Iranian militants seized the U.S. embassy in Tehran, *Nightline* eventually found a regular place in the late-night time slot. But the fortunes of the television networks were changing. Industry consolidation, competition from the burgeoning cable networks, and changing tastes of the audience combined to put the network evening news on a downward spiral that continues to this day.

Local Television News

While the television network news divisions were establishing their dominance as an information source for the U.S. population, local stations also were experimenting with televised news. WPIX in New York City was licensed as an independent station by the owners of the *New York Daily News* in 1946. The station's managers decided their niche would be local news, and by 1948 WPIX offered two local nightly newscasts, one at

7:30 p.m. and another at 11:00 p.m. The station staffed its newscast, *Telepix Newsreel*, with the first local television news anchor, a weathercaster, and a sportscaster—a model that continues to this day.[11] WPIX specialized in breaking news coverage of local events, including plane crashes, fires, political events, and celebrity visits. Covering breaking news was an advantage WPIX held over the network newscasts that were still airing days- or weeks-old film for their national and international coverage.[12]

Another local news pioneer, KTLA in Los Angeles, started as an experimental station in 1939 and was licensed for commercial broadcasting in 1947. It was first owned by DuMont, then by Paramount, but it went independent by 1948. West Coast television station managers felt their region was ignored by the network news organizations. They also felt that network news produced in New York was "stale" by the time it aired three hours later in their market; the KTLA staff turned that into an advantage. Using relatively sophisticated technology for the day, the news staff used small, portable cameras and mobile live transmitters to cover local events in real time.[13] Another independent station in Los Angeles, KTTV, also offered a local newscast in 1948. Competition between the two stations set off the first local TV news wars.[14]

In 1949, a three-year-old child named Kathy Fiscus fell into an abandoned well in a Los Angeles suburb. KTLA and KTTV were on the story within minutes and provided continuous coverage for more than twenty-seven hours with live reports from mobile television equipment at the site. There were probably no more than 20,000 television sets in the entire Los Angeles market at that time.[15] Nonetheless, the eventually unsuccessful rescue effort provided local viewers, who watched with neighbors or on sets in store windows, with a sense of the power of local television coverage to command attention.[16] Unfortunately, none of this precedent-setting local television news coverage exists in television news archives. The only visual record resides in still photographs and a bit of newsreel coverage produced by British Pathé, whose cameras arrived on the scene near the tragic end of the rescue efforts.

Throughout the 1950s, as television sets became household fixtures, local television continued to develop in markets across the country. Local newscasts were typically fifteen minutes in length, to complement the fifteen-minute network news programs that aired at the dinner hour and at 11:00 p.m.

The 1960s saw the continued development of local news as a separate entity from the network broadcasts. Local stations began to understand the value of local news as a means to sell local advertising, the revenue from which they could keep rather than share with their parent networks. By the 1970s, news consultants were advising local stations to adopt "action news" or "eyewitness news" formats and to encourage friendly banter and hometown references among the attractive anchors, weather announcers, and sportscasters. By the early 1980s, local news broadcasts were enormously profitable. Many stations expanded their news operations and added additional time slots for local news.

The development of satellite newsgathering (SNG) in the mid-1980s provided the means for local news operations to expand their newsgathering. The creation of the Hubbard Continental U.S. (CONUS) network based in St. Paul, Minnesota, enabled those major-market stations that could afford a satellite truck and a transmission antenna to capture news from virtually anywhere. Local CONUS news stations could decrease their reliance on the networks for news from outside their own markets. Individual local stations teamed together and shared news content with each other regardless of their network affiliation. The CONUS network stopped newsgathering operations in 2002, but today CONUS offers an online archive of stories its member stations generated and shared.[17]

Local news operations did not escape the industry upheavals of the 1990s and early 2000s, however. Station ownership changes, network affiliation switches, industry consolidation, technological advances, and other developments took their toll on local stations and led to many archival losses.

Public Broadcasting

The U.S. public broadcasting infrastructure was established in 1967. At the urging of a Carnegie Commission report that year, Congress authorized the Corporation for Public Broadcasting (CPB) built around the nonprofit National Educational Television network stations already in operation around the country. In 1969, CPB created a new organization to manage program distribution among the interconnected stations, the Public Broadcasting Service (PBS). By 1972 there were more than two hundred public television stations in the United States.[18]

The congressional hearings in the summer of 1973 into what would become President Richard M. Nixon's Watergate scandal provided an opportunity for the new PBS network to cover an ongoing, major public-affairs event live. The PBS coverage was anchored by Robert MacNeil and Jim Lehrer and featured evening recaps along with the daylong live transmission of the hearings and anchor commentaries. The popularity of the Watergate coverage set the stage for the next development: *The MacNeil/*

Lehrer Report. PBS's signature thirty-minute news program was first broadcast in 1976. PBS expanded the newscast to a full hour with *The MacNeil/ Lehrer NewsHour* in September 1983.[19]

Cable Television Networks

Community antenna television (CATV) was first set up in the late 1940s to deliver over-the-air television via coaxial cable to remote or mountainous communities that could not receive traditional broadcast signals. By the 1970s, however, cable television operators realized it was not just broadcast TV–deprived viewers who might be interested in receiving programming via cable. Taking advantage of advances in terrestrial and satellite signal distribution technology, Home Box Office (HBO) started in 1975. Cable-Satellite Public Affairs Network (C-SPAN) began live broadcasts of the House of Representatives in 1979, and C-SPAN2, devoted to live coverage of the U.S. Senate, launched seven years later. Ted Turner's Cable News Network (CNN) launched on June 1, 1980.

CNN's around-the-clock news operation soon set the standard for a new type of televised news programming. By the end of 1980, CNN could be seen on more than six hundred cable systems around the United States, reaching 4.3 million homes.[20] CNN2, the sister service that aired news headlines, a business report, weather, and sports in a continuous thirty-minute loop, entered the cable scene in 1982 and was soon renamed *CNN Headline News*.

CNN's success in the United States prompted Ted Turner's goal of turning the network into a global news service. By 1988, CNN was available in fifty-eight countries,[21] and many Americans turned to CNN for international coverage rather than the traditional broadcast networks. Breaking domestic news also was CNN's forte. Echoing Los Angeles station KTLA's coverage of a child trapped in a well in 1949, CNN produced breaking and live continuous coverage of the rescue of "Baby Jessica" McClure, a toddler who had fallen down an abandoned well in Midland, Texas, in October 1987. The "Baby Jessica" coverage helped solidify the network's reputation as a breaking-news superstar.

Additional cable networks established their presence as news providers during the 1990s, but with more channels and more competitors, it was more difficult for any one service to maintain dominance. Financial news channels, left-leaning and right-leaning news channels, sports news channels, entertainment news channels, and many more niche offerings created lots of news content but also splintered the news audience and added even more to television networks' woes.

WHY TELEVISION NEWS WAS LOST

As was true for newsreel and radio companies, television news operations focused their archival efforts on storing stock footage and collections of materials that could be reused for future broadcasts. The archives, when they existed at all, were a business resource with little or no attention paid to creating a collection for preservation purposes. This attitude had a devastating impact on the historical record of television news in the United States.

Early television programs were transmitted live, and there was no means of capturing them unless a film camera was pointed at a video monitor and synchronized to the monitor's scanning rate to capture the broadcast (called a kinescope recording). The quality of the picture was not very good, but it was the only means for the networks to distribute programming to affiliates for broadcast at a different time than the live offering. Kinescope recordings were made for live, high-profile entertainment programming rather than for regular news broadcasts. Very few U.S. news broadcasts on kinescope have survived.

Television news footage was shot on 16-millimeter film and was typically logged into the station's collection as stock footage after being used for the day's news broadcasts, if it was kept at all. Stations' film libraries were typically located in basements or backrooms under less-than-ideal conditions, meaning that even with acetate safety film, deterioration was inevitable. And when space ran out, film cans of old news were tossed to make way for new news. The sheer quantity of film generated by the network news operations worked against the goal of maintaining a complete archive. The thirty-minute network news broadcasts often were compiled from more than two hours' worth of film that had been shot and developed each day.

Ampex introduced professional quality black-and-white videotape good enough for broadcast in 1956. For the first time, it became practical to regularly capture live broadcasts as they were aired rather than through the occasional kinescope capture. The two-inch quadruplex videotape format quickly became the industry standard for recording entire programs. The color version of the technology was introduced in 1958. But the Ampex tape machines were the size of a bedroom armoire, and the two-inch tapes were expensive. Most broadcasters erased and reused the tapes over and over, so very few early programs on tape were archived.

Additional industrial and professional analog videotape formats followed in the 1960s and 1970s, employing different standards. Brands and formats included Sony one-inch, half-inch, three-quarter-inch U-Matic;

Early Ampex videotape recorder, ca. 1959. *Courtesy Department of Special Collections, Stanford University Libraries*

Ampex two-inch High Band, two-inch Super High-Band and one-inch A Format; and Phillips half-inch VCR tape. As television stations switched formats, they were not concerned about transferring content from the older formats onto new types of tape. And as different formats of tape machines broke or space ran out, the older formats were more likely to be tossed than archived. Even with the new tape formats for use in the studio, field camera operators still shot the day's images on film, which continued to pile up after being edited into the evening broadcast.

The switch during the mid-1970s through early 1980s to electronic newsgathering (ENG), which used three-quarter-inch videotape in cameras portable enough to record directly on magnetic media, resulted in the most significant loss of the now-superseded television news film collections. Film was a one-and-done format and required wet lab processing and shelf space to store. And the film collections invariably consisted of numerous short rolls of film stored many to a can, with poor or nonexistent labeling. In contrast, videotape in the camera could be used over and over. Once field camera operators switched from film to tape, film cans in station basements became an even larger target for elimination. For local stations, less than 10 percent of local television news film (covering 1950 to 1975) has survived because so much was discarded after the ENG revolution.[22]

Digital video formats were introduced in the early 1990s. Sony, Panasonic, and JVC all offered professional quality digital cameras, but they employed multiple competing standards. High-definition digital video was introduced in 1997 and continued the pattern of incompatible standards and formats. The dizzying array of formats for capturing news images, editing the footage into broadcasts, logging the images and sounds into the broadcast production system, and keeping track of everything over time led to the situation we have today: the legacy of network and local television news is severely compromised because so much of it was generated using systems and technologies that are now long outdated or gone.

Local Twin Cities broadcaster and current executive director of the Minnesota Broadcasters Association Jim duBois explained why local television stations didn't archive their content or think about the monetization possibilities: "To make that archive of any use, someone would have to log it and good luck with that—that would be expensive. As for demand, how long would a local news story be in demand outside the local marketplace? And even within the marketplace, who would want it? I can really understand why a network's archive would be valuable because they are covering stories of national prominence. But stuff here—traffic accidents, fires—I mean, who cares?"[23]

In a 2007 survey of local television station staff about their archives, the following were among the reasons given for why their film libraries were nonexistent: "All film either sold to private collectors or disposed"; "16mm was thrown away in the landfill while our film director was on vacation in 1972"; "WBRE-TV lost all film archive in the flood of '72"; and one station's chief engineer wrote their film was "thrown out and thus destroyed by stupid former employee."[24]

Of course, natural disasters plagued television news archives, just as with archives of other formats. As the only television station in western Colorado for the first twenty-five years of broadcasting and a fixture for half a century, KREX-TV in Grand Junction, Colorado, had compiled a comprehensive history of the region. In 2008, the seventy-seven-year-old building housing the KREX studios was destroyed by a fire, with losses of decades of file tapes, irreplaceable photographs, and other archival materials. As reported in the industry trade publication *Television Week*, "The Sunday morning fire wiped out five decades of recorded history of the area in western Colorado, as well as reels of tapes that reporters and the news operation had saved of their best work."[25] The fire is just one example of how many dangers threatened the preservation of news.

HOW TELEVISION NEWS WAS PRESERVED

The Library of Congress (LOC), memory institutions, academic centers, individual collectors, and the stock footage industry all have played a role in salvaging what television news content we have. However, the internal news libraries of the television networks and local stations have a checkered history in their service as guardians of their own history.

Network News Libraries

Much of the archiving effort within television news operations was focused on creating stock footage libraries to avoid the need to go out and capture original film every time a broadcast needed a clip of the White House Rose Garden or the Manhattan skyline. Rarely was the entire news broadcast captured. That said, the network news companies do have archives that document a portion of their work over time.

The NBC TV Film Library was established in 1936. In a document produced for film library clients in 1952, the library was said to contain the film shot for and used in NBC's earliest television experiments.[26] NBC TV Film Library contained more than fifteen million feet of film, which was being added to at the rate of two-and-a-half million feet of new film each year.[27] The film was being stored in ten fireproof vaults in a library annex in New York City. "Practically every foot of film that has ever been made by NBC's far-flung staff of expert motion picture camera men is in the Library."[28]

The guide to the NBC film library was an extensive card file that described in great detail the contents of each clip. Produced and maintained by a staff of sixteen library workers, the card file was kept current until 1985, when the cards were microfilmed and then tossed.[29] The switch to ENG meant the end of the film library index system.

Today, the NBCUniversal Archives online allows for searches of stock footage and news coverage back to the 1930s.[30] A search for news content from the 1930s returns twenty-one items, the oldest being a clip of the iconic Jesse Owens hundred-meter race during the 1936 Olympic Games in Berlin. Some of the footage is from the Universal newsreel library; other footage is from various production units within NBC television. Using the online stock footage database today, it is clear that the contents of the extensive card files were transferred to the database because the digital records include detailed descriptions of each clip in the collection. But the stock footage library consists of individual clips, not entire newscasts as they aired.

CBS founder William Paley told his news employees to create a stock footage library in 1953. The archive consisted of film that was being shot for evening newscasts and news series such as Edward R. Murrow's *See It Now*. Moving forward, the stock footage library archived images and sound for coverage of presidencies, wars, space exploration, the civil rights movement, popular culture, and any other topic that might be the subject of news. According to Roy Carubia, CBS News manager of archives, the network also (atypically) recorded full broadcasts of programs such as *CBS Reports*, *Person to Person*, and *See It Now*. The earliest CBS network evening news program in the archive is Douglas Edwards's first news broadcast on May 3, 1948—a fifteen-minute program.[31] Today the archive includes three million assets, with materials in every conceivable format: kinescopes, film, every version of videotape and digital formats. CBS works with a number of external vendors to make that content available and license materials for users. The content generates income for the network and is a way to monetize the effort in maintaining the archive.

Broadcast and cable networks still maintain their stock footage news collections and most have lucrative arrangements with third-party vendors to monetize the archival materials they have. However, the material most likely to be in demand could be considered the "greatest hits" of broadcast news. All of the high-value archival content from the networks' collections was digitized early on once the technology was available, and that high-value content continues to provide a steady stream of licensing revenue.[32] Most network news organizations stream content on their websites or through YouTube channels. However, the steady day-to-day coverage that is likely to be of most interest to historians and researchers is largely not digitized or accessible to outsiders.

Documentarian Ken Burns has been working with CBS News archival film from the Vietnam era for a number of years. He is trying to match veterans' letters about certain battles or events with the news footage that was shot by CBS news crews. CBS News Archives manager Carubia explained that the cans of film that Burns is using contain many small rolls of film, much of it reflecting the rushed film processing practices required at the time. CBS crew would process the film while in flight from Saigon to New York and would do things like use masking tape for splices. This creates a nightmare for anyone trying to use that collection now.[33]

In 2013, CPB, the parent corporation for PBS, chose one of the flagship public broadcasting stations, WGBH in Boston, to partner with the LOC to preserve the legacy of the national public broadcasting system. The station was an early innovator in television archiving. The American Archive of Public Broadcasting was built on the foundation of the CPB's inventory of public broadcasting stations that it conducted between 2010 and 2012. Approximately 40,000 hours of public broadcasting programs were digitized in the initial effort, focusing on some of the most vulnerable formats such as two-inch quad videotape.

The Associated Press (AP) started its own video news wire in 1994, but television stations had been subscribers to the regular AP wire content

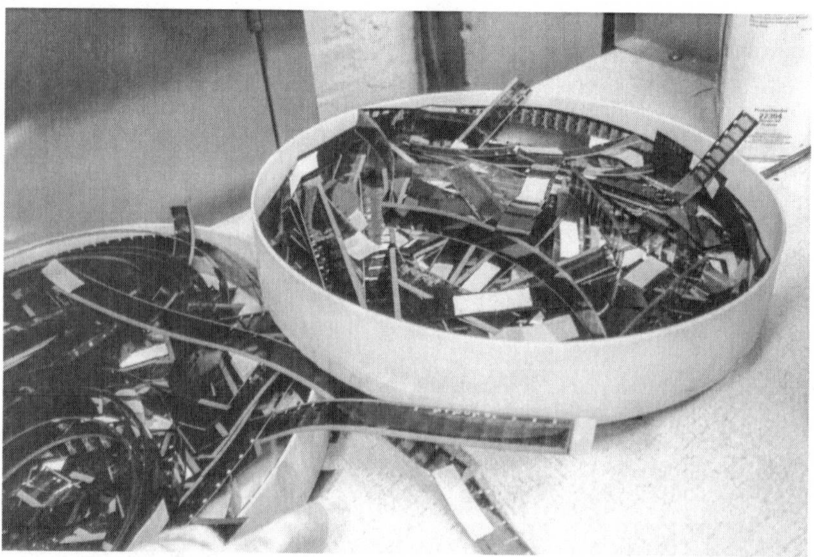

Snippets of spliced film from CBS News Vietnam War coverage. *Hansen Photo/CBS News Archive/New York*

for decades. Today, the AP Archives include all AP broadcast content since 1994, along with several other wire services' broadcast content from 1963 to 1998. All of it is accessible to AP television news members.[34] In 2015, the AP uploaded to YouTube video clips with news events dating back to 1895 through its archival British Movietone newsreel partner for general public access.[35] As of 2016, the AP YouTube channel offers more than 1.7 million clips.

Local Television

A number of scholars and professional associations have attempted to inventory the archives that might still exist in local television stations around the country. In a 2007 Rochester Institute of Technology thesis titled "Uncovering Local History: 16mm TV News Film Remaining in U.S. Television Stations," author Rob Jason Fain summarizes local television archiving efforts, following surveys conducted since the 1980s.[36] The sad conclusion from the surveys analyzed in Fain's thesis is that the majority of local television news is lost to posterity.

That said, there are efforts to encourage local stations to try to salvage what remains. The Association of Moving Image Archivists (AMIA) produced a guide funded by the National Historical Publications and Records Commission, the funding arm of the National Archives and Records Administration, titled *Local Television: A Guide to Saving Our Heritage*, in 2004.[37] The guide was a practical, step-by-step handbook to help local station managers conduct an inventory of their vintage footage and even included a twenty-question quiz to help determine the station's "heritage quotient." Station staff earned more points depending on how they answered questions such as:

> The vintage footage at our station would fill: a) a few boxes; b) several shelves or c) a whole room
>
> When we need to find footage we: a) throw up our hands. We really can't hope to find anything; b) look at the labels for dates or titles, or ask the old guy down the hall; or c) search a database for names, topics, dates, etc.
>
> Our vintage materials physically reside: a) wherever they happen to be; b) in one place that we don't use for anything else; or c) in a physically and environmentally secure space.
>
> The worst thing about our vintage materials is: a) it is long gone; b) it is a financial drain; or c) it is underutilized.[38]

Despite the tongue-in-cheek nature of the quiz, the questions do provide insight into the types of issues facing local television stations trying to preserve their archival content.

In 2009, the CPB contracted with Oregon Public Broadcasting to manage a pilot project to demonstrate the feasibility of coordinating the archiving activities of local public broadcasting stations. Twenty-four local public radio and television stations identified, restored, digitized, and made accessible nearly 2,500 hours of content from their archives related to the civil rights movement and World War II veterans' stories. During the project, many local stations reported that their archival material was in the process of decay, which spurred CPB to conduct a nationwide inventory of local public broadcasting archival holdings.[39] This effort resulted in creation of the American Archive of Public Broadcasting.

Academic Institutions

Academic libraries did not start systematically collecting materials related to television until after the establishment of media studies programs in the 1970s and 1980s. As was the case for film and newsreels, the materials to support the academic study of television were found in books and journals rather than the actual broadcasts themselves. If laser disc or videotape collections were found on campus, they typically were housed in audiovisual centers or similarly equipped spaces outside the traditional academic library. Individual faculty members teaching in media studies or journalism programs may have been early adopters of home video recorders, using the new machines to capture broadcasts over the air, but these personal stashes would not have been recognized as part of a formal library collection for a myriad of reasons, not the least of which would have been copyright concerns.

One academic institution, the University of Georgia, does have a collection of the thousands of broadcast news programs entered into the annual Peabody Awards starting in 1940. The Grady College of Journalism, as the administrator of the prestigious industry award for excellence in radio and television (and now web) public service, recognized its obligation to maintain a record of its history. The collection consisted of film, two-inch quad videotape, and every other format for capturing public affairs broadcasts as they aired. Unfortunately, students in the Grady College had access to the collection and rummaged through the entries, excising film clips, erasing over tape, and causing other types of damage.[40] Once transferred to the University of Georgia Library in 1980, however, the collection came under archival stewardship. The collection has been restored and tens of thousands of award entries are available in a variety of formats through the library's Walter J. Brown Media Archives and Peabody Awards Collection.[41]

The year 1968 marked a major milestone in individual and academic institution efforts to capture and archive television news. A Metropolitan Life Insurance company executive in Nashville, Tennessee, Paul C. Simpson, was a voracious news consumer. He followed the evening news broadcasts by watching several television sets in his living room at once and by listening to one through an earpiece.[42] In the first sentence of his 1995 memoir, Simpson says he remembers hearing, during an evening news broadcast sometime in 1967, psychiatrist and 1960s drug culture guru Timothy Leary encouraging young people to discover themselves by taking LSD. Simpson wanted to find that broadcast to confirm exactly what had been said.[43]

Simpson contacted the three network news divisions to ask if he could visit during a routine business trip to New York in March 1968. During his tours, he asked to see the archives of the evening news broadcasts. To his surprise, he was told by staff at all three networks that the tapes were kept for just two weeks before being taped over. Simpson then started calling around the country to ask whether any other institutions were archiving the news as it was broadcast. The Department of Defense was taping broadcasts and sending excerpts to commanders in Vietnam so they could see how the war was being covered at home. Calls to universities, the FCC, and the LOC helped Simpson conclude, however, "that nowhere was the national news being preserved in a systematic way."[44]

What followed was an extraordinary effort to establish the first archive in the country dedicated solely to television news. Simpson was a graduate of the Vanderbilt University Law School in Nashville. Simpson contacted Vanderbilt Libraries associate director Frank Grisham, who suggested Simpson draw up a proposal for consideration by university faculty and administrators. Simpson took a leave from his job at Metropolitan Life and devoted himself to preparing a proposal, exploring funding options, and working out the logistical issues that would be involved. He traveled to Chicago to meet with people at the Ampex Corporation, who offered to help with equipment and tape. The Vanderbilt committee met and approved the proposal in July 1968, and the group decided that the upcoming national presidential nominating conventions would provide a good experimental project to show that regular taping could be done.

A local Ampex dealer in Nashville helped set up three videotape recorders in the rare book room of the library, which could be locked to better to secure the equipment at night, and Ampex provided ten rolls of tape.[45] Together, Simpson and Grisham sat in the room and taped the nightly news and the full presidential convention coverage, starting on August 5, 1968. Of course, the startling coverage of the violence that erupted at the Democratic National Convention in Chicago made for a perfect test case of the value of recording the news.

Having established the feasibility of capturing television news broadcasts, Vanderbilt University, Simpson, and a number of his generous friends provided funds to keep the project afloat. By 1971 the archive had attracted funding from a number of foundations and the university had endorsed its continued operation on the Vanderbilt campus. That year, James P. Pilkington was appointed administrator of the archive and production began on the *Television News Index and Abstracts*, a tool that became vitally important for access to the collection as it grew. A lawsuit filed by CBS in 1973 threatened to end the archive's over-the-air taping of broadcast news programs, but the Copyright Act of 1976 clarified that such taping was considered acceptable if the content was strictly limited to educational uses. CBS dropped the lawsuit in December 1976.

The Vanderbilt Archive continues to digitally record news content from ABC, CBS, NBC, CNN, and Fox News, and it has sponsorship

Vanderbilt Television News Archive in 1981. *Courtesy Vanderbilt University Special Collections and University Archives*

agreements with major educational and memory institutions that help fund its efforts, including the LOC. It published the monthly guide, *Television News Index and Abstracts* from 1972 to 1994, after which the indexing, abstracting, and search function moved online. Although much news content is now accessible through other online sources, the Vanderbilt Television News Archive continues to serve an important preservation function in that its content is time stamped and authenticated, a crucial factor for serious scholarship. The archive's wary relationship with the television networks regarding copyright has limited its attempts to do more to market and publicize the collection, but the value of the Vanderbilt effort is undeniable.

The University of California, Los Angeles Film and Television Archive was originally established as the National Television Library in 1965 when the president of the foundation for the National Academy of Television Arts and Sciences (NATAS) offered the university what was the largest collection of kinescopes, films, and television ephemera then in existence.[46] Included in the collection were broadcast news entries from NATAS national Emmy awards competitions. These were typically not an entire broadcast, however, but an individual story or package that had been entered into the various national Emmy judging categories. Starting in 1965, the UCLA Archive also got the entries for the regional Emmy competitions from the local Los Angeles stations, typically one full news broadcast a year. Though few in number, these submissions did capture momentous events such as the Watts riots, earthquake and disaster coverage, and other important local news.[47]

The UCLA Broadcast NewsScape Archive of International Television News is another collection managed by the UCLA Library on behalf of the Department of Communication Studies. The archive captures and digitizes more than one hundred news programs from forty-six television channels with program-level metadata and actual content from 2005 to present. The capture process relies on closed-caption texts, onscreen texts, detected visual shapes, and other attributes of the audiovisual stream. The collection grows by one terabyte with fifty-six million new searchable words each month. All material captured by the NewsScape Archive must be used within the provisions of the copyright law that allow for educational use of such content by those authorized to have access to the collection—primarily UCLA-affiliated users. The library lends DVDs of content, and it charges fees to cover the costs of operating the archive.[48]

Although C-SPAN itself launched in 1979, it was not until 1987 that attention was paid to archiving the public affairs network. The private, nonprofit public service network initially provided gavel-to-gavel coverage of the U.S. House of Representatives. Robert Browning, a faculty member at Purdue University in Indiana, started the archive as a project in the School of Liberal Arts. C-SPAN has now expanded to three networks providing public affairs programming from a variety of government and educational sources. The archives at Purdue contain every C-SPAN program aired since 1987 and can be accessed through the C-SPAN Video Library.[49] C-SPAN itself assumed responsibility for the archival operations and the facilities were moved from the Purdue University campus to the Purdue Research Park in West Lafayette in 1998.[50]

The Moving Image Resource Collections (MIRC) at the University of South Carolina (USC) also has local television content. When the MIRC was established, three local television stations in South Carolina donated their stock footage and outtakes newsfilm collections. One collection also included the scripts for the broadcasts as they aired. The dates of the material generally cover the 1950s to 1980s, with the most comprehensive materials covering 1963 to 1979. The television film collections are maintained in humidity- and temperature-controlled vaults. Nevertheless, the MIRC staff learned that the red strips of film that separated individual items on the newsfilm reels hastened vinegar syndrome so they had to go through all the cans and replace those with white strips of film that didn't decay.[51]

Many other universities have collections of television news content that were donated or purchased over the years. But because there is no union catalog or master list of such collections, it is questionable whether a researcher will find the appropriate collection when it is needed. And in many cases, the institutions that house these collections have not had the resources to fully catalog and properly store the materials.

The Library of Congress

Broadcast evening news content was not systematically collected by the LOC for reasons of format, space, and copyright considerations. Television content was not a priority for acquisition until after passage of the 1976 Copyright Act, which established the American Television and Radio Archives. The law allowed libraries to tape broadcasts without violating copyright.[52] CBS, ABC, and PBS did not start depositing copies of their evening newscasts with the LOC until after the 1976 changes in the law. NBC never deposited copies because it felt the network's General Counsel's office would be able to defend any copyright claims that arose.[53]

In 1977, the LOC convened a symposium for those institutions and individuals who managed television archives in the United States. The television archivists had been frustrated with the refusal of the Society of

American Archivists to allow them to form their own committee within the SAA.[54] As a result of that LOC gathering, the American Film Institute convened a Television Archives Advisory Committee (TAAC) that met for the first time in January 1979.[55] The TAAC provided television archivists with a way to keep their momentum going in their efforts to recognize television as an important archival concern.

The LOC reorganized its structure for managing sound and moving images and established the Motion Picture, Broadcasting and Recorded Sound Division in 1979. At that time, the television collection consisted of 15,000 cataloged programs—primarily special event coverage, presidential television appearances beginning with Truman, coverage of the Kennedy assassination, and some obscure DuMont and National Educational Television documentaries.[56] The new division had the ambition to fill in the collection with materials that were not well represented and to begin systematically collecting television content going forward.

A number of gift agreements led to transfers of thousands of program films and tapes to the LOC during the following years. Through these types of gifts and acquisitions, the LOC today has early broadcasts of NBC's *Meet the Press*, CBS's *See It Now*, *Face the Nation*, *CBS Reports*, and *60 Minutes*, ABC's *Issues and Answers*, and similar types of public affairs programming.[57] A pamphlet titled "Moving Images at the Library of Congress" provided to visitors to the collection in 2016 stated: "The television collection at the Library of Congress offers a broad but uneven view of the history of broadcasting in the United States. Issues such as technology, copyright, and early acquisition policies have left surprising gaps in the collection, but through copyright deposits, gifts, donations and purchases, the Library's television collection continues to grow."

The television networks stopped depositing copies of their newscasts with the LOC in the early 1990s. The former head of the library's Motion Picture, Broadcasting and Recorded Sound Division said that by that time, the rapid change in the physical formats for deposit was a huge issue. For instance, there were fifty or sixty different formats of videotape in use, and the networks and other depositors kept trying to send the cheapest format with the least suitability for long-term archiving purposes. The LOC also had problems maintaining all of the machines that were required to play all of those recording formats. Finally, the backlog of content it was receiving (200,000 items per year) was going to take more than thirty years to process by the division's four staff members. So the LOC's network news deposit effort was abandoned.[58]

The Motion Picture, Broadcasting and Recorded Sound Division today holds master copies of the news broadcasts being captured by the

Vanderbilt Television News Archives, for which it pays $100,000 per year. Obviously, the first decades of the nightly news programs are not part of the collection. The division also houses an extensive collection of NBC network radio and television paper documents but little NBC network television news content. In 2004, the LOC funded the Preserving Digital Public Television project through its National Digital Information and Infrastructure Preservation Program to focus on the importance of digital preservation for public broadcasting, which resulted in the creation of the American Archive of Public Broadcasting described earlier.

Museums and Historical Societies

The Museum of Broadcasting (MOB), founded by CBS leader William S. Paley, opened to the public in New York in 1976. The first president of the MOB, Robert Saudek, was a former network television producer. To get the collection started, Saudek asked his former television and radio colleagues to contribute tapes of old shows.[59] To avoid copyright problems, the museum, now named the Paley Center for Media, has a standard donor agreement, which states, in part, "the Donor is giving to the Paley Center title to the physical tapes or records delivered, but is not transferring to the Paley Center any title to, or any artistic, literary or other proprietary right or copyright in, the Collection Programs themselves."[60] The New York and Los Angeles locations have viewing rooms where users can request any of the items in the collection. However, due to copyright and other issues, the majority of the collection cannot be used off-site or streamed online.

The Museum of Broadcast Communications (MBC) in Chicago has a national focus, although a large part of its effort is directed toward the local and regional radio and television legacy of the upper Midwest. Bruce DuMont, who had an award-winning career in radio and is the nephew of Allen B. DuMont, founder of the DuMont Television Network, started the museum in 1987. The collection includes radio and television news programming in addition to vast entertainment collections. As an example of the fragility of such institutions, however, the MBC's website includes a plea for funding to help restore an initial version of the museum's website that crashed under requests to stream the more than 8,000 program episodes the museum had digitized and made available for free. The website, offering just 10 percent of the museum's collection, was thought to be lost forever in 2013, but museum staff learned that it could be recovered and restored for $40,000, for which they were soliciting donations.[61]

Historical societies have played an important role in archiving the local broadcast news collections that have survived. Minnesota broadcast pioneer KSTP-TV has been family owned for its entire existence. The company's radio station, WMAD, went on the air in 1923 when founder Stanley E. Hubbard was twenty-six years old. He bought a television camera in 1939, but his attempts to launch a local station in the Twin Cities were stalled by World War II. The television station, by then titled KSTP, was established in 1948 with regularly scheduled newscasts as part of the programming from the very start.[62] Perhaps because of the stability of family ownership over the company's entire history, the archive of news content was complete when station officials approached the Minnesota Historical Society (MHS) in 1988 about getting help cataloging the collection. The switch to ENG meant that the news film archives were no longer in high demand and were becoming a storage problem.

The MHS was interested but didn't see how it could accept the collection without any direct benefit to the society. By 1994, the two parties had negotiated a model arrangement whereby the physical property ownership and copyright for all of the content is transferred to the society twenty-five years after program creation. The MHS agreed to properly store, preserve, and provide public access to the collection. With a gift from the Hubbard Family Foundation, the MHS created the KSTP/Hubbard Broadcasting Media Center, which has the facilities to manage the archive. The KSTP-TV newsroom has full access to the archive in MHS's care. "With materials going back to 1948 it is the only television collection in the state with materials predating 1975."[63]

A review of the materials on MHS's website reveals that the archive consists primarily of film or video clips, many without sound, as opposed to recordings of broadcasts as they aired on the local KSTP station. Although the stock footage collections are invaluable as a record of what was being captured by the film and video photographers at the time, they do not provide a viewer with any sense of whether or how those images were actually used in a broadcast that was seen by the public.

Another local television collection resides in the Mississippi Department of Archives and History. Capturing a unique record of the civil rights movement, according to the Department's website, "The WLBT Newsfilm Collection (1954 to 1971) documents two decades of intense social and political change in Mississippi. It primarily consists of more than 520,000 linear feet (635 16mm reels) of black-and-white and color film footage from WLBT, the NBC affiliate in Jackson, Mississippi. The collection is made up of the outtakes of the film shot, not the segments that were broadcast on the news program. Some but not all of the reels have sound tracks."[64]

In 2003, the National Television and Video Preservation Foundation (NTVPF) was set up as a private effort with a small budget to provide funding for efforts similar to those that had been successful through the National Film Preservation Foundation, established the previous decade. The effort on behalf of television and video, however, was unsuccessful in generating interest and funding. After providing small grants to three dozen mostly noncommercial and independent sector grantees, the NT-VPF folded in 2008.[65]

Individuals

Individual collectors have played an outsized role in the preservation of television news. Whether journalists or individual news enthusiasts, much of the televised material we have available today is due to the efforts these people exerted to save television news. The collection of 1,171 *Meet the Press* broadcasts from 1947 to 1984 in the LOC can be traced to the program's original host, Lawrence Spivak, who kept personal copies and later donated them to the LOC.[66]

Robert Dotson, whose long-running series *The American Story with Bob Dotson* appeared on NBC's *Today Show* from 1975 to 2015, posted a personal note to the Facebook page of the American Journalism Historians Association that captures the efforts of individual journalists well:

> Over the years, I saved more than six thousand American stories, whenever my bosses, looking to save space, tossed them out. I preserved not just the stories themselves, but all the video we shot over forty years, crisscrossing the country, traveling more than four million miles. Before hard drives and Cloud technology all those segments were stored on film or videotape, maintained at my expense in air-conditioned rooms—first in my basement then, as the collection grew, in warehouses. That great wealth of American stories, all of the scripts, research and video are now available to students and researchers at the Dotson Archive in the University of Oklahoma.[67]

When Ted Koppel, longtime host of ABC's *Nightline* series learned that the network was discarding its archive of the program, he took possession of the tapes that covered decades of his work. He made a personal donation of all his materials to his alma mater, Syracuse University, in 2011. The news release issued by Syracuse at the time of the donation said: "The videotapes include the complete collection of 'Nightline' and 'The Koppel

Report.' Koppel will also donate correspondence, photographs, cartoons, awards and notebooks, including those from when he was a Vietnam War correspondent."[68] Because of copyright restrictions, however, the collection may be used only on the Syracuse campus in a library reading room.[69]

Individual enthusiasts also have played a role in capturing television news off the air. A librarian in Philadelphia, Marion Stokes, casually began taping television programs in 1977.[70] Stokes thought local and network television news was especially important and when the cable news phenomenon blossomed, she also began recording MSNBC, Fox, CNN, CSNBC, and C-SPAN around the clock, with as many as eight television recorders running at a time. When she got too old to continue the effort individually, she hired an assistant to help run the tape recorders. She continued her effort for thirty-five years, right up until her death in 2012 at the age of eighty-three. The collection of VHS tapes eventually numbered 140,000, which she stored in her own home and in several apartments she owned.

Roger Macdonald, the television archivist at the Internet Archive, heard about the Philadelphia librarian's collection and contacted Marion's son. The Internet Archive had been recording national television news, but its collection of pre-2009 news was spotty and mostly relied on donations of content. Macdonald recognized the Stokes archive was a treasure trove and worked out an arrangement to have the 140,000 tapes shipped to San Francisco. The collection is stored in a temperature-controlled warehouse and is slowly being digitized to be made available through the Internet Archive's website.

TELEVISION NEWS PRESERVATION CHALLENGES

Preserving the film, tape, and digital record of television news poses many challenges, and machine obsolescence is one of the most pressing. Although it isn't economically feasible to go back and digitize all of the materials in television archives, managers recognize that some content will be lost forever if it isn't migrated to new formats. For example, the two-inch quad videotape is high on the list of archive managers' migration priority list. The Cold War–era tape machines are cumbersome, and the technicians who knew how to run and service them are retired or deceased. Carubia, the CBS News Archive manager, has one working two-inch tape machine and a second one he is cannibalizing for parts. The LOC has two functioning two-inch machines, with a dozen others used for parts at the Packard Campus.[71] Those two institutions are frantically transferring the remaining two-inch tape content in their collections to digital formats before the machines that do work stop functioning altogether.

CBS News Archive videotape collections. *Hansen Photo/CBS News Archive, New York*

When Indiana University conducted its census of audio-visual holdings, the authors also included the availability of playback equipment as part of the survey. What they learned was disturbing. For example, a typical replacement head assembly for a one-inch videotape machine cost $16,000 in 2013, according to the director of the study. One Ampex part for two-inch videotape machines must be replaced every three months; the cost in 2012 for that part was $5,200. Other replacement parts for two-inch machines are not available at any cost.[72] In 2016, the world's last manufacturer of one-inch VCR machines, so popular as home recording and playback devices in the 1980s, announced it was ending production of the machines.[73] Similar stories can be told about many other obsolete machines.

Physical issues with film also raise problems. The black-and-white and Ektachrome color reversal emulsion films used by the television news divisions were less stable than negative-positive emulsions. And because the film was chemically processed under time deadlines for broadcast as soon as possible, the manufacturers' recommended specifications for stable film developing were rarely followed.[74] This means that the film is more likely to fade and deteriorate over time.

Film can with multiple rolls of damaged film. *CC BY 4.0/Asia Harman/Indiana University*

As is true for all acetate film, vinegar syndrome is a constant threat if film is stored under less-than-ideal temperature and humidity conditions. And any film stored next to a can or a roll of film that is suffering from vinegar syndrome gets attacked by the gases as well. It was not unusual for as many as fifty short rolls of film to be stored in one metal film canister when television stations were still using that medium, making vinegar syndrome even more problematic.[75]

Just as with film, videotape is subject to deterioration over time if not stored properly. Videotape was never engineered to provide a permanent record, and archivists do not recognize magnetic tape as an archival recording medium. Sticky-shed syndrome in videotapes, analogous to the vinegar syndrome that affects acetate film, happens when the binder that holds the iron oxide magnetic coating to the plastic tape base deteriorates, resulting in dusty particles shedding from the tape as it is handled or run through a playback machine. Tape decay also happens when the magnetization of the oxide coating on the tape weakens over time. Even when videotape in any format is archived, the quality of the images and sound degrade to the point where much of the content is rendered useless if the physical storage conditions are not ideal.

TELEVISION ARCHIVE USERS

It is not just news professionals and historians who use news archives. Government agencies such as the FCC use television news broadcasts as evidence for regulatory purposes. For example, the agency has for some time tried to enforce a "news distortion doctrine" as part of its regulatory oversight of broadcast licensees. The doctrine allows litigants to charge that a station's news coverage is distorted and violates a licensee's obligation to serve the public's interest, convenience and necessity. Although there are significant First Amendment concerns about the agency's attempt to regulate news content, the rules about evidence for such enforcement actions are clearly stated in FCC documents.

First, the claimed distortion "must be deliberately intended to slant or mislead." The FCC and the courts require "evidence other than the broadcast itself, such as written or oral instructions from station management, outtakes, or evidence of bribery."[76] In other words, there must be evidence that the top management knew the broadcast was distorting information. The second element of bringing a successful claim requires the litigant to show that the distortion involved a significant event, "not merely a minor or incidental aspect of the news report."[77]

These requirements make it clear that the FCC or individuals claiming that a news program violated the agency's news distortion doctrine must have access to the broadcast archives. And the archival content must consist of the broadcast as it was delivered to the audience in a specific newscast, not just the stock footage or outtakes in the station's internal library. Also, the materials that would demonstrate prior knowledge of distortion among the top management of the station would almost certainly require the station to have a system of archiving production documents, e-mail messages, scripts, and other types of materials that would shed light on the process of creating the story at issue.

Given our descriptions of the way that television content has—or mostly has not—been archived, it would be very difficult for a litigant or for the FCC to uphold a claim of news distortion since the archival record would be incomplete. In fact, this aspect of the agency's activities has been the subject of much discussion, scholarly comment, and legal decision making.[78] The example, however, provides an insight into the myriad of uses for which news archives might be needed.

NOTES

1. William T. Murphy, *Report on the Current State of American Television and Video Preservation*, vol. 1 (Washington, DC: Library of Congress, 1997), www.loc.gov/programs/national-film-preservation-board/preservation-research/television-videotape-preservation-study/.

2. William T. Murphy, *Los Angeles Public Hearing*, vol. 2 (Washington, DC: Library of Congress, 1997), Edie Adams's testimony before the panel of the Library of Congress, Los Angeles, CA, March 6, 1996, www.loc.gov/programs/national-film-preservation-board/preservation-research/television-videotape-preservation-study/los-angeles-public-hearing/.

3. Gary Edgerton, *The Columbia History of American Television* (New York: Columbia University Press, 2010), 33.

4. Harold A. Lafount, "Uncle Sam's View of Television," *Television News*, March–April 1931, 29.

5. Edgerton, *Columbia History*, 15.

6. Edgerton, *Columbia History*, 14.

7. Murphy, *Report*.

8. David Sheddon, "Early TV Anchors," Poynter.org, last updated April 4, 2006, www.poynter.org/2006/early-tv-anchors/74607.

9. Sheddon, "Early TV Anchors."

10. Christopher H. Sterling and John M. Kittross, *Stay Tuned: A History of American Broadcasting*, 3rd ed. (Mahwah, NJ: Lawrence Erlbaum Associates, 2002), 412.

11. Craig M. Allen, *News Is People: The Rise of Local TV News and the Fall of News from New York* (Hoboken, NJ: Wiley-Blackwell, 2001), 5.

12. Allen, *News Is People*, 6.

13. Allen, *News Is People*, 8.

14. Allen, *News Is People*, 8.

15. Patt Morrison, "The Little Girl Who Changed Television Forever," *Los Angeles Times*, January 31, 1999.

16. Mark Willliams, "Paramount's KTLA: The Leading Station in Early Los Angeles Television," in *Television in America: Local Station History from across the Nation*, ed. Michael D. Murray and Donald G. Godfrey (Ames: Iowa State University Press, 1997), 334; Pete Noyes, *Who Killed the Big News? A Memoir* (Los Angeles, CA: Pete Noyes, 2014), 8.

17. CONUS, www.conus.com/.

18. Charles L. Ponce de Leon, *That's the Way It Is: A History of Television News in America* (Chicago, IL: University of Chicago Press, 2015), 179.

19. James Day, *The Vanishing Vision: The Inside Story of Public Television* (Los Angeles: University of California Press, 1995), 278.

20. Ponce de Leon, *That's the Way It Is*, 179.

21. Ponce de Leon, *That's the Way It Is*, 191.

22. Murphy, *Report*.

23. Jim duBois (executive director, Minnesota Broadcasters Association), interview with authors, May 5, 2016.

24. Rob Jason Fain, "Uncovering Local History: 16mm TV News Film Remaining in U.S. Television Stations" (MA thesis, Rochester Institute of Technology, 2007), 23.

25. Michele Greppi, "Fire Darkens Colo. Stations: KREX, KFQX Set to Restore Signals in Wake of Blaze," *Television Week*, January 28, 2008, 4.

26. NBC-TV Film Library Handbook, National Broadcasting Company History Archives, file P421, 3, Library of Congress, Motion Picture, Broadcasting and Recorded Sound Division.

27. NBC-TV Film Library Handbook, 5.

28. NBC-TV Film Library Handbook, 7.

29. Dan Einstein (television archivist, UCLA Film and Television Archive), interview with Hansen, February 19, 2016; Daniel Einstein, *Special Edition: A Guide to Network Television Documentary Series and Special News Reports, 1955–1979* (Lanham, MD: Scarecrow Press, 1987).

30. NBCUniversal Archives, "NBC Radio Archives—Historic Broadcasts," www.nbcuniversalarchives.com/nbcuni/home/nbcradio.do.

31. Roy Carubia (manager of archives, CBS News), interview with authors, April 22, 2016.

32. Carubia interview.

33. Carubia interview.

34. Associated Press, www.aptn.com/news.

35. Todd Spangler, "British Pathé Uploads Entire 85,000-Film Archive to YouTube in HD," *Variety*, April 18, 2014.

36. Fain, "Uncovering Local History."

37. *Local Television: A Guide to Saving Our Heritage* (Hollywood, CA: Association of Moving Image Archivists, 2004).

38. *Local Television.*

39. Alan Gevinson, "A Brief History of the AAPB," American Archive of Public Broadcasting, http://americanarchive.org/.

40. Fay C. Schreibman, "A Succinct History of American Television Archives," *Film & History* 21, nos. 2–3 (May/September 1993): 90.

41. "Peabody Awards Collection," http://gilfind.uga.edu/vufind/Record/376 1721.

42. Frances Goins Wilhoit, producer, "Vanderbilt Television News Archive," (Bloomington: Indiana University School of Journalism, Center for New Communications, 1978), cassette tape T81:0421 in Paley Center for Media in New York, viewed by authors April 24, 2016.

43. Paul C. Simpson as told to Patricia G. Lane and F. Lynne Bachleda, *Network Television News: Conviction, Controversy, and a Point of View* (Franklin, TN: Legacy Communications, 1995), 7. Actually, the program aired on *NET Journal* on the Nashville public television station on November 20, 1967 (*The Tennessean*, TV listings, November 20, 1967, 30). Produced by WGBH in Boston, it was titled "LSD: Lettvin vs. Leary" and featured a debate between Leary and an MIT professor who opposed drug use. The program can be found in WGBH's archive (incorrectly date-stamped as November 30, however) at http://openvault.wgbh.org/catalog/V_0669B2FE8ADC4F80A8D89CB58D02BBC0

44. Simpson, *Network Television News*, 9.

45. Simpson, *Network Television News*, 21.

46. *UCLA Film & Television Archive: 50 Years* (Los Angeles: Regents of the University of California, 2015), 13.

47. Einstein interview.

48. Sharon E. Farb and Todd Grappone, "UCLA Broadcast NewsScape Archive of International Television News," presentation at Center for Research Libraries conference, Global Resources Roundtable: Beyond the Fold: Access to News in the Digital Era, Chicago, IL, June 27, 2013; "NewsScape," http://tvnews.library.ucla.edu/.

49. C-SPAN.org, www.c-span.org/.

50. Purdue Research Park, "Company Profile: C-SPAN Archives," www.prf.org/researchpark/companies/c-companies/C-SPAN%20Archives.html.

51. Amy Ciesielskii (local TV news collection curator, USC Moving Image Research Collections), interview with Hansen, March 28, 2016.

52. Murphy, *Report*.

53. Patrick Loughney (director, Packard Humanities Institute), interview with authors, June 7, 2016.

54. Sarah Ziebell Mann, "American Moving Image Preservation, 1967–1987," (MLIS thesis, University of Texas at Austin, 2000), 30.

55. Mann, "American Moving Image Preservation," 45.

56. Arlene Balkansky, "Through the Electronic Looking Glass: Television Programs in the Library of Congress," *The Quarterly Journal of the Library of Congress* 37, nos. 3–4 (summer/fall 1980), 458–75.

57. Sarah Rouse and Katharine Loughney, *3 Decades of Television: A Catalog of Television Programs Acquired by the Library of Congress, 1949–1979* (Washington, DC: Library of Congress, 1989).

58. Loughney interview.

59. Gail Horowitz, "Museum Preserves Old TV Programs," *TV/Radio Week*, December 25, 1977, 26.

60. Paley Center for Media, "Paley Center Donation Agreement and Terms: Section 3," 2002.

61. Museum of Broadcast Communications, https://squareup.com/store/museum-of-broadcast-communications/.

62. Erin Peterson, "The Pioneers," *Murphy Reporter*, spring 2015, 9.

63. *Local Television*, 32.

64. Mississippi Department of Archives and History, "WLBT Newsfilm Collection," www.mdah.ms.gov/arrec/digital_archives/newsfilm/.

65. Jan-Christopher Horak, "The Gap between 1 and 0: Digital Video and the Omissions of Film History," *Spectator* 27, no. 1 (2007): 32; Internal Revenue Service Form 990 for National Television and Video Preservation Foundation, 2002, www.guidestar.org/profile/13-4141025; Gregory Lukow (chief, National Audio-Visual Conservation Center, Packard Campus), interview with Hansen, April 7, 2016.

66. Rouse and Loughney, *3 Decades of Television*; Library of Congress, Meet the Press Collection, https://memory.loc.gov/ammem/awhhtml/awrs9/meet_press.html.

67. Bob Dotson Facebook post, American Journalism Historians Association Public Group, March 24, 2013, www.facebook.com/groups/24811577199/search/?query=dotson; Linda Miller, "Longtime TV Newsman Gives Collection to OU; Bob Dotson's Donation Includes Tapes, Photos from 33-Year Career," *The Oklahoman*, February 16, 2003.

68. Glenn Coin, "Anchorman Ted Koppel to Donate Personal Collection of Videotapes to Syracuse University," *Syracuse University News*, June 10, 2011.

69. "Ted Koppel Collection: A Description of the Collection at Syracuse University," https://library.syr.edu/digital/guides/k/koppel_t.htm.

70. Sarah Kessler, "This Former Librarian Single-Handedly Taped 35 Years of TV News," *Salon*, November 22, 2013, www.salon.com/2013/11/22/this_former_librarian_single_handedly_taped_35_years_of_tv_news_newscred/.

71. Hansen tour of Library of Congress National Audio-Visual Conservation Center, Packard Campus, Culpeper, VA, April 6, 2016.

72. Mike Casey, "Why Media Preservation Can't Wait: The Gathering Storm," presentation at AMIA conference, Richmond, VA, November 8, 2013, www.avpreserve.com/wp-content/uploads/2013/11/casey_amia2013.pdf.

73. Elizabeth Weise, "World's Last VCR Manufacturer to Cease Production," *USA Today*, July 22, 2016.

74. Murphy, *Report*.

75. Steven Davidson and Gregory Lukow, eds., *The Administration of Television Newsfilm and Videotape Collections: A Curatorial Manual* (Los Angeles, CA: American Film Institute, 1997).

76. Galloway v. FCC, 778 F.2d 16 (D.C. Cir. 1985), 20.

77. Galloway v. FCC, 20.

78. Clay Calvert, "Toxic Television, Editorial Discretion and the Public Interest: A Rocky Mountain Low," *Hastings Communications and Entertainment Law Journal* 21, no. 1 (fall 1998): 163–204; Mark Emery, "Regulating Televised News: A New Season for the Public Interest Standard," *Notre Dame Journal of Law, Ethics and Public Policy* 19 (2005): 737–88; Chad Raphel, "The FCC's Broadcast News Distortion Rules: Regulation by Drooping Eyelid," *Communication Law and Policy* 6 (2001): 485–539; Nariessa L. Smith, "Consumer Protection in the Marketplace of Ideas: A Proposal to Extend the News Distortion Doctrine to Cable Television News Programs," *Thurgood Marshall Law Review* 40 (2014–2015): 223–72.

7

THE DIGITAL TURN

> Experts on computer technology believe the day will soon be here when it will be possible economically and technically speaking to read into a computer the entire content of all news articles. This will be accomplished, they say, by optical scanning of printed material or through the use of the signals which would be used to create the printed material in the first place.
>
> —Andrew Fisher, *New York Times* executive director of daily operations, 1966[1]

In the 1957 movie *Desk Set* Spencer Tracy plays an efficiency expert hired by a television network to convert its print-based reference library to an "electronic brain machine called EMMARAC . . . the Electromagnetic Memory and Research Arithmetical Calculator."[2] It took some time for the news industry to catch up to Hollywood's vision of digital news storage and retrieval. Technological innovations in news organizations were usually confined to some new forms of analog recording media or methods intended to improve the same production techniques that had always been used. With the dawning of the digital age, however, news content storage and retrieval options would radically change.

The digital shift in production methods set the stage for the full-on digital revolution in news that started in the 1990s. Eventually, the digitally produced output of print news publications and broadcasts would be used to craft new news products. The particular preservation issues of these Internet and application-delivered news products are discussed in chapter 8.

This chapter examines the ways that the shift to digital production methods affected news organizations' news content archiving. We also focus on the impact of new digital conversion methods on news preservation and access—the methods that turned analog news assets into ones and zeroes.

NEWSPAPERS

The *New York Times* was still a good decade away from converting its "hot type" (using molten metal poured into typesetting frames) press room to "cold type" (using computer-generated copy to create photographic plates for the printing press) when proposals describing computer-based story retrieval systems were delivered to upper management.

The *New York Times* had been in the information-access business since 1913, when its internally produced index to news stories was cumulated quarterly and sold to the public for the first time as the *New York Times Index*. The *Index* allowed searchers to use keywords to look up articles, which would then need to be found on microfilm or in bound volumes of the newspaper.

On June 15, 1966, a committee convened "to construct a comprehensive information retrieval system that would meet all current and anticipated demands by users on the staff and outside clients and that would furnish the content of published Indexes at the same time."[3]

The committee noted that one of the incentives for finding an electronic alternative to the clip files currently used by the newsroom was that "clippings and sometimes entire files are missing, that clippings are not in chronological order, that subject files are often too general and inclusive, and that help in pinpointing material is not always available."[4] This next iteration of the *New York Times Index*, it was envisioned, would add an abstract of the news article to aid retrieval and, it was hoped, to provide key information without the user having to find the source article.

Support for exploring enhanced information retrieval services grew. A memo on February 13, 1967, from Harding F. Bancroft, the *New York Times* executive vice president to publisher Arthur Sulzberger, underscored the urgency and the perceived potential. "The important thing is to shift our Morgue [traditional news clip library] operations to a twentieth century approach. The Morgue is a tremendous asset but a depleting one because of the substantial loss of material. The sooner we get to a system whereby loss is eliminated, the better off we will be. And we should not hesitate to spend a lot of money on it not only as an essential resource of The Times now but as an income-producing potential in the future."[5]

On December 4, 1967, Robert S. November, an employee in the *Times* promotions department and a member of a committee looking into full-text retrieval for their information resources, wrote a memo to John Rothman, head of the corporate archives and information initiatives. In it he listed the requirements expected of a full-text system. He wanted one that would retrieve the entire news story, unlike the current news index, which referred users to the date and page where the story would be found in hard copy or on microfilm. A satisfactory solution would allow the user to quickly see the full story, to display the full page, because the placement and play of the story on the page could be important, and to make it possible to obtain a hard copy of the story.

November reported that they had "found a system which satisfies these requirements." He went on to describe a system consisting of a "closed circuit TV and hard copy printers. With this system every page of The Times containing news or editorial matter would be put on a form of microfiche. At every one of 10 locations there will be a keyboard and a TV set. An inquirer can type out a date and page and will see it on his screen within 10 seconds. He can zoom in on the story he wants, and if necessary, push another button and get a hard copy print out."[6]

In April 1973, the in-house publication *Trends of the Times* announced in an article titled "Faster Clip" that "the morgue may not be dead yet, but its days are numbered." It described the new Times Information Bank service this way:

> It's a marvelous array of computers, cathode ray tubes (called CRT by those in the know), electronic printers and other hardware programed [sic] to allow someone seeking information on a given subject to obtain it almost instantaneously. It works like this. Each day several hundred stories, reports and columns from The Times and other newspapers and magazines are abstracted and indexed. These abstracts are put on magnetic tape and processed into the Information Bank system. A reporter seeking information sits at a CRT terminal equipped with keyboard and viewing screen. He or she types the topic request and—bingo—on the screen appears the relevant abstract.[7]

Finding the full text of the article, however, still required the second step of locating the microfiche, described in the *Trends* article as "4 x 6 inch microphotographs; a single microfiche contains the entire contents of a weekday Times."[8]

This technological leap from analog (clipping files) to digital (computer access to story abstracts) was far from successful, at least in the view of the newsroom. Peter Millones, assistant managing editor, outlined the concerns in a December 1973 memo to managing editor A. M. Rosenthal. Among the problems with the new research system was access to limited numbers of terminals that required reporters to leave their desks—and phones. Challenges included inadequate indexing, three-to-four day lag time for information to get into the database, and the need for reporters to "change their habits so that they more nearly resemble researchers."[9] Ultimately, the biggest problem was the fact that the limited information—just keywords and an abstract—rarely met a reporter's needs for broader background and full context. They ended up having to go to the printed clips or microfilm to see the complete story.

Within a few years of the Information Bank's launch, a technology that would enable true full-text retrieval of news stories (without the added step of going to the microfilm) was moving into newsrooms. Computer typesetting, called "pagination," began to replace the laborious work of placing metal slugs into typesetting trays. *New York Times* editor Allan Siegal outlined three advantages in a 1976 internal staff memo titled "Questions and Answers about the Electronic Newsroom."

One advantage was that "electronic writing and editing give news people greater control over the finished product."[10] The transfer of typewritten copy from the newsroom to the typesetters laying out the story often resulted in typos or awkward hyphenation. With this new technology, the phototypesetting would be direct from the editors. "No error will be able to get into the copy unless we ourselves let it slip by."[11]

Second, there would be a reduction of time between deadlines and the press runs because the labor-intensive typesetting step would be eliminated. This gave reporters more time to make the story as complete and current as possible.

And it was Siegal's third advantage that signaled the upcoming change for news archiving. "Once a story is in the computer's memory, it can be called out repeatedly, in an endless variety of formats, at the touch of a few buttons."[12] The move from hot type to cold type enabled digital capture of the raw material of the news story and presaged the move in newsroom libraries from clipping and filing physical newsprint stories to digital storage and retrieval systems.

The Toronto *Globe and Mail* introduced the first truly full-text digital newspaper content storage and retrieval system in 1976.[13] Researchers seeking news content were able to locate articles that contained the terms for which they searched and to retrieve, in one step, the entire contents of the stories on a computer screen. Major vendors such as Lexis/Nexis, Vu/Text,

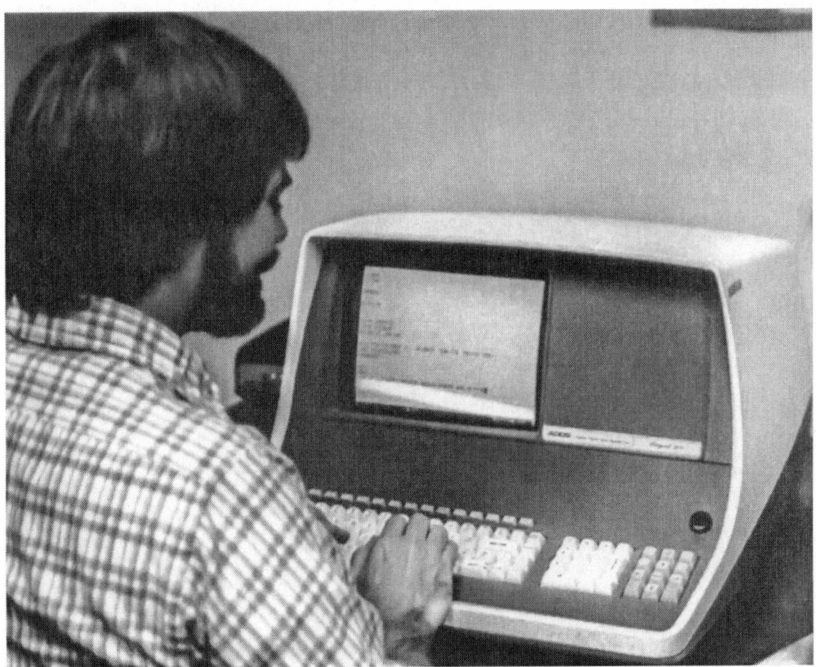

Librarian at the *New York Times* Information Bank terminal in the M. D. Anderson Library, 1980s. *Courtesy University of Houston Digital Libraries*

DataTimes, BRS, DIALOG, and Dow Jones News Retrieval established their digital databases of full-text newspaper content in the early 1980s by signing agreements with news producers to capture and sell newspapers' digitally produced content.

Some of these systems were established by newspaper groups that recognized a way to get into the information vending business, to monetize their news content after original publication, and to provide economies of scale for their newspapers to support in-house news research services. For example, Vu/Text was a Knight-Ridder operation. Newspapers without their own vendor operations partnered with long-established database vendors (BRS and DIALOG), which were anxious to offer full-text news resources to their longtime customers.

These early digital systems allowed searchers to identify individual stories that had appeared in the print newspaper. A librarian at Philadelphia's Free Library described the value of this kind of full-text retrieval of newspaper content: "There's really no substitute for the data-base, because the *Inquirer* has no printed index. Aside from Vu/Text, there's no alternative except to thumb through old issues of the paper looking for the article you need."[14]

The disadvantage was that the database captured only the text. Any visual content that appeared in the print newspaper (pictures, graphs, tables, comics) was noted, but the database did not contain a digital version of those materials. Furthermore, the version of the database that the news librarians sent to the vendor was not a complete reproduction of the text that appeared in print. Newspapers with multiple editions through the day or zoned editions would send just one version to the vendor.

After a Supreme Court decision regarding copyright for freelance material, newspapers started stripping out all of the stories written by freelancers before sending the text to the vendor.[15] Many newspapers limited the number of wire-service stories they sent, and no newspaper sent agate material such as box scores, funeral notices, stock market listings, calendars, classified or legal-notice advertising, or similar materials. None of the display advertising was included either. In other words, the version of the newspaper that appeared in the "full-text" databases was in no way an accurate replication of what had appeared in print.

As vendors improved their interfaces and search capabilities and as costs came down, newspaper databases became the sine qua non of access to news archives for libraries, historical societies, and individual searchers. However, most database news content does not extend back any further than the mid-1980s, when pagination systems were introduced in newsrooms. The text-only versions are also absent any visual cues about the importance or play of the story. Design attributes of the newsprint version of the story—such as headline size or placement on the page ("above the fold" being more significant, perhaps, than stories that ran at the bottom of the page)—are lost.

The growing information industry was volatile. The *Times* sold its information services (the abstract/microfiche-based Information Bank and early full-text database) to Mead Data Central in 1983, triggering a flurry of memos among *Times* executives about the folly of now paying for access to their own archive files. Competition for exclusive access to certain newspaper databases, shifts in corporate ownership, and a growing number of new entrants to the full-text delivery service ranks made it difficult to track who had which news databases available and for what range of dates. None of the vendors of full-text online news still in business today rely solely on newspaper content to stock their database offerings.

How Digital Newspaper Stories Were Lost

The transfer of the digital output of news publication to a digital archive was not entirely loss free. *Times* librarians alerted their management in 1984 that a week's worth of their 1973 story abstracts were missing from the Information Bank database. Librarian Linda Amster said in a memo: "At this point . . . the integrity of the Abstracts data base is in question: we can no longer be confident that there actually are no articles when the 'no abstracts available' message is displayed, or that the number of abstracts cited for a given subject reliably correlates with the number of articles written."[16]

The memo's closing paragraph summed up concerns about reliance on these new digital databases to provide access to the news record: "If the integrity of the data base cannot be demonstrated, we shall have to re-evaluate our plans for weeding the Morgue, since they are based on the assumption that the InfoBank will serve as a reliable back-up for discarded files."[17] It was clear, at least on the part of the custodians of the newspaper's content, that a backup system was needed.

As for wholesale loss of archives, computer crashes rival the destructive loss of records due to fires or floods. In 2002, the Columbia *Missourian*'s server crashed. Housed in the University of Missouri's journalism school, the server had contained fifteen years' worth of newspaper stories and seven years' worth of digital images. "Although a backup did exist, the system that was holding the material had become obsolete, rendering the information irretrievable."[18]

Weeding digital files or the decision—for lack of time or space—to stop archiving some content also affected the thoroughness of the news archive. Tom Pellegrene, manager of news technology at the Fort Wayne *Journal-Gazette*, said in the early 1990s that they were working with very limited server space. They decided to stop archiving obituaries. In this case, their backup system was the local library: "Our local public library has a wonderful database of everything we did, and we can still get them off our microfilm, but there are several years there we wish we had back. Fortunately, our loyal opposition [Fort Wayne's afternoon newspaper, the *News-Sentinel*] had a different plan during this time, and on deadline we sometimes look for their obit first, then go to microfilm for our version," said Pellegrene.[19]

But the biggest challenge to preserving digital stories results from changes from one publishing system to another. A librarian at a Midwest newspaper described a situation that occurred after her newspaper purchased a new electronic archiving system in 2001. Their previous database stored all locally produced stories dating back to 1994. When a new publishing system was installed, the contract called for converting their existing database into one that would integrate into the new publishing system. However, that conversion was far less than satisfactory. "Many stories had text stripped out; fields were all jumbled; some important fields [such as corrections to stories] were omitted altogether. A portion of the database [essentially two years of data] was not converted at all and to this day remains a black hole in our database."[20]

Compounding the problem was the fact that the system on which the newspaper's previous database had been housed died before the transfer to the new archiving system. As a cost-savings gesture, the service contract had not been renewed. As a result, reporters had to work for about six months without access to the library database, and staff and reporters resorted to manually looking through hard copy of newspapers to try to find the information they needed.[21]

NEWS PHOTOGRAPHY

The digital turn for capturing photographs began with Steven Sasson's pioneering work creating a digital camera at Kodak's Apparatus Division Research Lab in the mid-1970s. Not until 1991, however, was Kodak's digital camera refined enough to be offered to the public. High cost (the initial version was $13,000) and storage restrictions kept most newsrooms from switching from their film-based cameras to digital.[22]

However, because of the switch from hot type to cold type, digital photography was already in place in many newsrooms through the use of scanners to digitize film negatives for placement in pagination systems. The Associated Press (AP) started issuing their photographers a compact portable photo film negative scanner called the Leafax in the mid-1980s for use in the field. The AP announced in 1990 that newsrooms would need a digital darkroom to receive the AP's high-speed digital photo transmission service, called Photostream. This further accelerated newsrooms' move from analog to digital photo processing and publication. Within two years, nearly all of the AP's 1,000 photo clients had these digital darkrooms, called the Leaf Picture Desk.[23]

This switch from analog to digital transmission vastly increased the number of photos sent to the AP's clients. According to Hal Buell, former director of the AP Photography Service and leader of the AP's shift to digital, the service went from sending out 120 photos a day in analog format to 2,000 daily digital transmissions. In an interview, Buell attributed this "waterfall of photos" to "better equipment, better training, better transmission, and better coverage." He also acknowledged there is a downside to digital photography that can affect archiving and retrieval. "Lots of good stuff gets

Associated Press Leafax photo film negative scanner, 1980s. *CC BY-SA 3.0/US/Morio/CP+/2014*

lost. There is a lot of duplicative material. One day someone will need to go in and weed. Because there are so many photos, there is not enough time to write good photo captions."[24] The absence of descriptive photo captions makes it more difficult to locate appropriate images.

How Digital Photos Were Lost

In individual newsrooms, the routine for shifting from filing physical photographic prints, negatives, or metal cuts to digital images was a preservation challenge. The *Wisconsin State Journal* and *Capital Times* library director, Ron Larson, described the impact of the digital darkroom on library workflow in an article for *News Library News* in 1994.[25] According to a survey of news librarians he conducted regarding digital archiving practices, he discovered twelve of the twenty newspapers that responded had a digital darkroom, but only two of them had any type of digital archiving system for their images.

In Larson's own newsrooms, experimentation with digital imaging had begun but managers had turned down multiple requests for additional computer storage equipment for the photos. They set up a stop-gap archiving system until, according to Larson, a "full-fledged archiving system was on the market. This required the library to connect to photographers' individual computers so that the library could receive the images for indexing and storage, and for the library to send images back to the newsroom for later publication."[26] This, in theory, was a good temporary solution but, as Larson reports, there were problems. One issue was that photographers were not consistent about sending the images; the library had to go in and find them. To save space on the storage discs, the images had to be compressed, which added yet another step. The software used to find images once they were in the storage system was inadequate. Larson said "many keywords could not be found when conducting searches."[27] The storage media, called optical discs, were of sufficient concern that a dual storage system to digital audio tapes (DAT) was instituted "primarily for backup purposes to guard against discs going bad."[28] No wonder Larson concludes his 1994 report, "Indexing and filing digital images is more time consuming for the library compared to the traditional filing and indexing of prints."

Another digital image preservation issue is that the ease of snapping a digital photo is matched by the ease of deleting it. According to a 2006 study on digital camera use: "A lower proportion of digital images is saved compared to film. Digital images are deleted at the scene, in the newsroom and before being archived. Photojournalists . . . expressed anxiety about their news organization's irregular archiving policies and the obsolescence of archival technology."[29]

This concern was echoed in comments made by a photographer in a 2007 survey about digital image archiving: "'I have used negs and slides for 20 years. . . . My concern is that digital may erase future historical images and rob generations of important images not felt as important now."[30]

Time magazine photographer Dirck Halsted offered a perfect example of this concern in a 1999 interview on PBS. He describes "a little piece of photographic lint" that he remembered once the presidential sex scandal between Bill Clinton and Monica Lewinsky broke in early 1998. Seeing Lewinsky, he recalled her face and knew he had photographed her earlier. His researcher looked through thousands of older images in the archives, eventually finding a photo of Lewinsky embracing the president at a fund-raiser two years earlier. But, Halsted said, what was most interesting to him was that there were photographers from other agencies at the fundraiser that day who also probably had shots of Lewinsky that had been discarded and forgotten. Here is Halsted's take on the dangers of digital cameras:

> We see photographers who work covering . . . things that are history, throwing two-thirds to three-quarters of their pictures away . . . just to clear the space with no sense [of] "well, maybe tomorrow, maybe one of these people will turn out to be really important," and you don't

> know it today. The still image is still the most powerful tool that we have insofar as how we remember things. We're in the memory business. We're losing our photographic heritage and the question is, how can you enable people to collect those memories? That's the question.[31]

RADIO AND TELEVISION

> For all its advantages, the transition to digital workflows has also come with its challenges: bloated storage, unprotected assets and proprietary formats.
>
> —*Digital Archiving for Filmmakers*, 2010[32]

The digital turn for broadcast news—both radio and television—happened on two fronts. In terms of the broadcasting signal, the switch from analog channels to digital began for television in the early 1990s. In 1996 the Federal Communications Commission (FCC) authorized an additional channel to television stations, allowing them to experiment with digital broadcasting along with their analog signals. By 2009, the FCC ended permission for analog transmission. Digital broadcasts became the rule, and television's digital turn was complete.

Digital radio broadcasting has not been fully embraced in the United States. While many radio control rooms and studios have digital equipment, there is not yet the mandate for digital transmission of radio signals as there is with television, although the FCC has permitted radio stations to simulcast analog and digital channels. With a digital audio receiver, a user can program the equipment to display weather updates, news content, and related information if the radio station is making that content available. Many automakers now include digital-enabled radios as standard equipment.[33]

By the end of the 1980s, television stations began purchasing digital editing equipment that allowed the conversion of analog recordings on videotape to digital content that could be edited on a computer. A decade later, the introduction of professional quality digital video cameras meant that users no longer had to convert video from analog to digital form. Digital content came straight from the camera.[34]

Seeing the advantages of digital recording, many broadcast stations began the process of converting some analog content to digital audiotape and digital video discs. But this is complicated by the legacy of multiple recording formats. CBS News Archives director Roy Carubia runs a complex enterprise, overseeing a collection of more than three million assets. When requests come in for items from their stock library footage (which date to 1953) or sound clips from radio (which date to 1933), they automatically convert the analog recording to digital. The fact that dozens of recording media have been used over the years is the challenge. Different equipment is required to handle the different formats and, as Carubia explained in an interview, the tape often outlasts the equipment needed to render it. As much as he wishes all of the analog assets in his archive could be digitized, the estimated $168 million price tag means he will continue with the slow process of digital conversion when material is requested.[35]

Now it is easier to track and log content as it enters the system because television news production has fully migrated to digital processes. For example, all CBS television news shows since 2013 are immediately captured in the digital archive system. Four full-time employees log and add metadata to the 230 hours of news content that come into the system each week. The material from the server is migrated onto digital tape and is also saved on a mirror server in another location outside Manhattan. The database that provides access to the archive content has migrated at least twice, with little loss of information from one version to the next.[36]

How Digital Broadcasts Were Lost

> The harsh reality is that these vaults have been more burial ground than archive, prompting one pundit to label them as "a place old clips are sent to die through lack of use, an offline video cemetery."
>
> —*Digital Archiving for Filmmakers*, 2010[37]

Digital broadcast archives face obsolescence issues, just as their analog counterparts do. Unless early digital tapes and discs have been migrated to the most recent formats, the machines used to play those archival copies will soon be unavailable or inoperable. For example, a digital videocassette tape called D3 was widely used in the television industry starting in the early 1990s. The D3 format is now obsolete, and the videocassettes themselves are particularly vulnerable to damage. The British Broadcasting Corporation started migrating 340,000 digital D3 tapes in its archive in 2007 before both the tapes and the machines to play them became unusable. By 2014, less than a third of the content had been migrated to digital file–based storage. As one writer said about the project, "it is more than questionable whether there are enough D3 head hours left in existence to read all the information back clearly and to an archive standard."[38]

Reels of D2 and D3—two types of obsolete digital videotape. *Courtesy GREATBEAR analogue & digital media ltd.*

Even when content is migrated from obsolete to more recent systems, the differences in technical standards, such as data compression rates from one version to another, can cause data loss. This is especially disastrous for digital video and sound files, which tend to be very large and challenging to move and store. Digital video will remain an expensive medium in terms of download, navigation, and seeking time. It will be crucial to find appropriate methods for long-term digital video preservation to avoid losses similar to those that affected television film and analog videotape.

CONVERTING ANALOG ARCHIVES TO DIGITAL

The digital turn changed news output and how it could be preserved. But it also created new methods for conversion of analog news objects such as stories, photos, film, and audio into digital forms.

Digitizing Printed and Microfilmed Newspapers

Microfilm was a space-saving solution for many newspapers. Contracts with microfilm service vendors provided newspapers with a secure way of photographing their complete publication, replacing the need to maintain cumbersome bound volumes.

Sending microfilm to the Library of Congress (LOC) for copyright deposit requirements ensured that cover-to-cover copies of publications were maintained. But microfilm, as discussed in previous chapters, had problems as a long-term storage medium. As for its use as a way to find information from past newspapers, without an index or some kind of referencing scheme to unlock the location of relevant articles, scrolling through newspaper microfilm files was cumbersome and frequently frustrating.

But as computer storage costs dropped and the sophistication of optical character recognition (OCR) technology grew, a new method for making previously published newspapers searchable arrived on the scene. Two Bell and Howell divisions, among the largest of the services that provided microfilming for newspapers, merged to become ProQuest in 2001.[39] Among its first initiatives was scanning and digitizing the microfilm archives of several large U.S. newspapers.

When analog microfilm is digitally scanned, the content on each of the scanned pages becomes searchable. This is not without issues. As Sandy Levy explained in an article for *News Library News* in 2003, "The job of digitizing microfilm itself is tremendous. Broadsheet newspapers are cumbersome, and the print is tiny. The quality of the scanning is vital, or there's no point in doing the work. Some old microfilm is nearly impossible to read, so it's a struggle for the scanners to work."[40] As the computer programmers' old saying goes, "garbage in, garbage out." If the quality of the item being scanned has deteriorated, the output from scanning it will be unsatisfactory. For this reason, Levy concludes, "Newspapers that have kept print copies have a big advantage, and newspapers that are preparing to do this [scanning] in the future would do well to save electronic versions [PDFs] of the full pages."[41]

News organizations have been archiving portable document file (PDF) versions of their print newspaper content since the early 2000s.[42] Most use an external vendor to produce and manage the PDFs, and these comprise the e-version of the printed newspaper that is available to subscribers. Advertising departments rely on PDF versions of printed newspapers to verify ad placements, as well, because PDFs capture the page design of content in the printed newspaper. In 2009, the LOC ran a pilot program to explore the feasibility of accepting PDFs in place of microfilm for copyright deposit. However, the pilot did not result in a permanent process and is still under discussion, despite newspaper organizations' impatience with the cost and inefficiency of continuing to produce and send microfilm.[43]

The option of digitally scanning both old hard copy issues and old microfilm images in their collections has led many memory institutions to shift their focus away from microfilm as the preferred archival medium. Although digital capture of fragile newsprint or deteriorating microfilm may seem like a good alternative to keeping bound issues or microfilming the pages, the notion of a "preservation" version of *anything* in digital form is highly problematic.

A Canadian company, Cold North Wind (CNW), was among the first to create a market for scanned newspaper archives. Founded in 1998, it took CNW four months to scan the complete publishing history of the *Toronto Star*.[44] CNW's website, Paper of Record, quickly grew to include millions of scanned newspaper pages. Unlike ProQuest, which targeted the largest newspapers for its scanning and digitization service, CNW was interested in making smaller, regional papers' content accessible. As CNW's founder Bob Huggins explained, smaller papers were more willing to share their content in exchange for a fully functional digital archive.[45]

Paper of Record's growing range of scanned content and its growing user base attracted Google, which bought CNW in late 2008. This became the foundation of Google's News Archive. Over the next several years, Google scanned millions of microfilmed news pages from two thousand titles from around the world and covered material spanning two hundred years.

According to Carly Carlioli, editor at the *Boston Phoenix*, one of the newspapers included in the scanning project, Google's method of providing a scanned image of the whole newspaper page seemingly solved one problem: "It threaded a loophole for newspapers, who, in putting pre-internet archives online, generally would have had to sort out tricky rights issues with freelancers—but were thought to have escaped those obligations due to the method with which Google posted the archives."[46] (Instead of posting the articles as pure text, Google posted searchable image files of the actual newspaper pages.)

Considered a boon to smaller newspapers that would never have the budgets to support an ambitious scanning initiative, Google found that even for a well-funded technology powerhouse, there were considerable challenges with digitizing newspaper pages. Again, Carlioli explains that "Google reportedly used its Maps technology to decipher the scrawl of ancient newsprint and microfilm; but newspapers are infamously more difficult to index than books, thanks to layout complexities such as columns and jumps, which require humans or intense algorithmic juju to decode."[47]

In early 2011, Google announced it would no longer be adding new scans of old newspapers to its News Archive and on August 14, 2011, without any notice, Google shut down the Google News Archive website altogether.[48] The combination of copyright issues, pressure from publishers, and complexity of providing cleanly scanned pages was apparently too much to manage.

After complaints from historians, genealogists, and many others about the loss of the database, CNW founder Bob Huggins resurrected Paper of Record, charging an institutional membership fee for libraries or a monthly rate for individuals to gain access. The company no longer added content to the database, but at least the scanned newspaper content that had originally been accessible through the service was once again available.[49]

Digitizing Photo Collections

Once the digital production of photographs was fully incorporated in newsrooms, internal photo databases were created. These digital photo archives were parallel to, but not incorporated with, the text archives that were generated from "cold type" publication. Predigital prints were not part of the database. As photo prints from the analog archives were retrieved and used in an issue of the newspaper, they would be scanned by the photo desk and therefore become part of the digital photo archive. But the cost of scanning—both in staff time and equipment—precluded most newsrooms from converting their entire archive of photo prints to digital format.

As discussed in chapter 3, some newsrooms, in their dual desires for reducing storage space and saving processing costs, fell for "get scanned quick" schemes like the Rogers Photo Archive debacle. Others have donated their analog photo collections to local memory institutions in the hopes that they can take on the cost of conversion. However, budgetary constraints have curtailed many of these scanning efforts.

One example of a photographic scanning project funded by memory institutions is the collection of 55,000 digital images shot by Chicago *Daily News* photographers between 1902 and 1933. The *Daily News* ceased publication in 1978, but in the interest of saving space, 80,000 glass negatives weighing about ten tons were donated to the Chicago Historical Society in 1960. In collaboration with the LOC's American Memory project, 55,000 of these glass negatives were selected to be scanned. Several factors determined which negatives were scanned; those deemed the most unusual and the ones for which long-term survival was most tenuous were chosen. Because glass plate negatives are more fragile than film negatives, their use by researchers was restricted, providing further justification for their scanning. Since the collection had been culled by the staff of the Chicago *Daily News* over the years, project coordinators felt that whatever remained would be of value. With great care in transferring corresponding information about each image and triplicate digital versions, this digitization project has opened up access to images that had been saved but had not been accessible because of their fragile nature.[50]

Digitizing Radio

Private collectors and former radio station staffers continue to serve as amateur archivists for radio content of all types. A former staff member of WCCO radio in Minneapolis, Minnesota, is responsible for recovering and digitizing a huge cache of tapes from that CBS-affiliated station's history. According to Jim duBois, executive director of the Minnesota Broadcasters Association,

> at the WCCO transmitter site in Coon Rapids is a complete archive of their on-air audio product from late 1966 through 1989. It is on ten-inch reel tape. . . . There are thousands of reels in the basement. Tom Gavaras, who operates . . . radiotapes.com, has been making regular visits to the site and is digitizing it. He takes a handful of reels home. . . . There is not a handy way of indexing everything on the tape because there is no time code—each tape can hold several days of audio, so it's hit and miss—but he's done a lot of digitization. . . . It is every second of [local and network] audio from late 1966 to 1989.[51]

A number of the projects to digitize analog radio archives discussed in chapter 5 provide insight into the process as it is taking place in radio stations around the country. Public radio stations, in particular, have taken the lead in developing best practices and technical standards for these digitizing efforts, with the help of grant funding from public and private sources and with assistance from the LOC's Radio Preservation Task Force.

Digitizing Newsreels, Television Film, and Analog Video

Film digitization is controversial as a conservation method for a variety of reasons. Purists argue that a digital copy does not capture the nuance of the original film as it was projected onto the screen. Archivists also have serious concerns about technical obsolescence. Which digital format should be used for copying, and who will ensure that the machines and software to render those digital copies will be available in the future?[52] Who will be responsible for migrating today's cutting-edge digital copy to tomorrow's even newer format? Rob Stone, curator of the Moving Image Collections at the LOC described it this way: "A visitor from another planet could arrive here and probably be able to reverse engineer a piece of film—you hold it up to light to see the images, there are holes on the edges that means it moved through a machine of some kind. That could not be done with any form of magnetic media. You look at a piece of videotape or a digital disk and there is no way to understand it. If you don't know what it is, you don't know what it is."[53]

Nevertheless, the LOC is digitizing its film and analog video collections and encouraging digital deposit of materials going forward. The Packard Campus houses the humidity- and temperature-controlled vaults where the broadcast materials are stored. The staff there is in the process of digitizing vast amounts of its analog content, including 35-millimeter and 16-millimeter film and two-inch, one-inch, three-quarter-inch and half-inch videotape. The video ingest center has gear racks equipped with robotic arms that automatically load videotape cassettes into decks of players, push the play button, and remove the tapes after they have been transferred to digital formats.[54] The Packard Campus staff is also attempting to migrate early digital broadcast formats to more recent and archive-approved formats before the machines that can read those early digital discs and tapes become inoperable.

The LOC and the National Archives are deeply involved in creating the standards for broadcast archival stewardship going forward. Both institutions

"Scanity" digital scanner for converting 16- and 35-millimeter film. *Courtesy Cinelicious*

have an incentive to do so as guardians of thousands of miles of film and videotape. Since archives of video content require special handling of deteriorating physical objects and obsolete, barely functioning playback equipment, there are special challenges in migrating analog content to archival digital formats. That said, a 2016 post in the LOC blog on digital preservation stated:

> the basics are already well understood and championed by other communities where expertise in this area is profound: data storage research, all forms of computer sciences, information and knowledge management, emulation and migration specialists, and research repositories have a deep history in long-term data preservation. . . . Increasing the engagement of the analog film and video world with the digital preservation community, and vice versa, will yield tremendous benefits on both sides of the divide.[55]

Indiana University has made a particular mark in the area of physical preservation of video formats. The 2009 "Media Preservation Survey" conducted by university staff concerned about the state of the collections on campus identified a number of issues that required attention. Indiana University had more than 560,000 audio, video, and film objects in more than fifty formats. Nearly all were found to be "actively deteriorating, some quickly and catastrophically."[56]

In 2015, Indiana University (IU) announced it was providing $15 million over five years to "digitize, preserve and make universally available—consistent with copyright or other legal restrictions—all of the most critical media objects judged important by experts across the university's eight campuses by IU's bicentennial in 2020."[57] The project includes efforts to generate standardized workflow and metadata cataloging processes along with the physical transfer of media content to digital form. Broadcast news materials are among the items in the IU collection, and the work they are doing is establishing "best practices" for the future.

NOTES

1. Memorandum from Andrew Fisher to Lester Markel, August 2, 1966, New York Times Company records, "General Files—Computers 1966–1969," New York Times Corporate Archives, MssColl 17802, box 103, file 9, Manuscript and Archives Division, New York Public Library.

2. "Desk Set Script—Dialog Transcript," *Drew's Script-O-Rama*, www.script-o-rama.com/movie_scripts/d/desk-set-script-transcript-hepburn.html.

3. "Report from Committee on the Information Retrieval Project," New York Times Company records, "General Files—Information Bank 1964–1999—General 1964–1969," New York Times Corporate Archives, MssColl 17802, box 187, files 4–7.

4. "Report from Committee on the Information Retrieval Project."

5. Memorandum from H. F. Bancroft to Arthur "Punch" Sulzberg, February 13, 1967, New York Times Company records, "General Files—Morgue 1947–1994," New York Times Corporate Archives, MssColl 17802, box 168, files 3–5.

6. Memorandum from Robert S. November, December 4, 1967, New York Times Company records, "General Files—Information Bank—1964–1995—General—1964–1969," New York Times Corporate Archives, MssColl 17802, box 187, files 4–7.

7. "Faster Clip," *Trends of the Times*, April 1973.

8. "Faster Clip."

9. Memorandum from Peter Millones to A. M. Rosenthal, December 1973, New York Times Company records, "General Files—Information Bank 1964–1995—General 1970–1995," New York Times Corporate Archives, MssColl 17802, box 188, files 1–3.

10. Allan Siegal, "Questions and Answers about the Electronic Newsroom," 1976, New York Times Company records, "General Files—Information Bank 1964–1995—General 1970–1995," New York Times Corporate Archives, MssColl 17802, box 188, files 1–3.

11. Siegal, "Questions and Answers."

12. Siegal, "Questions and Answers."

13. David A. Rhydwen, "Computerized Storage and Retrieval of Newspaper Stories at Globe-and-Mail Library, Toronto, Canada," *Special Libraries* 68, no. 2 (1977): 57–61.

14. Doran Howitt, "Databases Target Micro Users, New Online Services Offer Full-Text," *InfoWorld*, May 21, 1984, 36.

15. *New York Times Company, Inc. v. Tasini*, 533 U.S. 483 (2001). Freelancers were paid once for the story that ran in the newspaper but not for any uses of their work that lived in the digital archive and generated ongoing income for the news organization and the vendor. The Tasini decision said freelancers' work was copyrighted and they deserved to be compensated when their stories were digitally accessed; most news organizations decided to strip freelance content out of their databases rather than pay.

16. Memorandum from Linda Amster to James L. Greenfield, 1984, New York Times Company records, "General Files—Information Bank 1964–1995—General 1970–1995," New York Times Corporate Archives, MssColl 17802, box 188, files 1–3.

17. Memorandum from Linda Amster to James L. Greenfield.

18. Lene Sillesen, "Minus Proper Archives, News Outlets Risk Losing Years of Backstories Forever," *Columbia Journalism Review*, July 21, 2014.

19. Tom Pellegrene, e-mail message to Paul, June 22, 2016.

20. Source requested anonymity, e-mail message to Paul, June 23, 2016.

21. Source requested anonymity, e-mail message to Paul.

22. "When Was the First Digital Camera Made, How Much Did It Cost, and Who Invented It? The History of the Digital Camera," *Bright Hub*, April 28, 2009, www.brighthub.com/multimedia/photography/articles/33452.aspx.

23. Jim Rosenberg, "Wirephoto Update," *Editor & Publisher*, March 1992, 31–33.

24. Hal Buell (photography service director, Associated Press), interview with authors, April 24, 2016.

25. Ron Larson, "A Follow-up on the Photo Survey's Minimal Response with a Look at an Interim Approach to Electronic Pictures," *News Library News* 16, no. 2 (1994): 15.

26. Larson, "A Follow-up."

27. Larson, "A Follow-up."

28. Larson, "A Follow-up."

29. Lucinda Davenport, Quint Randle, and Howard Bossen, "Now You See It; Now You Don't: The Problems with Newspaper Digital Photo Archives," *Visual Communication Quarterly* 14, no. 4 (2007): 218–30.

30. Davenport, Randle, and Bossen, "Now You See It."

31. *American Photography: A Century of Images*, episode 3, "Photography Transformed, 1960–1999," Public Broadcasting Service, October 1999, www.pbs.org/ktca/americanphotography/filmandmore/filmandmore.html.

32. Beth Marchant, ed., *Digital Archiving for Filmmakers* (New York: Access Intelligence, 2010), 2.

33. Federal Communications Commission, "Digital Radio," last updated November 4, 2015, www.fcc.gov/es/consumers/guides/digital-radio; Sterling and Kittross, Christopher H. Sterling and John M. Kittross, *Stay Tuned: A History of American Broadcasting*, 3rd ed. (Mahwah, NJ: Lawrence Erlbaum Associates, 2002).

34. Wikipedia, "Non-Linear Editing System," last modified July 2, 2016, https://en.wikipedia.org/w/index.php?title=Non-linear_editing_system&oldid=727909397.

35. Roy Carubia (manager of archives, CBS News), interview with authors, April 22, 2016.

36. Carubia interview.

37. Marchant, *Digital Archiving*, 49.

38. "D1, D2 & D3—Histories of Digital Video Tape," The Great Bear, www.thegreatbear.net/video-tape/d1-d2-d3-histories-digital- video-tape.

39. Paula J. Hane, "Bell & Howell Becomes ProQuest Company," *Information-Today*, June 11, 2001.

40. Sandy Levy, "Digitizing Microfilm: An Overview," *News Library News* 26, no. 1 (2003): 1, 8–9.

41. Levy, "Digitizing Microfilm," 8.

42. Kathleen A. Hansen and Nora Paul, "Newspaper Archives Reveal Major Gaps in Digital Age," *Newspaper Research Journal* 36, no. 3 (2015): 290–98.

43. Danielle Coffey, "The Perils of Preservation: The Library of Congress' Transition from Microfilm to Digital Newspaper Records," *Newspaper Association of America Public Policy Bulletin*, February 25, 2016.

44. Bruce Gillespie, "All the News That's Fit to Scan," www.brucegillespie.com/Articles/Allthenewsthatsfittoscan.html.

45. Gillespie, "All the News."

46. Jared Keller, "Google Shuts Down Newspaper Archive Project," *The Atlantic*, May 2011.

47. Keller, "Google Shuts Down Newspaper Archive Project."

48. Wikipedia, "Google News Archive," last modified May 29, 2016, https://en.wikipedia.org/wiki/Google_News_Archive; Robert B. Townsend, "'Paper of Record' Disappears, Leaving Historians in the Lurch," *AHA Today,* April 17, 2009, http://blog.historians.org/2009/04/paper-of-record-disappears-leaving-historians-in-the-lurch.

49. "Paper of Record," https://paperofrecord.hypernet.ca/default.asp.

50. Library of Congress, "Photographs from the Chicago Daily News," http://memory.loc.gov:8081/ammem/ndlpcoop/ichihtml/build.html.

51. Jim duBois (executive director, Minnesota Broadcasters Association), interview with authors, May 5, 2016.

52. Thomas Nachreiner, "Future-Proof? How Audiovisual Archives Adopt Digital Technologies," in *Digital Memories: Exploring Critical Issues*, ed. Daniel Riha and Anna Maj (Oxford: Inter-Disciplinary Press, 2015), 1–13.

53. Hansen tour of Library of Congress National Audio-Visual Conservation Center, Packard Campus, Culpeper, VA, April 6, 2016.

54. Hansen tour.

55. Abbey Potter, "Demystifying Digital Preservation for the Audiovisual Archiving Community," *The Signal: Digital Preservation*, February 22, 2016.

56. Mike Casey, *Media Preservation Survey: A Report* (Bloomington: Indiana University, 2009), v.

57. Indiana University Newsroom, "IU Marks Official Launch of Media Digitization and Preservation Initiative," news release, October 29, 2015, http://news.iu.edu/releases/iu/2015/10/media-digitization-preservation-initiative-opening.shtml.

8

DIGITAL NEWS

> How will digital records be kept alive across decades, centuries, and millennia? If history is a matter of what is stored, and if what is stored is a matter of the media available (stone, papyrus, DNA, bone, film, floppy disks), then changes in media infrastructure will mean changes in the historical record. Obsolescence of the basic media of the historical record is a fact any historian must confront, but our digital moment makes this problem particularly urgent.
>
> —John Durham Peters, "Proliferation and Obsolescence of the Historical Record in the Digital Era," 2015[1]

For fourteen years, Gawker Media was an independent online journalism trendsetter that was once hailed as the future of media. The news-gossip site established the use of a blogging voice with an attitude in online writing that influenced the style that now dominates in the digital world. The site had admirers and a large number of detractors for its take-no-prisoners approach to stories that many other mainstream media organizations wouldn't touch. It was, in many ways, the digital equivalent of the gossip magazines of an earlier age, such as *Graphic* and *Confidential*. It also was the career incubator for many journalists who went on to mainstream digital sites throughout the 2000s. In 2016, reeling from a number of lawsuits brought by angry subjects of stories on the site, the company declared bankruptcy and was sold to media giant Univision.

Gawker's other specialized sites—Deadspin, Jezebel, Gizmodo, and Jalopnik—would continue under Univision ownership. But the mothership, Gawker.com, would be shuttered. The announcement led to a call for action to archive the Gawker site and save the content that had such an outsized influence on online journalism. Activists suggested that the Library of Congress, the New York Public Library, the New York Historical Society, or a major academic institution should take the site out of the hands of the private owners to ensure that it survived beyond the market forces that killed it. The activists conceded that there were difficult questions about copyright and continued liability if a memory institution took over the site. But they argued that the content had historical value as an example of vernacular material that would be invaluable to future historians trying to understand the early days of online publishing and American society in the early 2000s. In fact, the Internet Archive stepped up and ensured that the archive was saved.[2]

Once the production of news moved from the physical world of newsprint, film, and analog radio and television signals to the digital world of ones and zeroes, many of the early characteristics that distinguished one form of news delivery from another disappeared. Chapter 7 described some of the early digital experiments and efforts that led news organizations to abandon traditional production and distribution processes. As the move toward digital production accelerated, news organizations faced a changing archival landscape.

EARLY VIDEOTEX EXPERIMENTS

Two-way electronic information services, called videotex, were being developed in the early 1970s. Users who purchased a special set-top box could attach it through the telephone line to their television set and connect a keyboard that allowed them to receive text and crude graphic images on their TV screen and send messages back to the system to select content or scroll through the offerings. A number of news organizations were early investors in the systems. Perhaps the best-known was the Knight-Ridder venture (with AT&T) called Viewtron.

After years of development, Viewtron launched tests of the system in Coral Gables, Florida, in 1983.[3] Viewtron carried news from Knight-Ridder newspapers and the Associated Press and allowed subscribers to shop

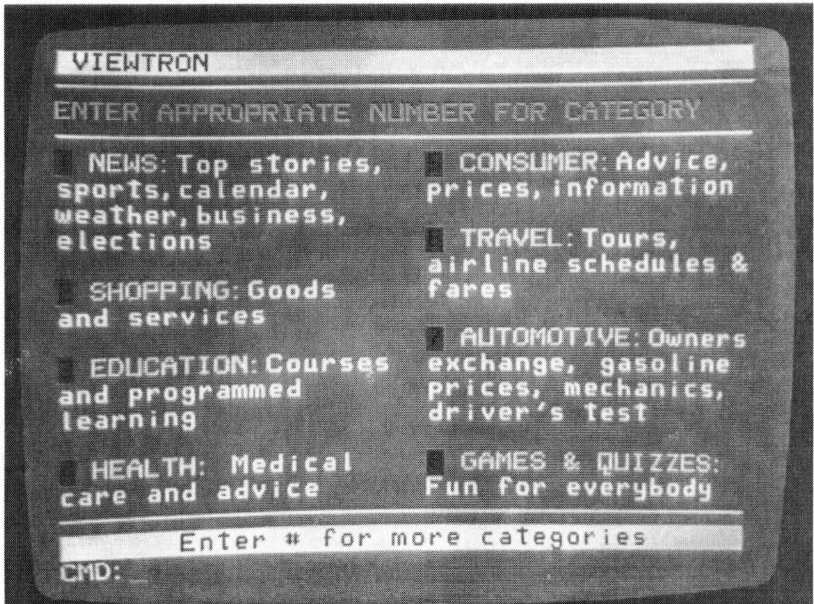

Screen capture from Viewtron videotex service, early 1980s. *Courtesy David Carlson/ University of Florida*

and bank through the telephone lines that ran from terminals to the TV set. The Knight-Ridder chain poured millions of dollars into the experiment, thinking it was going to eventually become the electronic newspaper that futurists were predicting. However, Viewtron was cumbersome and expensive for users (terminals cost $600, fees were $12 per month, plus an additional $1 per hour of connectivity). And although it was innovative, the system didn't offer much beyond what people could easily get from their newspapers at the time. The early versions did not allow users to send messages to one another; once that feature was introduced, users spent more time messaging than reading the news. Plus, the system tied up users' telephone lines and televisions while they were connected.

Viewtron never attracted the audience it needed to become economically feasible, and Knight-Ridder pulled the plug in 1986. By that time, the company had lost $50 million.[4] This high-profile and expensive failure made Knight-Ridder—and the entire media industry—extremely wary of any new consumer-oriented electronic news systems to come. Short of a few videos from AT&T or television stations covering the developments that demonstrate Viewtron at the time, there are no archives of content from videotex service providers.[5]

COMPUSERVE AND COMPETITORS

The pioneering consumer online service company CompuServe started in 1969 in Columbus, Ohio, as a mainframe computer time-sharing business. In July 1980, CompuServe began hosting a digital text version of the local newspaper, the *Columbus Dispatch*. A year later, seeing an opportunity to distribute their content without developing their own digital platform to do so, the *New York Times*, *Virginian-Pilot* and *Ledger Star*, *Washington Post*, *San Francisco Examiner*, *San Francisco Chronicle*, and *Los Angeles Times* joined CompuServe. Additional newspapers followed, bringing the total number of titles available to subscribers to eleven by 1982.[6] Reading an entire newspaper using this method was impractical, however. Because the company charged members by the hour, the text of a 20-cent print-edition newspaper would cost as much as $30 because it took two to six hours to download.[7]

Despite the disadvantages, other consumer online vendors such as America Online (AOL), AT&T's Interchange, and General Electric's GEnie followed suit and started inking deals with newspaper and magazine publishers and broadcasters throughout the 1980s. One vendor, Prodigy, was a 1984 joint venture between broadcast giant CBS, computer manufacturer IBM, and retailer Sears, Roebuck and Company.[8] But CBS left the venture in 1986 when the company divested of properties deemed to be outside of CBS's core broadcasting business. As the timing of this divestiture demonstrates, the failed Viewtron experiment weighed heavily in media companies' decision to back away from digital ventures.

These consumer online services required subscribers to dial in to the online site using their home or office phone line and a personal computer equipped with a modem. This meant users had to install a second phone line if they didn't want to tie up the primary phone for hours while the modem was connected. The services also offered e-mail, chat rooms, and online shopping, banking, and games. But the data transmission speeds over the copper telephone wires were painfully slow, and the services could not provide anything beyond the simplest graphic icons. Moving images were out of the question.

Newspaper and magazine publishers, initially skeptical about the consumer online market's potential, hedged their bets by allowing some text content from their print publications to appear online. However, the familiar layout, design, and visual images from the print publications were lost. This led to the term "shovel ware," referring to the way the text content produced for the printed page was shoveled over to the consumer online service companies. Because the digital text being sent to the online companies was no different from that being used to produce the printed publication, no one found any reason to archive the news content that was appearing on CompuServe and its counterpart services.

Based on computer software advances, some of the early consumer online vendors also started offering a graphical interface to their subscribers, including AOL. The company had developed proprietary software called Rainman that reformatted news content that providers sent to the system and allowed some graphics to appear on the screen.[9] By 1993, the service was providing content from, among others, *Time* and *Omni* magazines, the *Chicago Tribune* and the *San Jose Mercury News*, which called its AOL online site Mercury Center.

The Mercury Center AOL site set the pace for newspapers nationally. Headquartered in the booming Silicon Valley region of California with a tech-savvy audience eager for the next new thing, the site managers understood that they could provide content in the online version that the printed paper could not. Described in a 2011 article in *Columbia Journalism Review*, "The site could, of course, include the content of the day's print paper, but that seemed secondary. The emphasis would be on *more*—more stories, listings, and advertising, too."[10]

By 1994, the site had dramatically expanded the definition of what a newspaper company could provide. In addition to offering subscribers the opportunity to have, for instance, an online chat with the mayor or to read the full text of speeches and press releases, the site had made available the archives of all the stories that had appeared in print since 1985, when the newspaper established its database of digitally produced news stories. According to the *Columbia Journalism Review* article, "The archives, which came with an additional fee, had proven to be particularly popular. [Site developers] had thought their greatest appeal would be to schoolchildren working on reports. But the traffic was heaviest during the day, suggesting that the biggest users [of the archive] were business people eager for information about their industries and competitors."[11]

Large media organizations were taking notice. A December 27, 1993, memo to top *New York Times* editors Max Frankel and Joe Lelyveld from staffer Richard J. Meislin (who was named the senior editor for information and technology in 1994) laid out the stakes for the newspaper as it approached the launch of its own AOL site:

> In roughly three months, The Times will launch its first electronic product for the general public on America Online. This will be different from

> every other secondary marketing effort The Times has made. . . . Make no mistake about it: for the half-million people who subscribe to America Online, and millions more who hear about it, this will be the first face of The New York Times newspaper in the electronic world. It will be appearing in an environment that is both textual and visual. . . . The New York Times newspaper stands to have its reputation either enhanced or tarnished on a grand scale.[12]

As it turned out, the *New York Times* AOL site, so touted in the 1993 memo, offered just a small selection of content from the newspaper, never caught on with AOL subscribers, and was shuttered in 1995. The Mercury Center, an online newspaper leader, saw the future in an opportunity to move away from AOL's proprietary software using something new, the World Wide Web.[13]

THE WORLD WIDE WEB

> For all its openness, the web has proven to be a leaky vessel for historical preservation, with much of its treasure trove lost in a maze of altered web pages, broken links and deleted sites.
>
> —Eric Auchard, "The Black Hole: How the Web Devours History," 2009[14]

It may be difficult to understand now, but the Internet preceded the World Wide Web by more than twenty years. Originally called ARPANET, the Internet was built by the United States Department of Defense in 1969 as a nuclear attack–proof system of communication using networked computers in multiple locations connected by a data-transmission technology called packet switching. The early Internet was entirely text based and was primarily used for sharing reports, information, and communications among a small cadre of individuals housed in government and academic institutions—those who could afford the mainframe computer infrastructure to connect to the network. Commercial traffic on the Internet was banned until 1991.[15]

It wasn't until the introduction of the World Wide Web and its user friendly interface—the web browser—that the Internet moved out of military bunkers and the ivory tower. An English computer scientist, Tim Berners-Lee, working at CERN in Geneva, Switzerland, in 1990 wrote the computer code for a new way to connect to the Internet. Based on that work, Berners-Lee is credited with inventing the World Wide Web. The browser he invented was released to the public in 1993.[16] Also in 1993, Marc Andreessen and Erica Bina at the University of Illinois introduced Mosaic, a web browser that morphed into Netscape Navigator in 1994. Navigator quickly became the world's most popular web browser.

In January 1995, the Mercury Center became the first commercial newspaper site in the United States to migrate to the web. Users could click on a headline from the homepage and go directly to that story, something revolutionary at the time. In addition to the news content, the site offered News Hound, a digital "clipping service" that allowed users to personalize the stories they wanted saved to their electronic inboxes, and continued to provide premium subscribers with digital access to the newspaper's print archives. It was these services that attracted users and made them willing to pay. In 1996, the Mercury Center was named the nation's best newspaper on the web by *Editor & Publisher* magazine.[17]

While newspapers were working on their digital presence, broadcasters were experimenting as well. In 1993, author and technologist Carl Malamud launched Internet Talk Radio, which was the first online talk radio show. Each week Malamud interviewed a computer expert. The program was distributed as audio files that computer users fetched one by one rather than as a streaming service, which became more familiar after the World Wide Web caught on. In late 1994, Malamud's Internet Multicasting Service launched RTFM, a multicast Internet radio news station. In January 1995, RTFM's news programming was expanded to include live audio feeds from the U.S. Congressional House and Senate floors.[18] Unlike so many early digital media sites, many of these early programs are archived at the World Wide Cobweb—Internet Talk Radio Archives at http://museum.media.org/radio.

At 2 a.m. on Thanksgiving Day, November 23, 1995, ABC News streamed its overnight television program, *World News Now*, over the Internet. To view the program, users needed video conferencing software on their computers and a very fast Internet connection. There were just a half dozen Internet viewers scattered around the world who could see it. But watching live television on a computer screen without a satellite link was historic and presaged the coming revolution in delivery of television and radio through digital means.[19]

The rush to the Web accelerated as newspaper organizations began to see their monopoly on classified advertising disappear in the wake of online classified ad site start-ups such as Monster.com (1994), Craigslist (1995), and Cars.com (1998). Broadcasters initially used their websites as a promotional medium, profiling their on-air personalities and community relations efforts. But as advertising revenue plummeted through the early 2000s, news organizations began to understand that they were facing a fundamental disruption to their business models and that their online presence needed to become more than shovel ware or merely a public relations element of their news operations.

Ironically, the lesson that the pioneering Mercury Center had learned early on—that the archives of the newspaper were a major attraction for their online site users—failed to carry over to their own web content. It is almost impossible to find any early news website content today. If a screenshot does exist, it is just that—a static screenshot—with none of the links or interactive content. Once again, as has been true for every other innovation in news delivery, the early history of online journalism is all but lost.

WHY NEWS ON THE WEB (AND BEYOND) WAS LOST

> The archival axioms of permanence and provenance don't remap well into the digital domain, where everything is as fragile as the next spike, brownout or coronal mass ejection.
>
> —Rick Prelinger, "Silence, Cacophony, Crosstalk," 2016[20]

Although many newspapers and broadcasters expanded their websites during the late 1990s and early 2000s, most still considered the web audience to be a small subset of their core audience. It was not unusual for the web content producers to be physically isolated from the main newsroom, sometimes on another floor of the main building or in another building altogether.[21] And because website content producers weren't following traditional newsroom routines to enter their stories into the traditional news production systems, the content they generated was not captured by the legacy newsroom archiving processes.

Digital content presents a variety of new issues and challenges to archival staff trying to capture, preserve, and manage such collections. The first issue involves preservation of the physical media on which data are written: floppy discs, digital tape, CDs, DVDs, and server hard drives. When ones and zeroes stored on these media degrade, it is called bit rot. Bit rot has become a huge problem for the data from early forms of digital storage as they age. The second issue is that in order to read any data that survive, there must be machines and software to read and translate that data into a comprehensible form. This involves addressing both technological obsolescence of the machines and the unavailability of software over time. All these issues pose thorny problems for individuals and institutions trying to preserve digital information.[22]

New Content, Old Problems

As information science professor Peter Lyman outlined in a 2002 piece about archiving the World Wide Web, digital preservation also is plagued by some of the same cultural, technical, economic, and legal problems that have always affected archives.[23] This is especially true for the news content that is now generated second-by-second by thousands of producers, both legacy news organizations and brand-new entrants.

According to Lyman, a cultural problem is that people can't—or don't want to—recognize the value of the content at the time it is being created. Most legacy news organization managers had long-entrenched attitudes that kept them from understanding the truly disruptive nature of this new form of news delivery. The culture of capturing web content as it was being created simply was not in place. When the manager of the Minneapolis *Star Tribune* website was interviewed in 1996 about the lack of an archive for the site, he said there was no need because the site was "a service, not a publication."[24] Yet that manager lamented in the same 1996 interview that there were no captures of the newspaper's earlier digital site hosted on the AT&T Interchange system. According to the manager, that pioneering work had been "written on the ether."[25]

Major news organizations celebrating the twentieth anniversary of their web launches in 2016 found that they had no screen captures of their sites' first day. The *New York Times*'s site launched on January 22, 1996. The first screen capture of the site, however, is from November 12, 1996, found on the Internet Archive's Wayback Machine rather than the media organization's own archive. The *Wall Street Journal* launched on April 28, 1996. The first screen capture of its homepage is from June of that year. At an academic conference in the mid-2000s, a panelist from the *San Jose Mercury News* ruefully admitted that the organization had no capture of its groundbreaking site on the day it launched. One attendee at the session, a journalism professor from San Jose State University, raised his hand and said he had taken some screenshots from that first day in 1995. After the session ended, the professor was surrounded by people asking for copies of the screenshots, including the journalist from the newspaper.[26]

Technical problems, according to Lyman, refer to the fact that by the time people start to recognize the cultural value of archiving something, the hardware and software for doing so is obsolete. Just as the introduction of a mind-boggling variety of new videotape technologies complicated television archivists' efforts, the dizzying array of software and hardware needed to produce news on the web created a disincentive to archive the day-to-day and minute-by-minute content.

The *Miami Herald*'s first web manager, Rich Gordon, actually downloaded the entire site to his computer hard drive the day after the *Herald-Link* site launched on May 12, 1996. On the twentieth anniversary of the launch, Gordon posted a link to his archival capture on Facebook.[27] When asked how he had that archival content, he said, "The next day [after the site launch], I guess the history major in me made me realize I wanted to keep a copy. So I just downloaded the whole site to my hard drive. It was easy in those days—all the pages were just flat HTML. Wish I'd made a habit of it—as far as I can remember, it's the only day I did that. The real miracle is that I was able to find it this week on an old CD-ROM that I made when I left the *Herald*!"[28] But the type of data capture and migration reflected in Gordon's example is not the norm.

For economic problems, Lyman asks, "Who has the money to do this?" Although a few online news sites were initially profitable, notably the Mercury Center, the introduction of news on the web coincided with the collapse of news organizations' traditional business models. News organizations were caught up in simply surviving in the new economic reality of the news marketplace. By the early 2000s, newspapers were laying off the traditional guardians of the archives, the news librarians, and closing their news libraries.[29] Television and radio stations, which never had invested in extensive news archives to begin with, were equally unable or disinclined to devote resources to archiving web content.

Music blogger Carter Maness wrote a 2015 piece titled "All My Blogs Are Dead." "We assume everything we publish online will be preserved. But websites that pay for writing are businesses. They get sold, forgotten and broken. Eventually, someone flips the switch and pulls it all down. . . . For media companies deleting their sites, legacy doesn't matter; the work carries no intrinsic value if there is no business remaining to capitalize on it."[30] Maness said that his writing resume is oddly incomplete and unverifiable because so much of his work has disappeared from websites that went out of business.

Finally, legal problems, according to Lyman, refer to the copyright and intellectual property laws that affect what can and cannot be archived in the first place. We will discuss this in more detail in the next chapter, but suffice it to say that web publishing introduced a huge number of new

HERALDLink

Sunday, May 12, 1996
Last update: 2:20 a.m. EDT

SectionSkim

Section
- Front Page
- USA
- Americas
- World
- Sports
- Living/Arts
- Business
- Florida
- Keys
- Dade/Miami
- Broward
- ActionLine
- Opinion
- Voices
- Tropic
- Travel
- Home

Services
- Help!
- News Library
- FactLine
- Subscribe

NETSCAPE Now!
This site is Netscape enhanced

Disaster in the swamp

109 killed -- no survivors -- in DC-9 crash

They used airboats and helicopters. They dodged snakes and alligators. But the rescuers who desperately searched the Everglades muck for survivors of South Florida's worst plane crash soon came upon the grim reality:

None of the 109 people on board a ValuJet DC-9 survived Saturday when their plane slammed into the earth west of Miami International Airport. Today, the grimmest of tasks continues -- assessing the crash toll by combing the Everglades debris.

Full Story and info-graphic

WELCOME to HeraldLink

The Miami Herald's news, information and Internet access service

This is an "extra" providing coverage of the crash of Flight 592 -- and giving you a sneak preview of the rest of our information service. Some things won't work 100% correctly, but we hope you find it interesting.

Today's Weather

Click only on a need to know basis
LeadStory.com

Homepage of Miami HeraldLink's 1996 launch. *Courtesy Rich Gordon/Northwestern University*

legal problems for archival practices. Content for a news website is stored in many different places, comes from many different sources, including many outside the news organization's own newsroom, and provides links to hundreds if not thousands of additional sites over which the news organization has no control whatsoever. Even if the news organization had the will, technology, and money to archive its website, what legal restrictions would affect the use of that archive? Who would sort out all of the copyright and intellectual property issues that would arise?

The Nature of Digital News Content

As digital news content has expanded beyond the text and images of early websites, there are additional complications to any archiving scheme. One troubling example is the issue of archiving the dynamic content that is so characteristic of good online news sites—interactive maps; voter guides; multimedia stories with their combination of text, audio, video, and graphics; animations; databases of content that users can tailor to their interests. This type of content is made up of dynamic elements that require many different types of software and content repository links to work.

The *Philadelphia Inquirer*'s 1997 "Blackhawk Down" project is an early example of a multimedia news package. The groundbreaking series explored the consequences of the U.S. military's 1993 intervention in Somalia. The project included text, videos, audio, maps, and other types of content that were recognized at the time as a stellar example of what online news could be. Although the site still exists, many of the multimedia features no longer function because the software that rendered the video, audio, and animations is long out of date.[31] More recent examples of lost multimedia news packages abound. A 2009 *Washington Post* series that explored fatal medical helicopter crashes is still accessible but none of the multimedia maps, interactive crash time lines, or trend infographics work.[32]

News applications, or news apps as they are called, are another example of an archiving nightmare.[33] An example of a news app is ProPublica's *Dollars for Docs*, which allows users to search for doctors who have received payments from drug companies for talks, research, and consulting.[34] A news app has multiple components: a database, the data in the database, the unique graphical interface that appears in the web browser that allows the user to interact with the database, one or more text-based stories, and photos or illustrations.[35] Just as a floppy disc cannot be inserted into a USB port on a computer, these news app elements cannot be captured in existing news archives that only handle text. In addition, apps are likely to be developed outside the news organization's existing content management system (CMS) used for the organization's website.

In a study of news app developers, researcher Meredith Broussard quoted one interviewee as saying, "Almost any news programmer generally loathes their organization's Content Management System; its codified formats and rigid workflows often feel more like strictures to our project. And so we do our work outside the CMS."[36] Another interviewee in that study said, "News apps are the artisanal cheeses of the journalism world." Although unique and exciting, they are expensive to produce and very difficult to store.[37] When the *Washington Post* produced a news app about the Affordable Care Act in 2013, it was an excellent example of this kind of content. But after a change in the CMS, the information in the app is now unreadable.[38]

User-generated content presents another huge problem for website archiving. Many news organizations have delegated management of their online comments sections to third-party vendors, meaning that the comments are not stored in the newsroom's computer systems. As many comment sections have devolved into vitriol and name-calling, there is questionable value in archiving them anyway. However, for the sites where the comments do still provide a respectful narrative from readers or viewers on the news they see, such content would be invaluable for future researchers. But that content is not being archived inside the news organization itself, and future access to it depends on the goodwill and financial stability of third-party vendors who have no dedication to the archival obligations of news producers.

As social media sites such as Facebook, Twitter, SnapChat, and Instagram have sprung up, news organizations have moved some content to those platforms as well. Journalists are encouraged, and sometimes required, to maintain a presence in these fora; many news followers get their news from these social sites rather than from a news website or traditional newspaper, radio, or television program. A 2016 study by the Pew Research Center found that roughly two-thirds of social media users get news on those sites.[39]

Social media sites exist far outside the boundaries of the news organization's own computer systems and processes. Even if a news organization wants to archive that content, there are restrictions on their ability to do so since they are captive customers of these outside vendors who set the rules.[40] The Library of Congress (LOC) started archiving Twitter posts in 2010 (obviously including tweets from news organizations), but that content is still not accessible to the public because there are no provisions or budget in place to help make the staggering amount of data available.[41]

Web-Specific Issues

Beyond these news-specific issues, however, is the plain fact that a website is made up of digital objects, the boundaries of which are ambiguous at best. Any attempt to archive even a single webpage must address the fact that the page might be made up of perhaps twenty links to other pages and to sound, image, or interactive database files, some of which are not stored on the organization's own server. And the web is not a fixed collection of artifacts, even when they can all be identified. Webpages are often generated on the fly, customized on demand from content, databases, and software code that may be buried deep within remote parts of the web. For example, think about advertisements that are sent from remote servers and tailored to specific users based on their individual shopping habits. This means that one user sees different ads on the same content page of the site than does another. So although there might be a record that a "digital ad artifact" appeared at a certain place on the page, the actual *content* of that ad is not fixed in any way.

Also, websites, if they truly reflect the key unique aspect of digital production, change continually. What should be preserved? Single captures of one point in time on one day? Or would the archivist want to capture the site when it was at its "best," however that might be determined? The chimerical characteristics of webpages mean that the archival notion of provenance (where did something come from?) and authenticity (is it what it claims to be?) is rendered all but moot.

For an entire website or a single page to be archived, the underlying computer code that renders that site or page (i.e., that makes it possible for the user to view the site or page as it appeared when it was served) must be archived as well. As previous chapters have outlined, news organizations have been woefully inattentive to the issue of migrating their archival content from one version of storage and display to another. This is equally true for their digital content.

We conducted a study of archival practices at ten different news organizations in 2014. Eight were traditional news operations that had produced a printed newspaper for decades and now also supported a website (most started in the mid-1990s). One surveyed publication had abandoned its newsprint operation in 2008 and had become a web-only publisher. And one was a born-digital operation started in 2007 that never had a printed version.

The legacy newspapers had complete back files of their newsprint and were still microfilming their content to send to the LOC for copyright. But not one of the ten publications, including the born-digital operation, had a complete archive of its website. Most could go back no earlier than 2008. For the legacy operations, that means that the first decade (at least) of their web presence was gone forever. The chaos of changing content management systems, shifting organizational homes within the operation, news library staff cuts, and other events meant that every one of the operations had an incomplete archive of the web publication.[42]

Andy Jackson, the technical lead at the UK Web Archive, conducted a study of ten years of web content (2004–2014) from the UK Web Archive. He aimed to learn whether content from the URLs for archived sites could still be found on the "live" web. He discovered that after one year, half of the archived content was either gone or had been changed so much as to be unrecognizable. After ten years, almost no content was still found at its original URL.[43] As more and more news content appears *only* on the web, the lack of web archiving creates an even larger vacuum in our historical record.

Another issue that complicates digital news preservation is that so many different versions of the digital content now exist. The content that resides in the newsroom's internal content management system is used to create the printed newspaper or newscast and a subset of that content is sent to the vendor for the online version of the newspaper or broadcast (Lexis/Nexis, Factiva, etc.). The news website consists of a different set of digital content, some of which resides far outside the newsroom proper. If the newsroom supports mobile interfaces for people to get the news on their phones or tablets, that is yet *another* version of the digital content. The PDF version of the printed version of the newspaper or the digital files of the newscast as it was broadcast are additional formats to address.[44]

Disappearing Content

In addition to the technical issues that impede digital news archival efforts, a major concern involves deliberate actions to alter or erase news content. Individual stories, photos, videos, or entire websites have disappeared because they were taken down deliberately. News organizations have always dealt with the issue of how to correct a story after publication. Corrections columns in the newspaper or on-air statements saying "station XYZ regrets the error" have been used for decades. But the ability now to make a story or an entire site disappear altogether as if it never existed does serious damage to the accuracy of the record. Former *New York Times* editor Bill Keller said in 2013 that the *Times* got about four requests a week from the public for stories to be purged from the digital database. But the paper's policy is to update stories, not to erase them.[45]

The online news and entertainment site Buzzfeed reportedly removed more than four thousand posts from its site in 2014. When questioned about it, the site's spokesperson said the posts no longer met the site's updated editorial standards.[46] But that doesn't change the fact that the posts had been available on the web for years and now were gone. And it ignores the fact that those early posts would have been invaluable to anyone studying the evolution of the site's editorial standards over time.

A screen capture from September 11, 2001, shows a plane smashing into the World Trade Center in New York with the text surrounding the image in the Italian—the screen capture is from the website CNNitalia.it. The site's editor, Mario Tedeschini-Lalli, explained in a 2015 article that

> there is no way you may know that CNN had an Italian language website (which I happened to edit), unless you actually read it between 1999 and 2003. The CNNitalia.it domain is still there, but it points to a single bilingual page explaining that "CNNitalia.it is no longer in service." Which is like saying that its full four years of coverage—including 9/11—are nowhere to be found, just like almost all of the journalism produced by myself or by the digital newsrooms I managed in the last 18 years. . . . The same happened to other "language sites" of CNN targeting Brasil [sic], Norway, Sweden, Denmark, and the Hispanic countries of Latin America.[47]

Judicial orders also threaten the historical record. In 2015, a New Jersey judge ordered the *Bergen Dispatch* to remove an online news article that related to a child custody case. The paper's response said, in part, "we have confirmed that Bergen County does currently remain part of the State of New Jersey and that currently New Jersey is still part of the Union of States that is governed by the United States Constitution and Bill of Rights. As such, Bergen County citizens continue to enjoy the right to freedom of speech and the right to a free press."[48] The judge backed down but this was not the only example of a news site being ordered to remove content.[49] The issue of deliberately deleted websites is discussed in more detail later in this chapter.

DIGITAL NEWS PRESERVATION TODAY

> Digital information lasts forever, or five years, whichever comes first.
>
> —Jeff Rothenberg, "Ensuring the Longevity of Digital Information," 1995[50]

A large community of organizations and institutions now recognizes that we are in danger of creating a digital black hole for future generations who will find huge gaps in the records of this time and place. Collaborative groups such as the National Digital Stewardship Alliance, the MetaArchive Cooperative, the Digital Preservation Network, and the International Internet Preservation Consortium, to name just a few, are trying to establish technical standards, develop archiving protocols, and encourage innovation in an effort to ensure the survival of digital information.

News Organizations

As has been the case with every other format of content, news organizations are still mostly inattentive to archiving their web-only news. A 2014 survey conducted by the Reynolds Journalism Institute/Journalism Digital News Archive project at the University of Missouri asked both legacy and born-digital news organizations about their archiving practices (among other things) for digital content delivered on the web. From their 476 respondents, the researchers learned that the majority had no written policies for how to archive and handle their web content, and most did not send that content to any type of external memory institution. The content management systems being used to produce that web content either do not provide adequate support for archival processes, or the workflow that is in place ignores that part of the process.[51]

EidosMedia, a Milan-based content management system (CMS) provider whose publishing software is used by a number of large U.S. news operations (and others around the world), is a case in point. In an interview, Rob Schmitt, EidosMedia client solutions manager, described the dilemma this way: "We always talk about archiving. But everyone's looking forward and no one's looking back." The company's publishing system, Méthode, includes an archiving function as an optional part of the CMS. But as Schmitt explained, "Clients must add metadata to make the information meaningful in their system. That requires a lot of overhead to tag and make it meaningful. Reporters don't see the value and are pressed for time—they don't see why they have to tag it." Schmitt added, "All of our news clients used to have a staff of librarians. Now if they have *one* it is unusual." That means that even when the news organization installs the archive function in Méthode, the staff in place is not sufficient to use it effectively.

When EidosMedia works with clients to install Méthode, "We ask where are your archives? [We're told] 'Under Jim's desk. He retired five years ago.'" And the archived content news organizations *do* have is spread across many different locations. "Their video is with vendors such as BrightCove, Bella, Invado; the photos are in another system; print pages are in the main CMS; the web stuff is just put up there and they use the web as the archive. There is no archive for all the iterations."[52] Even for a sophisticated system such as Méthode, however, the archive function captures individual digital objects, *not* the way those objects were rendered on the website. This is the equivalent of newsreel, radio, and television archives keeping individual film or sound clips but not the program as it was presented to the audience.

A Politico.com journalist participated in a panel discussion at an academic conference in 2013 along with colleagues from other born-digital news organizations. The Politico journalist described the site's important work during the historic 2008 presidential campaign that led to the election of the first African American president. When asked whether that work was being properly archived for posterity, the journalist said, "Well, theoretically it is all findable somewhere and everything lives on the Internet forever." None of the other panelists had an official archival process in place, either.[53] If your archival strategy is to assume everything is on the Internet, you don't have an archival strategy.

Those same panelists, however, did acknowledge that when digital news providers track story developments and make changes throughout the day (called a "write-through"), the earlier versions disappear with no record of how the story changed over time except to include a note saying the story has been updated. The Politico panelist said that she sometimes insists that the staff start a fresh story page when the write-throughs to an original story have been so voluminous that the story no longer offers a coherent account.[54]

In some ways it is difficult to understand why news organizations are still doing such a poor job of archiving their web content. Organizations such as NBC News, CNN, and the Associated Press are using their websites to *market* the digital video archive of what ran on the air, but are not archiving the website content itself.[55] As long ago as 1995, Mercury Center managers discovered that site users were willing to pay a premium for access to archived stories from the newspaper. The content of today's websites will presumably be equally valuable to news consumers in the future, but there will be nothing to sell because it won't have been archived.

Even when an organization does try to archive its site, however, link rot is a major problem. Link rot is the term used to describe disappearing links caused when a site or page was renamed, moved, deleted, or had even a single character in the URL changed. The Journalist's Resource website developed a list of "linking best practices" to help news sites avoid link rot after learning in 2015 that its own site (tiny compared to most) had more than ten thousand internal and external links, ten or more of which broke every week.[56] The first rule was simply "don't link too much." But that undermines one of the key distinctions of digital news: the ability to point to evidence and sources outside the specific story the journalist creates.

Library of Congress

In 2000, the U.S. Congress enacted legislation directing the LOC to facilitate the development of an infrastructure to support long-term preservation of digital content.[57] The bill allocated $100 million for the National Digital Information Infrastructure and Preservation Program (NDIIPP). The LOC was told to focus on materials created primarily in digital form for which there were no analog representations, referred to as born-digital content. Relevant for news archiving, the LOC commissioned a series of studies focused on documenting archiving practices for the web, digitally recorded sound, digital television, and digital moving images.[58] They learned that there were a number of U.S. and worldwide initiatives in public, nonprofit, and commercial sectors trying to address the challenges of digital preservation, but no one had come close to solving the problem.

The LOC started its web archiving activities shortly after NDIIPP was established. The LOC identified likely partners in the effort: national libraries of other countries such as Sweden and Australia, which had been pioneers in archiving websites; federal agencies including the National Archives and Records Administration, the National Library of Medicine and the National Agricultural Library; research libraries; news organizations; and the Internet Archive.[59]

The LOC made an agreement with the Internet Archive to harvest the websites of the 2000 national election campaigns. Using the method of automatically "crawling"[60] the sites to capture the content, the Internet Archive gathered material from more than eight hundred websites related to the election between August 1, 2000, and January 21, 2001.[61] That collection is still accessible in the LOC's Website Collections archive. These early efforts provided all partners with valuable experience in the problems and pitfalls, as well as the best practices, for archiving websites. By 2016 the LOC had twenty-two collections of archived websites and were still working collaboratively with the Internet Archive's software.[62]

In 2008, the LOC started capturing websites for what is now known as the Public Policy Topics collection. Michael Neubert, supervisory digital projects specialist, decided to include some news sites with a political and policy point of view (e.g., DailyKos.com, Townhall.com, Truthdig.com, Redstate.com) as part of the Public Policy Topics collection. The project started with weekly crawls to build a record of how these sites covered different types of news events over time. Neubert then worked with colleagues in the Newspaper and Current Periodical Room to expand the effort to a "General News on the Internet" collection. They included born-digital sites only, not the websites of legacy news operations such as the *New York Times* or CNN. They wanted general born-digital news sites with significant national presence: HuffingtonPost.com, BuzzFeed.com, Vox.com, TheVerge.com, and parody sites such as TheOnion.com.

After experimenting with weekly crawls of these sites, they decided it wasn't a good method of capturing the site content because the results seemed totally random and didn't ensure that the archive reflected what had actually appeared on the news sites each week. Around that time, Neubert learned from a colleague in Iceland about a method of using the Really Simple Syndication (RSS) feed from a site as a way to build a list of specific content that the crawler could be directed to capture each week. They changed their process, and that method appears to be working well. The LOC is now collecting content from thirty-six news sites and generates twenty terabytes of web content each month from its archiving work across all collections. The content from any of the library's website archives is not released for one year after capture as a matter of policy.[63]

In 2009 and again in 2014, the LOC convened news content creators, academics, memory institution representatives, and similar stakeholders to specifically address preserving digital news. Representatives from the Associated Press, CBS News, CNN, and WGBH were among the participants at these gatherings. The general consensus from the group was that archiving news content is beyond any one institution or organization's capabilities. That said, no archiving initiative will succeed unless the news organizations that create the content in the first place make a commitment to build the archival function into their routine workflows and practices, something that has not been the case in any earlier iteration of news production before and is not in place now. Libraries, memory institutions, and well-intentioned individuals cannot make any progress unless the content creators themselves step up.

Internet Archive

Brewster Kahle founded the Internet Archive, a public, not-for-profit organization, in 1996. The Internet Archive was an outgrowth of Kahle's commercial product, Alexa Internet, Inc., a software program that users installed on their web browsers. Alexa tracked where a web searcher and others using that browser had been and then suggested other places that the user might find useful or interesting. Alexa was acquired by Amazon in 1999, which helps explain Amazon's uncanny ability to suggest stuff you might want to buy based on what you and others like you have looked for or purchased previously.

Alexa's underlying mechanism allowed it to archive the websites it was crawling. This led Kahle to envision what became the Wayback Machine, an archive of as much of the public web as possible, as part of the Internet Archive. Essentially, the Wayback Machine uses a computer program referred to as a robot to crawl across the web making a copy of every page it can find. It generally captures a site once every two months, although there are many sites chosen by librarians and subject experts that are crawled much more often than that; news sites are now among those crawled more often. Users can find limited content from some news websites going back to 1996, but it is likely that the early captures are for one day in one month with months of gaps, and then one or two more captures followed by more gaps.

The Internet Archive now also offers individuals and institutions hosting websites a service called Archive-It.[64] Organizations around the world are using the Archive-It service to capture their sites on a regular basis, but it does not work well for sites that are updated continually, such as news

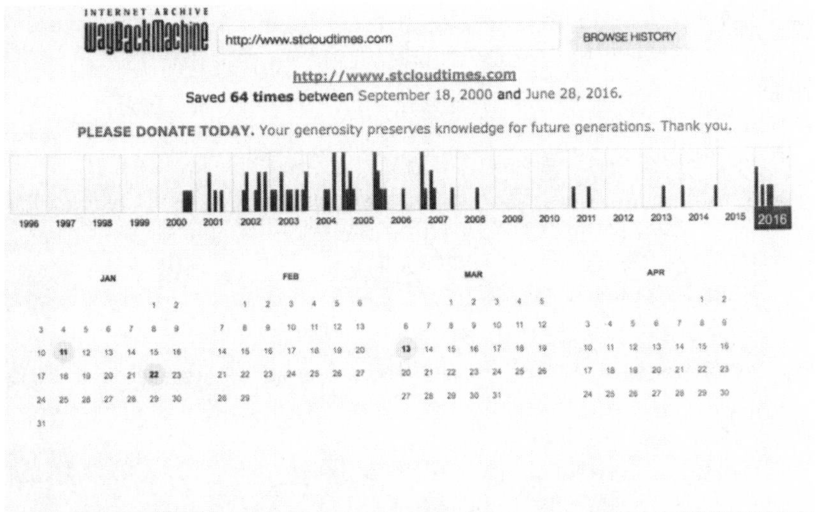

Wayback Machine dashboard indicating sporadic captures of *St. Cloud Times* website since September 18, 2000. *Hansen screen capture/Wayback Machine/Internet Archive*

sites. Finally, those who want to preserve a specific website at any given time can go to the archive.org/web portion of the Internet Archive, type in the web address (URL) of the site they want to capture, and click "save page now." Individuals trying to capture content from sites that are likely to be censored or removed for political or other reasons use this feature to archive sites that are in danger of changing or disappearing quickly.[65]

Because it is part of a nonprofit organization, the Wayback Machine's managers have successfully worked with news organizations to capture content without triggering copyright or intellectual property concerns. Website producers who don't want their site archived can install a simple piece of computer code to block the Wayback Machine's robot from visiting. Also, sites that require registration or charge fees for access are not included. Certain types of dynamic content (JavaScript, for example) will not render properly in the Wayback Machine. And if a website producer asks, the Internet Archive will remove archived content from the Wayback Machine. A large number of U.S. federal agency websites were removed after the September 11, 2001, attacks, especially those that had provided information such as the location of nuclear reactors or the condition of bridges and roadways.

The Wayback Machine is an amazing resource, but it does not constitute a strategy for web archiving for news organizations. First of all, the Wayback Machine does not capture an entire website. Visitors can get two or three clicks into a captured site, but then the system returns the "page not found" message. This is unacceptable for news organizations that want a complete capture of their site at a given time. Second, the Wayback Machine currently does not support full-text searching by keyword. The only way to find something is to enter the web address (URL) of the site you want; the search can be refined by date, but there are no other advanced search features. Wayback Machine director Mark Graham described current efforts to enhance the searchability of the sites archived in the Wayback Machine. The beta version of the feature in mid-2016 allowed a user to search for words that occur in a URL, a major improvement.[66] But if a news organization intended to use the Wayback Machine as its archiving solution, it would be a pale imitation of a complete, searchable archive similar to those that were established and maintained by their news librarians, stock footage managers, or photo archivists in the past.

Another feature of the Internet Archive is the Television News Archive. Since 2009, the Internet Archive has been capturing television news programs, including the major evening news broadcasts and many news programs and series from twenty different news channels. Because the Internet Archive is capturing both the video and the closed captioning from news broadcasts (essentially, the transcript of the program), this part of the archive is searchable by keyword, making it much more valuable as a research tool than the Wayback Machine. Newscasts appear in the archive the day after they air. For the large networks and the major news program producers, this part of the Internet Archive could serve as a way to retrieve clips from past broadcasts. However, if a user wants an entire program as it aired, the archive must send it on a DVD. The hundreds of local news stations around the country are not included.[67] And once again, the capture of content from any television station news *website* would have to be found in the Wayback Machine, not in the Television News Archive.

Radio station websites also are included in the Wayback Machine if they don't block the robot. Many old radio programs, including some classic newscasts, are part of the Internet Archive's Old Time Radio collection. Some early television programs and newsreel clips also are accessible through the Internet Archive if they have been digitized and if the rights owners don't object.

The Wayback Machine is a breathtaking repository of twenty years of website history. The Television News Archive is a major resource for research and examination. Even so, Internet Archive managers recognize what they are doing is simply demonstrating what is possible in the face of so much that is being lost.[68] They are continuing to experiment with improvements to the Wayback Machine, including developing software to automatically recognize broken links in WordPress sites and on Wikipedia pages and to direct users to a capture of that dead link in the Wayback Machine. Through a project called "Top News," they are scanning major news sites to archive everything, not just a few screen captures. A team of volunteers is capturing content that might be missed by the Wayback Machine's algorithm. And they are capturing and archiving the news feed from the Global Database of Events, Language and Tone, which "monitors print, broadcast, and web news media in over one hundred languages from across every country in the world."[69] Together, the new initiatives are generating one hundred million captures of news URLs per week in addition to the regular crawls by the Wayback Machine.

Memory Institutions, Academic Institutions, and Individuals

Preserving born-digital news content, whether it be websites, news applications, social media posts, virtual reality stories, or whatever digital format comes next (holographic news?) is going to require a collaborative effort.

One group trying to pull together the appropriate participants is the Atlanta-based Educopia Institute. They describe their work, in part, as follows: "Right now, most networks don't yet include all of the players necessary to bring about systemic change [in digital preservation]. Libraries, archives, museums, publishers, and researchers have largely worked within their own silos, but each is an essential player within a bigger system of knowledge creation and dissemination. Bridging these stakeholders to catalyze change is our core purpose."[70] Among other projects, Educopia prepared the publication *Guidelines for Digital Newspaper Preservation Readiness*, a 2014 how-to for newspaper organizations to evaluate their archival functions and start to build digital archiving into their workflows.[71]

Educopia also partnered with the University of Missouri's Journalism Digital News Archive at the Reynolds Journalism Institute to sponsor a series of workshops starting in 2014 that brought together news publishers, journalists, archivists, librarians, scholars, technologists, lawyers, and entrepreneurs to address the issues around preserving digital news. Titled "Dodging the Memory Hole: Saving Born-Digital News Content," the workshops have established an ongoing agenda of action items around six issues: (1) awareness of the problem, (2) the legal framework that must be in place for any progress, (3) policies that all parties must adopt, (4) resources that have to be brought to bear, (5) standards and practices for implementing those policies, and (6) the technology necessary to make digital preservation a reality.[72]

Stanford University Libraries has carved out a specific area of web archiving through its Stanford Web Archive Portal. The project attempts to capture at-risk sites defined as "political candidates' campaign websites, that live only for the duration of the election season; the websites of grant-funded projects, whose value to scholarship persists well beyond the period of funding; dissident political speech subject to government censorship; online news related to fast-breaking events, which is quickly amended and submerged; the orphaned web presence of important, deceased personages; and more."[73]

Individual academic institutions are working on other aspects of the web archiving puzzle through their libraries and through the research being conducted in their computer science, engineering, and related departments and disciplines. Legal scholars, communications researchers, and many others housed in universities or research institutions and in private corporations are recognizing the depth of the problem and the effort that will be necessary to address it.

One example of such work is a tool called Time Travel,[74] a collaboration between the Research Library of the Los Alamos National Laboratory and the Computer Science Department of Old Dominion University. Like the Wayback Machine, Time Travel helps you find and view versions of webpages that existed at some time in the past using the site's URL but allows you to specify the date and time for the past version of the site you want to see.

So a user could ask to see the January 21, 2009, capture of the *Washington Post* website at 3:00 p.m., the day former president Barack Obama was inaugurated for his first term. The Time Travel tool will locate the website capture closest in time from any of the web archiving sites around the world that use the computer protocol written by Time Travel's programmers. The capture of the *Washington Post* site done by the Stanford Web Archive at 11:00 p.m. that day is the best Time Travel match for that search.

Another example is a tool called Past Pages,[75] created by Ben Walsh, a former data journalist for the *Los Angeles Times*. The site captures the home pages of one hundred news organizations around the world every hour, going back to 2012. The screen captures are static; users cannot link to any of the stories on the page. However, the tool allows users to track how a story developed over the course of time as reflected on the news site home page. Such tools are constantly evolving and the pace of experimentation demonstrates the level of attention the web archiving problem is finally receiving.

"DARK ALLIANCE" CASE STUDY

> Persistence in the digital world does not happen by luck but through intentional action and explicit investment. The odds that bits will survive in a shoebox in an attic are pretty small."
>
> —Ann J. Wolpert, MIT Libraries director, "Archives and History," 2009[76]

Websites disappear for many reasons. Archiving ones and zeroes is a difficult task in and of itself. It is even more difficult when there is a concerted effort to make a website go away on purpose. That is what happened to the investigative journalism piece that Gary Webb produced for the *San Jose Mercury News* in 1996.[77] The series, "Dark Alliance," traced money fueling the U.S. Central Intelligence Agency–backed war against Nicaragua to the profits from the Los Angeles 1980s crack cocaine epidemic. Webb argued that the poor communities in Los Angeles paid the price of the crack explosion while the U.S. government protected those moving the drugs into the city so the profits could support the covert war.

The series appeared on the *Mercury News*'s website, the Mercury Center, in August 1996. According to the *Columbia Journalism Review*, "online newsletters and other Internet services made the series available to African American students, newspapers, radio stations, and community organizations."[78] After Webb appeared on African American talk radio stations, mentioning the web address for the series, the story caught on and created an uproar. The CIA launched an internal investigation, and politicians cited the series in calling for action.

But the *Washington Post*, the *Los Angeles Times*, and the *New York Times* attacked Webb and the *Mercury News* for what they argued were poorly sourced claims. In the face of criticism from the national media, the *Mercury News* retracted the story, deleted the "Dark Alliance" website, and destroyed thousands of undistributed CD-ROM versions of the site that the paper had prepared to promote the work. One of the reasons given by the executive editor for deleting the website was that the "Dark Alliance" logo, a photo of an African American man using a crack pipe superimposed on the CIA seal, was "too suggestive."[79] Gary Webb was forced to quit.

The "Dark Alliance" series, published the same year the Mercury Center was named the country's best news website, was an early example of the power of the web to not only widely distribute a story from the print newspaper, but to truly expand the storytelling by linking to images, sound files, reader discussion forums, and a huge library of background documents supporting the investigative work. But with the website gone, all of the links to that supporting material disappeared as well.

The 1997 *Columbia Journalism Review* analysis of the furor concluded that the "Dark Alliance" series was "an overwritten and problematically sourced piece of reporting." At the same time, by stimulating a national debate on U.S. government/drug trade/covert operations connections, "This regional newspaper accomplished what neither the *Los Angeles Times*, the *Washington Post*, nor the *New York Times* had been willing or able to do." And the *Post*'s reader representative, Geneva Overholser, said that rather than protecting the people from government excesses, "The *Post* and others showed more energy for protecting the CIA from someone else's journalistic excesses."[80]

Webb eventually found one of the remaining copies of the "Dark Alliance" CD in 2002 and was able to resurrect the website on a commercial web server. But he never found another job in journalism. Tragically, Webb took his own life in 2004. And his resurrected website disappeared once again because the company hosting it was bought out and the files were lost.

In 2005, Webb's family found the CD, and his son sent it to another website, Narco News, which posted the original pages on its own site with support from the Fund for Authentic Journalism. The expanded version of the site could not be re-created, but the content that remained was unchanged from what first appeared on the Mercury Center nine years earlier. In 2016, the site was still accessible.[81]

This example serves as a warning about the vulnerability of the historical record when it consists of ones and zeroes. As two digital information librarians said, "Effective curation of digital data will . . . help safeguard our ability to hold governments, institutions, corporations, or individuals to account. Ultimately, it is about preserving access to the truth (or at least a version of the truth)."[82]

NOTES

1. John Durham Peters, "Proliferation and Obsolescence of the Historical Record in the Digital Era," in *Cultures of Obsolescence: History, Materiality, and the Digital Age*, ed. Babette B. Tischleder and Sarah Wasserman (New York: Palgrave Macmillan, 2015), 79–96.

2. Christopher Bonanos, "Save the Trash! Why the Gawker Archive Is Important," *New York*, August 19, 2016; Krishnadev Calamur, "The Road to Gawker's End," *Atlantic*, August 18, 2016; Sydney Ember, "Gawker Is Said to Be Sold to Univision in a $135 Million Bid," *New York Times*, August 17, 2016; Joshua David Stein, "The Death of Gawker.com: Univision Basks in Acquisition While Writers Mourn," *Guardian*, August 19, 2016; Mark Graham (Wayback Machine director, Internet Archive) and Roger Macdonald (Television News Archive director, Internet Archive), interview with Hansen, August 25, 2016.

3. Howard Finberg, "Before the Web, There Was Viewtron," Poynter.org, October 27, 2003, www.poynter.org/2003/before-the-web-there-was-viewtron/17738/.

4. Michael Shapiro, "The Newspaper That Almost Seized the Future," *Columbia Journalism Review*, November/December 2011.

5. AT&T Archives, "Viewtron Introduction, from the Viewdata Corporation," last updated February 29, 2012, http://techchannel.att.com/play-video.cfm/2012/2/29/AT&T-Archives-Viewtron-Introduction.

6. Elizabeth M. Ferrarini, "The Electronic Newspaper: Fact or Fetish," in *Videotex—Key to the Information Revolution* (Northwood Hills, Middlesex, UK: Online Ltd., 1982), 45–57.

7. Steve Newman, "1981 Primitive Internet Report on KRON," uploaded to YouTube on March 26, 2008, www.youtube.com/watch?v=5WCTn4FljUQ.

8. Tom Shea, "Big Firms Team Up on Videotex Project," *Infoworld*, March 12, 1984, 13–14.

9. Leslie Walker, "AOL's Garden Might Flourish without Rainman," *Washington Post*, April 15, 2004.

10. Shapiro, "The Newspaper."

11. Shapiro, "The Newspaper."

12. Memorandum on launch of the *New York Times* on AOL by Richard J. Meislin to Max Frankel and Joe Lelyveld, December 27, 1993, New York Times Company records, "General Files—Electronic Newspaper—Online Computer Services 1993–1999," New York Times Corporate Archives, MssCol 17802, box 124, file 6, Manuscript and Archives Division, New York Public Library.

13. Shapiro, "The Newspaper."

14. Eric Auchard, "The Black Hole: How the Web Devours History," Reuters.com, February 27, 2009, www.reuters.com/article/columns-us-column-web-idUSTRE51Q3KE20090227?sp=true.

15. Jill Lepore, "The Cobweb: Can the Internet Be Archived?" *New Yorker*, January 26, 2015, 37.

16. The browser Berners-Lee invented was at first called WorldWideWeb, but it was eventually changed to Nexus to avoid confusion with the name that came to encompass the entire web; Nexus is not to be confused with the Lexis/Nexis electronic legal and news text database that was offered by Mead Data Central starting in the 1970s.

17. Shapiro, "The Newspaper."

18. Peter H. Lewis, "Internet Radio Station Plans to Broadcast around the Clock," *New York Times*, September 19, 1994.

19. Victor Dorff, "Internet Television—An Anniversary," *Huffington Post*, November 23, 2015, www.huffingtonpost.com/victor-dorff/internet-and-television-o_b_8602316.html.

20. Rick Prelinger, "Silence, Cacophony, Crosstalk: New Talking Points," (presentation at Orphans X: Sound, 10th Orphan Film Symposium, Culpeper, VA, April 7, 2016).

21. Shannon E. Martin and Kathleen A. Hansen, *Newspapers of Record in a Digital Age: From Hot Type to Hot Link* (Westport, CT: Greenwood Publishing Group, 1998); Shapiro "The Newspaper."

22. Kurt D. Bollacker, "Avoiding a Digital Dark Age," *American Scientist* 98, no. 2 (2010): 106.

23. Peter Lyman, "Archiving the World Wide Web," in *Building a National Preservation Strategy: Issues in Digital Media Archiving* (Washington, DC: Council on Library and Information Resources and the Library of Congress, 2002), 39.

24. Robert Schaffer (website manager, Minneapolis *Star Tribune*), interview with Hansen, summer 1996.

25. Schaffer interview.

26. Hansen personal recollection.

27. Rich Gordon, "Miami Herald Launch," May 12, 2016, http://richgor.github.io//MiamiHeraldLaunch96/.

28. Rich Gordon, email message to Paul, May 13, 2016.

29. Kathleen A. Hansen and Nora Paul, "Reclaiming News Libraries," *Library Journal*, April 1, 2002, 44–46.

30. Carter Maness, "All My Blogs Are Dead," *The Awl*, February 2, 2015, www.theawl.com/2015/02/all-my-blogs-are-dead.

31. "Blackhawk Down," *Philadelphia Inquirer*, 1997, http://inquirer.philly.com/packages/somalia/sitemap.asp.

32. "Fatal Flights: Fatal Medical Helicopter Crashes," *Washington Post*, 2009, www.washingtonpost.com/wp-srv/special/nation/medical-helicopters/fatal-crashes.html.

33. These should not be confused with the "apps" that people download to their phones or tablets that provide functionality for many types of activities: shopping, driving directions, games, and so on.

34. "Dollars for Docs," *ProPublica*, last updated March 17, 2016, https://projects.propublica.org/docdollars/.

35. Meredith Broussard, "Preserving News Apps Presents Huge Challenges," *Newspaper Research Journal* 36, no. 3 (2015): 300.

36. Broussard, "Preserving News Apps," 310.

37. Broussard, "Preserving News Apps," 310.

38. Kennedy Elliott, "The Federal Health-Care Exchange's Abysmal Success Rate," *Washington Post*, November 21, 2013, www.washingtonpost.com/wp-srv/special/politics/state-vs-federal-exchanges/.

39. Jeffrey Gottfried and Elisa Shearer, "News Use across Social Media Platforms 2016," *Pew Research Center's Journalism Project*, May 26, 2016, www.journalism.org/2016/05/26/news-use-across-social-media-platforms-2016/.

40. Sarah Fihe, "The Preservation of Social Media As a Record of Social History," (final research proposal, San Jose State University, May 5, 2013), www.eportsarahfihe.com/wp-content/uploads/2015/03/Final-research-proposal-Fihe-Sarah_285.docx.

41. Nancy Scola, "Library of Congress' Twitter Archive Is a Huge #FAIL," *Politico*, July 11, 2015, www.politico.com/story/2015/07/library-of-congress-twitter-archive-119698.html.

42. Kathleen A. Hansen and Nora Paul, "Newspaper Archives Reveal Major Gaps in Digital Age," *Newspaper Research Journal* 36, no. 3 (2015): 290–98.

43. Andy Jackson, "Ten Years of the UK Web Archive: What Have We Saved?" (presentation at the International Internet Preservation Consortium General Assembly, Palo Alto, CA, April 30, 2015).

44. Megan Waters Bernal, "Production and Distribution of Electronic News: Technology and Preservation Challenges," (presentation at Global Resources Roundtable—Beyond the Fold: Access to News in the Digital Era, Chicago, IL, June 27, 2013).

45. Genevieve Belmaker, "Erasing the Record, One Story at a Time," *The Quill*, July–August, 2013, 20.

46. J. K. Trotter, "Over 4,000 BuzzFeed Posts Have Completely Disappeared," *Gawker*, August 12, 2014, http://gawker.com/over-4-000-buzzfeed-posts-have-completely-disappeared-1619473070.

47. Mario Tedeschini-Lalli, "Reinventing 'Past' in the Digital World," *Medium*, December 18, 2015, https://medium.com/thoughts-on-journalism/wait-a-moment-that-s-cnn-right-82c1fcaf57a0.

48. Xeni Jardin, "New Jersey Judge Orders Newspaper to 'Remove a News Article.' The Paper's Response Is Awesome," *BoingBoing*, May 30, 2015, http://boingboing.net/2015/05/30/new-jersey-judge-orders-newspa.html.

49. Belmaker, "Erasing the Record"; Mark Hansen, "Judge Orders Florida Newspaper to Unpublish Information on Its Website," *ABA Journal*, December 7, 2015.

50. Jeff Rothenberg, "Ensuring the Longevity of Digital Documents," *Scientific American*, no. 127 (January 1995): 42–47.

51. Dorothy Carner, Edward McCain, and Frederick Zarndt, "Missing Links: The Digital News Preservation Discontinuity," (paper presented at International Federation of Library Associations conference, Lyon, France, 2014).

52. Rob Schmitt (client solutions manager, EidosMedia), interview with authors, April 25, 2016.

53. Hansen observation, Association for Education in Journalism and Mass Communication conference, Washington, DC, August 8, 2013, www.c-span.org/video/?314458-1/aejmc-hosts-panel-politics-journalism&start=4695.

54. Hansen observation.

55. George Winslow, "Mining Gold from Yesterday's News," *Broadcasting & Cable*, July 29, 2013.

56. Leighton Walter Kille, "The Growing Problem of Internet 'Link Rot' and Best Practices for Media and Online Publishers," *Journalists Resource*, February 16, 2015, http://journalistsresource.org/studies/society/internet/website-linking-best-practices-media-online-publishers.

57. Consolidated Appropriations Act, Pub. L. No. 106-554 (2000).

58. Laura Campbell, "The National Digital Information Infrastructure and Preservation Program (NDIIPP) and Its Implications for a Research Agenda for Digital Preservation," *Library & Information Science Research* 26, no. 84 (2002): 32–40.

59. William Y. Arms, *Web Preservation Project: Final Report: A Report to the Library of Congress* (Ithaca, NY: Cornell University, 2001), 5.

60. A web crawler is a software agent that traverses the web in an automated manner, making copies of the content it finds as it goes along. The library's goal is to create an archival copy—essentially a snapshot—of how the site appeared at a particular point in time. Depending on the collection, the library archives as much of the site as possible, including html pages, images, flash, PDFs, and audio and video files, to provide context for future researchers. The Internet Archive's

Heritrix crawler used by the library is currently unable to archive streaming media, "deep web" or database content requiring user input, and content requiring payment or a subscription for access. See www.loc.gov/webarchiving/faq.html.

61. Arms, *Web Preservation*, 8.

62. Library of Congress, "Collections with Archived Web Sites," www.loc.gov/websites/collections?loclr=blogsig.

63. Michael Neubert, email message to Hansen, May 25, 2016; Library of Congress, "Web Archive Collections," http://loc.gov/webarchiving/collections.html.

64. Molly Bragg and Kristine Hanna, "The Web Archiving Life Cycle Model," March 2013, https://archive-it.org/static/files/archiveit_life_cycle_model.pdf.

65. Lepore, "The Cobweb," 38.

66. Graham interview.

67. Local station content in nine "battleground states" was captured as part of a project to document the 2016 presidential primary contests and general election coverage.

68. Macdonald interview.

69. "The GDELT Project," http://gdeltproject.org/.

70. Educopia, "History," https://educopia.org/about-us/history.

71. Katherine Skinner and Matt Schultz, *Guidelines for Digital Newspaper Preservation Readiness* (Atlanta, GA: Educopia Institute, 2014).

72. Edward McCain, "Plans to Save Born-Digital News Content Examined," *Newspaper Research Journal* 36, no. 3 (2015): 342.

73. "Web Archiving," https://library.stanford.edu/projects/web-archiving.

74. "Time Travel," timetravel.mementoweb.org/.

75. "Past Pages," www.pastpages.org/.

76. Ann J. Wolpert, "Archives and History," MIT Video, April 24, 2009, http://video.mit.edu/watch/archives-and-history-9483/.

77. Dan Feder, "Gary Webb's 'Dark Alliance' Returns to the Internet," *Narco News Bulletin*, June 23, 2005, www.narconews.com/darkalliance/; Peter Kornbluh, "The Storm over 'Dark Alliance,'" *Columbia Journalism Review*, January/February 1997.

78. Kornbluh, "The Storm."

79. Feder, "Gary Webb's 'Dark Alliance.'"

80. Kornbluh, "The Storm."

81. "Dark Alliance," restored June 23, 2005, www.narconews.com/darkalliance/drugs/start.htm, from Mercury Center website, last updated September 16, 1996.

82. Lena Roland and David Bawden, "The Future of History: Investigating the Preservation of Information in the Digital Age," *Library & Information History* 28, no. 3 (2012): 220–36.

9

CHALLENGES TO NEWS ARCHIVE ACCESS

> Preservation without access is historical censorship.
> Access without copyright protection is theft.
>
> —"Roundtable on Television Preservation," 1989[1]

Each chapter about preservation challenges for news content has noted some key trends: (1) For the most part, the actual creators of the content rarely concerned themselves with preserving the news product; (2) When news was preserved, the material either used to create it or to store it often was insufficiently stable to ensure future accessibility; (3) But for the efforts of a wide array of organizations, foundations, libraries, memory institutions, and individual collectors, the body of news content that has been created during the past three centuries would be lost.

That said, the most important aspect of news preservation is whether and how it is *now* available for use by researchers, historians, journalists, librarians, and citizens.

The two quotes from the "Roundtable on Television Preservation" that open this chapter sum up the issues that apply to any of the news formats we have discussed. On one hand, an archive of news content is all but useless if no one knows about it or has access to it. On the other hand, the creators and stewards of that content have a legitimate intellectual property interest in managing how that content is used. For those who have research or creative interest in locating and using news content, access and copyright issues can be hurdles—in some cases—impossible to leap.

For the person seeking news content, regardless of time span or media form, there are four questions they must answer:

1. Who has an archive of the content I need?
2. How can I get access to that archive?
3. Are there tools that will help me find specific items in that archive?
4. I've found what I need; will I be able to use it the way I intend?

WHO HAS AN ARCHIVE OF THE CONTENT I NEED?

Finding a collection may be the most challenging of all the issues facing news archive users. Simply identifying that an archive exists and has the needed content is a major undertaking. Repositories of media content are widely scattered geographically and institutionally. The idea that one library, archive, historical society, museum, or other type of institution has a complete and uninterrupted run of whatever news content is sought is highly unlikely.

There is a long history of attempts to create news "union catalogs" (comprehensive listings of content held by libraries), most of them ultimately defeated by the sheer quantity of material to be tracked. Printed union catalogs are out of date by the time they come off the presses but can provide a starting point for someone attempting to learn whether a collection of news content exists in a major institution. For example, Brigham's 1947 *History and Bibliography of American Newspapers, 1690–1820* is still helpful more than seventy years later when looking for specific issues of early American newspapers or collections in libraries. Godfrey's 1992 *Reruns on File: A Guide to Electronic Media Archives* is a similar effort for radio or television broadcast collections. Newsreel collections might be located using *Newsreels in Film Archives*.[2]

As union catalog efforts have moved online, there are many more opportunities to keep such lists up to date, but it still is a daunting task for someone to identify a specific news archive in a specific collection. The Library of Congress (LOC) maintains a listing called "Newspaper Photograph Morgues"[3] that identifies state public institutions that house at least one photo collection. The WorldCat database is an example of an online catalog that compiles collection information from thousands of libraries. WorldCat's ArchiveGrid compiles information specifically for archival collections, including news collections.[4]

The International Coalition on Newspapers (ICON) database produced by the Center for Research Libraries (CRL) in Chicago is the most comprehensive source of information about significant newspaper collections in print, digital, and micro formats. As of October 2015, ICON listed more than 169,700 newspaper titles and more than forty-six million issues, dating from 1649 to 2015. These represent the holdings of more than three thousand institutions, including the LOC, CRL, and the American Antiquarian Society.[5]

The National Digital Newspaper Program (NDNP), a partnership between the National Endowment for the Humanities (NEH) and the LOC, is a long-term effort to provide permanent access to a national digital resource of newspaper bibliographic information and historic newspapers from all U.S. states and territories. This program builds on the legacy of the United States Newspaper Program (USNP), which organized the inventorying, cataloging, and selective preservation on microfilm of a corpus of at-risk newspaper materials from 1836 to 1922. The USNP, funded by the NEH and successfully conducted from 1982 to 2011 by libraries and historical societies across the United States, represented the first truly national effort to identify and properly document the location and nature of newspaper collections around the country. The NDNP project digitized those USNP microfilmed collections and made them accessible through the LOC's Chronicling America database.

In July 2016, the NEH and the LOC announced that they were expanding the chronological scope of the NDNP to digitize newspaper collections. Now, newspapers published between 1690 and 1963 can be added to the NDNP Chronicling America database if the institution scanning the newspaper or microfilm can prove that the content is not under copyright.[6] It is especially significant that the project extends the date beyond 1922, which was the cutoff point between items in the public domain (those published before 1923) that could be microfilmed and scanned and those still under copyright protection that could not be included in the database. This new chronological scope will greatly increase the number of historical newspapers that can eventually be accessed digitally.

Just as private collectors of various news media have been preservation heroes, individuals sometimes compile finding guides. Genealogist Miriam J. Robbins describes the impetus for her Online Historical Newspapers Website: "Have you ever wished you could find links to all the online historical newspapers in one place? A place where they were listed by county and city so you could find the newspapers your ancestors read? This is the purpose of the Online Historical Newspapers Website. It is meant to be used as an aid to genealogists, historians, and other researchers."[7]

Clearly, union catalog efforts are more fully developed for newspaper collections than for other types of materials due to the length of time such collections have existed. But there are current efforts to build a digital union catalog for the film and television content being digitized and preserved in archives around the world. The Media Ecology project received funding from the NEH in 2015.[8] Dartmouth College professor Mark Williams and computer applications developer John Bell are creating a tool to collect information about items in the moving image archives at libraries and universities. The effort is in its beta phase with a few pilot projects underway. The tool would represent a major accomplishment if successful.

The LOC's Radio Preservation Task Force, discussed in chapter 5, is trying to collect information to generate a digital database of radio collections around the United States. Again, many different institutions and individual collectors hold such material, and the task force has a monumental challenge ahead of it.

But as we have demonstrated through earlier chapters, news archive collections of many other types are squirreled away in literally thousands of different places, some accessible to the public, many not, and it requires highly developed sleuthing skills to find them.

HOW CAN I GET ACCESS TO THE ARCHIVE?

Let's assume someone has found an archive with the news content that is needed. How does that person get access to that archive? In many cases, the material is part of a commercial enterprise that is closed to the public. Think of the internal news archives for newspapers or television stations, for instance. Some news organizations used to have "public service" desks as part of their internal news libraries that would fulfill non-newsroom requests for material from the archive. But those days are long gone. Now, news organizations frequently refer archival news seekers to the local library.

Other times, the archive may be part of a collection available to the public, but because of copyright and other restrictions, the material may be used only in person and on site. So the person who needs that content must travel to that location and have the time to sit in a reading room or an audio-visual lab with a notebook or computer. Some of these collections also require membership or status as a researcher with an institutional affiliation to gain access.

Sometimes an archive is available, but the playback equipment needed to make the material accessible is not in working order or even available anymore. Or the collection consists of things like glass plate photo negatives, metal wire recordings, film clips spliced with masking tape, newspaper clippings in nine-by-four envelopes. The ability to make use of that material is severely limited. If the archive of news content has been digitized, such as some of the material accessible through the Internet Archive's Wayback Machine, there is always a chance the researcher will receive a dreaded "404—Not Found" error message, indicating that the link is lost.

The news collection might be accessible remotely if it has been digitized, but it might also sit behind a pay wall or require other forms of payment. Certainly all of the databases provided by information industry vendors require payment for their extensive digital back files. If a library subscribes on behalf of its users, access would be free, but library budgets to support this kind of subscription are tight and an individual may need to be affiliated with that institution to be able to use the library or archive's subscription to that vendor's databases. Or an archive might be part of an individual or hobbyist group's efforts, again requiring membership, affiliation, or payment to gain access.

For newsreel, radio, or television material, there are commercial vendors who are more than happy to make clips or stock footage available for a price—typically a steep one if the use is for anything other than educational purposes. The news organizations themselves have lucrative contracts with stock footage vendors to help monetize their collections.

Here is one example of how you might find an archive but may not be able to get access to it. The Los Angeles Public Library's collection of Los Angeles *Herald Examiner* photos includes 2.2 million items, but fewer than 60,000 are digitized. From the library's frequently asked questions (FAQ) page: "A large percentage of the photos from the Herald Examiner . . . are not on the Web. . . . Many of the Herald Examiner photos are 'wire service' photos which the Library cannot post since they did not originate at the Herald Examiner and are the property of the originating wire service. . . . All library users can search the online database. The photo collection itself is not available for patron browsing."[9]

Chapter 5 discussed the Amertape Recordgraph machine that used cellulose acetate film to record sound for radio broadcasts during World War II. Some of the recordings still exist but the machines themselves are scarce. If someone wanted to play one of the recordings on an original machine (if one could be found), there still would be problems. As described on the website of a British company, Poppy Records, that worked on the problem, "the loops which now survive in archives have become brittle with age and would be put at risk of damage if they were played on the original machines." But, the Poppy Records engineers declared, "A new playback machine has been designed for replaying archival material at the highest possible quality."[10] Of course, getting access to that new playback machine would require a trip to Bath, England. Just because someone finds an archive of news content doesn't mean the content he or she is seeking will be accessible.

ARE THERE TOOLS THAT WILL HELP ME FIND SPECIFIC ITEMS IN THE ARCHIVE?

Let's assume, however, that the searcher succeeds in getting access to the back files of the news content needed. How does someone discover the way that different news organizations covered a topic over time? How does a researcher find all of the news stories about a specific person or topic that appeared in one particular newspaper or on one broadcast news station? How does a searcher identify individual photos, illustrations, audio, or video clips that appeared in a newspaper or broadcast? All of these research questions depend on the existence of some type of index to news content.

The index to the *Maryland Gazette* for content from 1727 to 1746 was the first of its kind in the United States.[11] The *New York Times* and the *New York Herald* were among the major daily newspapers to produce indexes of their content starting in the mid-1800s. The *New York Daily Tribune* sold an index from 1875 to 1906.[12] The American Library Association expressed interest in encouraging the production of an index to national newspaper content as early as 1893.[13] In the 1930s, the Works Progress Administration funded a project to index the contents of twenty newspapers, which resulted in indexes for those papers going back as far as 1728.

However, for the smaller circulation dailies and weeklies in communities around the country, the searcher may or may not find help from a locally produced index. The news organization may have one, but it is likely to be for internal use by the news staff only. The local public library or historical society may have produced one, but it may not be complete. If a complete index does exist, the archival content to which it refers might be held in different memory institution collections or in different formats. An archive of old clip files may be available, but those were organized for use by the news staff and may not be as helpful to general searchers. Some of the microfilm of that newspaper may have been digitized, making it searchable, but once again, those files would not be complete.

The dream of an index that would capture the content of all the major U.S. newspapers has been partially met by the full-text searchable databases of news content through vendors such as Lexis/Nexis, Factiva, ProQuest,

NewsBank, and others. However, these databases typically include only the text that appeared in the printed newspaper. All visual content is missing. After a 2001 Supreme Court ruling that said freelance writers' copyright was violated when a newspaper publisher included freelance work in its database, newspaper companies stripped all of the freelance articles from their vendor archives.[14] So anyone looking for a freelance piece published in the newspaper won't find it in the so-called full-text database.

And these information vendors offer only those news titles that they know have commercial value. Several vendor representatives participating in a 2015 summit meeting about making newspaper content more widely available admitted that they have hundreds of newspaper title archives in their vaults that they have no interest in digitizing because the market would not support the initial cost of doing the conversion.[15] The role that libraries used to play in deciding which newspapers to include in their collections is now being played by information vendors who decide which newspaper archives to digitize and sell based on economic rather than cultural heritage criteria.

Indexes to broadcast content, when available, are in the form of searchable transcript databases. Database services such as Newsbank's Access Broadcast Transcripts provide the full text of newscast transcripts and some video content from the major broadcast networks. Gale's Infotrac Newsstand contains radio and television transcripts, as does Factiva. Lexis/Nexis's Broadcast Transcript database has links to the video of selected newscasts, but those links are only available for thirty days from publication date. The Internet Archive's TV News Archive has created a searchable database of the closed captions from news broadcasts and provides access to the clips related to the caption starting in 2009. As Ellen Miller, executive director of the Sunlight Foundation describes the Internet Archive's TV News Archive, "It expands transparency by making words and deeds captured on a historically hard-to-rewind medium easy to find and review. This searchable video library puts research tools once available to only a small media elite into the hands of average citizens."[16] But access to the full news program requires the searcher to request a DVD copy or to go to the location of a repository of the broadcast itself.

As for newsreels, even confirmation that the newsreel exists does not ensure that a user will be able to find what is needed. It might be possible for someone to locate a specific newsreel that ran in theaters on a particular date, although that's a challenge, given that so few complete issues survive. But if someone wants to find all the newsreel stories that might have been produced about a specific topic across all the different newsreel providers over time, that will be very difficult. The newsreel collections at the National Archives, for instance, are fairly well indexed. For a highly celebrated topic, there might be a way to search by name or topic (e.g., "Roosevelt," "Suez crisis"). For more obscure topics or types of images (e.g., women working in factories in the 1940s), the indexing that does exist is not likely to capture the content in that level of detail.

Indexes can be as vulnerable to loss and degradation as the media they index. When staff at the Moving Image Research Collections (MIRC) at the University of South Carolina first created a searchable index for the Fox Movietone collection in the early 1980s, they used computer database software designed for medical diagnoses, because it was one of the few database programs then available that could digitally handle multiple information fields. That early computer catalog has been migrated five times since, and current MIRC curator Greg Wilsbacher says that each migration has resulted in some lost information.[17]

Indexing efforts present substantial time and budgetary expenses. Even with the best intentions indexing projects are often sporadic, as this specific index to obituaries in the *St. Louis Post Dispatch*, compiled by the St. Louis Public Library, demonstrates. The obituary index is available for the years 1880 to 1930, 1942 to 1945, 1960 to 1969, and 1992 to 2011. If you are seeking an obituary outside these dates, you are on your own.

I'VE FOUND WHAT I NEED: WILL I BE ABLE TO USE IT THE WAY I INTEND?

Once you have the content you need, you have to figure out whether you can use it for the purposes you intended. Because of preservation concerns, you are unlikely to get access to an original printed issue of the newspaper, an original news photo negative, an original nitrate newsreel film, an original radio news sound clip captured on a reel-to-reel tape, an original television news film clip, or an original videotape of a television news broadcast.

Rather, you are likely to get access to a *copy* of the original item (microfilm of a newspaper, analog or digital copy of a photo, sound clip, film clip, etc.). If you want to make individual use of the item for historical or genealogical research, for example, the copy of the original item will probably suffice. However, if you want to reuse the content in a new publication or broadcast, the archive's copy may not be of high enough quality for you to make yet *another* copy for your purposes. The archive may offer to convert its original content to a high quality (probably digital) copy for each user on demand, assuming the archive has the ability to do so. Of course, that might require payment. But conversion on demand is not always possible because the original is too fragile or because the archive doesn't have the appropriate equipment. The best a user may get is to see or hear the copy of the original but not to get it in a form that would be acceptable for republication purposes.

A related issue is whether the user has to pay to reuse archival content. Information vendors (news database companies, stock footage houses, or news organizations themselves) and memory institutions all have different rules and policies regarding how content can be reused once you locate it. This introduces the issue of copyright and intellectual property law. Though we cannot cover all of the intricacies of copyright law here, there are some basic principles that apply to the reuse of copyrighted news media content.

Copyright protection was provided for in Article I, Section 8 of the U.S. Constitution: "The Congress shall have Power . . . To promote the Progress of Science and useful Arts, by securing for limited Times to Authors and Inventors the exclusive Right to their respective Writings and Discoveries." Since then, the law has been codified, amended, and is now articulated in title 17 of the *United States Code*. The owner of a copyright has the exclusive authority to, among other things, authorize reproduction of the work; distribute copies of the work to the public through transfer of ownership or by rental, lease, or lending; display the work (images, motion pictures or audiovisual content) publicly; or perform the work (sound recordings) publicly by means of a digital audio transmission.

There are some limitations to these exclusive rights, the most relevant of which is the "fair use" doctrine. Provided for in Section 107 of the 1976 Copyright Act, this doctrine allows the use of copyrighted content for commentary or parody. Since the 1976 copyright law was adopted, various organizations and scholars also have established guidelines for educational fair use. For example, a teacher can show an example of a newspaper website or a news broadcast in a classroom under the educational fair use guidelines. More commercially oriented uses, however, would run into problems under the fair use doctrine depending on the amount of copyrighted material being used, whether the use deprives the original owner of income, and a number of other factors that would be determined by a judge hearing a copyright infringement lawsuit.

Section 108 of the 1976 Copyright Act further delineates the rules and regulations for libraries', archives', and museums' regular and frequent reproduction and distribution of copyrighted works. The 1973 lawsuit brought by CBS against the Vanderbilt Television News Archive due to the archive's taping of broadcasts and making them available for educational uses was dropped after the revisions to the Copyright Act in 1976 clarified that such taping was allowable for preservation purposes.

However, most archivists, librarians, and museum curators believe that Section 108 is woefully out of date for the digital era.[18] As explained on the American Library Association website, under the provisions of Section 108:

> The library may make up to three copies of an unpublished work for purposes of preservation, including copies in digital form as long as that format is not made available to the public outside of the library or archives. The library may also make up to three copies of a published work to replace a damaged, deteriorating, lost, or stolen work (when an unused replacement cannot be obtained at a fair cost). The library may also make up to three digital copies to replace a work in an obsolete format as long as that format is not made available to the public outside of the library or archives.[19]

So, for example, a library cannot stream copyrighted archival content over the Internet because that would make the content "available to the public outside the library or archives." When the UCLA Film and Television Archive received from PBS the full run and the rights to the lesbian, gay, bisexual, and transsexual newsmagazine *In the Life*, the archive staff uploaded the entire series to YouTube. However, third-party content providers whose work was included in the programs (background music, photos, etc.) flagged the content as copyright violations and the archive had to take it down.[20] The LOC explains its inability to stream radio content from its National Recording Registry this way: "Due to copyright concerns, the Library of Congress is unable to post even sample audio of most National Recording Registry selections."[21] This is the reason that many individual news archive collectors do not want to donate their material to memory institutions—they know that users would have limited access to content if it is part of an institution subject to Section 108 restrictions.

Each form of news content discussed in this book has its own specific copyright characteristics. A general rule of thumb is that any work that was under copyright protection before 1923 is now in the public domain. But there are so many exceptions that it's not safe to make any assumptions about whether the material in a news archive can be reused for commercial purposes without going through a careful legal review. Even if the copyrighted content can be used, there are likely to be licensing fees if the use is for anything other than nonprofit or educational purposes. Advice to anyone who wants to use copyrighted archival news content outside of a fair use context? Get an attorney.

NOTES

1. Jeff Porro and Fay Schreibman, "Roundtable on Television Preservation: A Colloquium Convened by the Annenberg Washington Program: Rapporteur Summary," (symposium, New York, May 19, 1989).

2. Clarence S. Brigham, *History and Bibliography of American Newspapers, 1690–1820*, 2 vols. (Worcester, MA: American Antiquarian Society, 1947; Hamden, CT: Archon Books, 1962); Donald G. Godfrey, *Reruns on File: A Guide to Electronic Media Archives* (New York: Routledge, 1992); Roger Smither and Wolfgang Klaue, eds., *Newsreels in Film Archives: A Survey Based on the FIAF Newsreel Symposium* (Trowbridge, Wiltshire, UK: Flicks Books, 1996).

3. Library of Congress, Prints and Photographs Reading Room, "Newspaper Photograph Morgues," last updated March 2016, www.loc.gov/rr/print/resource/newsmorgues.html.

4. "About ArchiveGrid," https://beta.worldcat.org/archivegrid/about/.

5. Center for Research Libraries, "ICON Database," www.crl.edu/archiving-preservation/print-preservation/icon-database.

6. National Endowment for the Humanities, "Expanding Our Current Scope | NDNP," July 7, 2016, www.neh.gov/news/expanding-our-current-scope-ndnp.

7. "Online Historical Newspapers," https://sites.google.com/site/onlinenewspapersite/Home.

8. Mark Williams, "The Media Ecology Project," https://sites.dartmouth.edu/mediaecology/.

9. Los Angeles Public Library, "Photo Collection FAQs," www.lapl.org/collections-resources/photo-faq.

10. "Recordgraph Transcription Services," www.poppyrecords.co.uk/ADM001/S07.htm.

11. Barbara P. Semonche, *News Media Libraries: A Management Handbook*. (Westport, CT: Greenwood, 1993), 375.

12. T. F. Mills, "Preserving Yesterday's News for Today's Historian: A Brief History of Newspaper Preservation, Bibliography, and Indexing," *Journal of Library History* 16, no. 3 (1981): 476.

13. Semonche, *News Media Libraries*, 276.

14. *New York Times Company, Inc. v. Tasini*, 533 U.S. 483 (2001).

15. Authors' participation, "Framing a Common Agenda for Newspaper Digitization and Preservation: An ICON Summit," Stockholm, Sweden, April 14, 2015.

16. Brewster Kahle, "Launch of TV News Search & Borrow with 350,000 Broadcasts," *Internet Archive Blogs*, September 17, 2012, https://blog.archive.org/2012/09/17/launch-of-tv-news-search-borrow-with-350000-broadcasts/.

17. Gregory Wilsbacher (curator, Moving Image Research Collections, University of South Carolina), interview with Hansen, March 28, 2016.

18. Jane C. Ginsburg, Laura Gasaway, Maria Pallante, Richard Rudick, Shira Perlmutter, "Session 1: The Legal Landscape," *Columbia Journal of Law & the Arts* 36 (2013): 527–46.

19. American Library Association, "Section 108 Photocopying by Libraries and Archives," www.ala.org/advocacy/copyright/dmca/section108.

20. Mark Quigley (director, UCLA Film and Television Archive, Research and Study Center), interview with Hansen, February 19, 2016.

21. Library of Congress, "National Recording Preservation Board: Recording Registry," www.loc.gov/programs/national-recording-preservation-board/recording-registry.

10

WHAT NEXT?

> The archivist's job is to hack media so that it can be preserved against its will.
>
> —Rick Prelinger, "Silence, Cacophony, Crosstalk," 2016[1]

THE CURRENT STATE OF NEWS PRESERVATION

Several key themes arose in our examination of media preservation efforts during the last three hundred years. Which of these themes will resonate for news preservation efforts in the future? Will attention to saving today's news for tomorrow fall into the same traps as those efforts have in the past? As we have seen, news preservation is imperiled by the forces of benign neglect and advanced by heroic, but sporadic, efforts.

News Organizations

News organizations are still adapting to the effects the digital age has had on their news products and business models. Plummeting finances led to draconian reductions in newsroom staff over the last decade and the near total elimination of news library staffs. Without anyone overseeing the archiving function, there are few champions in newsrooms when production changes endanger the flow of news content into a suitable storage system.

No longer does a news organization deliver only one type of news product such as newsprint or news broadcast. Virtually every news organization produces, at the very least, its legacy content as well as an online version. Each of these content streams provides different experiences for users and different content to be preserved. Archiving considerations are more complicated than ever before. Questions about "version control" for continually updated stories, specific storage requirements for different media types (videos, animations, data visualizations), and use of third-party vendors for certain content (comment sections, ad servers) riddle the field. When production systems change, there can be wholesale loss of past website content.

News organizations have had little incentive to archive their news products as the monetization potential has never been sufficient to capture management's support. Most arranged with information vendors to market and deliver their archival content for a small cut of the generated revenue. However, as news websites have struggled to become significant revenue sources, many have elected to erect paywalls that block users' access to archives of content if they don't subscribe. Others have gone to a pay-for-play model, providing an article or two from an archive for free and then imposing a fee for additional items.

Downsizing newsroom staffs has been accompanied by the downsizing of physical facilities. When a news company sells off its former headquarters and moves into smaller spaces, one of the first assets to be off-loaded is the space-hogging archive.

Memory Institutions

Libraries and historical societies often have been the recipients of choice for news organizations' discarded collections. But this largesse is sometimes more than the receiving institutions can manage. Reductions in budgets, staff shortages, and adjustments to changing reading and researching habits all have made it increasingly challenging to offer access to these news collections. When the resources donated or sold to a memory institution include fragile material, the dual urges for preservation and for providing access can sometimes conflict. The institution usually chooses to limit access to ensure that the materials survive intact. As depositories of a community's media memory, libraries are probably the safest bet for news archive preservation, but they are no sure bet in terms of providing greater access to the content.

As more information is being privatized and put under the control of technology companies such as Facebook, Google, and Amazon and as publishers develop and sell information resources as part of monetization strategies, the role of the library is being challenged. Bernard F. Reilly, president of the Center for Research Libraries, calls for reenvisioning libraries' approach to collection development. Rather than functioning as "containers, capturing and enclosing discrete physical objects,"[2] Reilly challenges libraries to perform the following roles as they work on preservation and access:

> Triage: Identify and focus on preserving items truly at risk and not likely to be preserved by others.
> Drill down: Make transparent the processes of the information life cycle and supply chain.
> Differentiate: Understand the various requirements and practices of different types of researchers.
> Collectivize: Libraries should "speak with one voice" in negotiating access to information for their constituents from the marketplace of information vendors.[3]

Reilly's admonition to memory institutions is especially relevant for news archives, given all of their format complexities and intellectual property challenges. Rethinking the role that memory institutions play in the field of news archive preservation and access may lead to a greater focus on informational wayfinding in an increasingly complex information environment.

Foundations and Philanthropic Organizations

During the past few years, the alarm over the loss of digital media has become more pronounced. However, the will to move efforts from awareness to action can be difficult to sustain. An example is an initiative funded by Knight-Mozilla OpenNews, the Newseum, and an audio transcription service called Pop Up Archive. Their concern was that the news industry does "a poor job of preserving interactive databases and online data visualizations, and they are in danger of being lost to history."[4] The groups convened a conference in March 2014 called "Preserving Interactive News Projects." They generated a report, but, as the document's author noted a year later, "Sadly, there really hasn't been any follow-up, despite this being a tremendously important issue."[5]

Examples of ongoing archival projects include the University of Missouri/Educopia partnership, "Dodging the Memory Hole," which is working on ways to advance the cause of digital news preservation, the Media Ecology project at Dartmouth College to identify moving image archives, and the Library of Congress's (LOC) support of the Radio Preservation Task Force's attempts to locate regional radio files. But the call for investment in preservation efforts is challenged by competing projects and flagging attention.

ARCHIVAL CHALLENGES AND OPPORTUNITIES

> DNA could be used to store digital information and preserve essential knowledge for thousands of years, research has shown us.
>
> —*The Daily Telegraph*, 2015[6]

Access to news content in the future depends on decisions made today about whether and how to store the minute-by-minute output of the news industries and the user-generated content associated with that output. We know that much of the archival news content from the past is inaccessible because the storage medium that was used at the time did not survive intact or because the equipment needed to decode that content is no longer available or operable. The shift to ones and zeroes did not eliminate that problem; in some ways, it made it worse because no form of digital media is easily decoded without the machines and software to render the content.

The three main processes of archival work—preservation, conservation, and restoration—must be taken into account in any solution. The efforts of the LOC and other memory institutions to stabilize and preserve the newsprint, microfilm, nitrate and acetate newsreel and television film, audiotape, and videotape originals that captured news content fall into the preservation category. During the past two decades, these memory institutions have recognized that without this basic preservation action, there will be nothing left from the analog era of news to conserve and restore. As we have seen, digital news preservation is a more vexing challenge.

Researchers and individual inventors across a wide spectrum of disciplinary expertise are exploring new ways to preserve digital data. Scientists in Britain have used nanostructured glass to record and retrieve five-dimensional digital data through an ultrafast type of laser writing. Major documents from human history, such as the King James Bible and Newton's *Opticks*, have been saved as digital copies on a glass disc the size of a quarter. Scientists say the data could survive the human race and "could be highly useful for organizations with big archives, such as national archives, museums and libraries, to preserve their information and records."[7]

Strands of biological material can store data as well. In 2015, scientists demonstrated the feasibility of using a silica sphere to encapsulate data encoded onto DNA. They stored the 1921 text of the Swiss Federal Charter and a copy of Archimedes's *The Method* dating from the tenth century. When the data were decoded, the text was error free.[8]

In 2016, the computer giant Microsoft purchased ten million strands of DNA from a biology startup to further investigate the use of genetic material to store data.[9] One gram of DNA can store close to one billion terabytes of data and last for five hundred years or more. It takes just ten terabytes to contain the entire printed collection of the LOC.[10] An article on the *Ars Technica* website stated, "If the technology can be made cheap enough, it means that one day long-term data archiving could use the same technology as life itself."[11]

Conservation is the process of maintaining the preserved content in a usable form. Diligently migrating content from current storage systems to the next generation of technology is one way to try to ensure archival news content conservation; hence the effort to convert analog film, audiotape, and videotape to digital forms and to digitally scan microfilmed newspapers. Even then, once an analog news archive is migrated to a digital form,

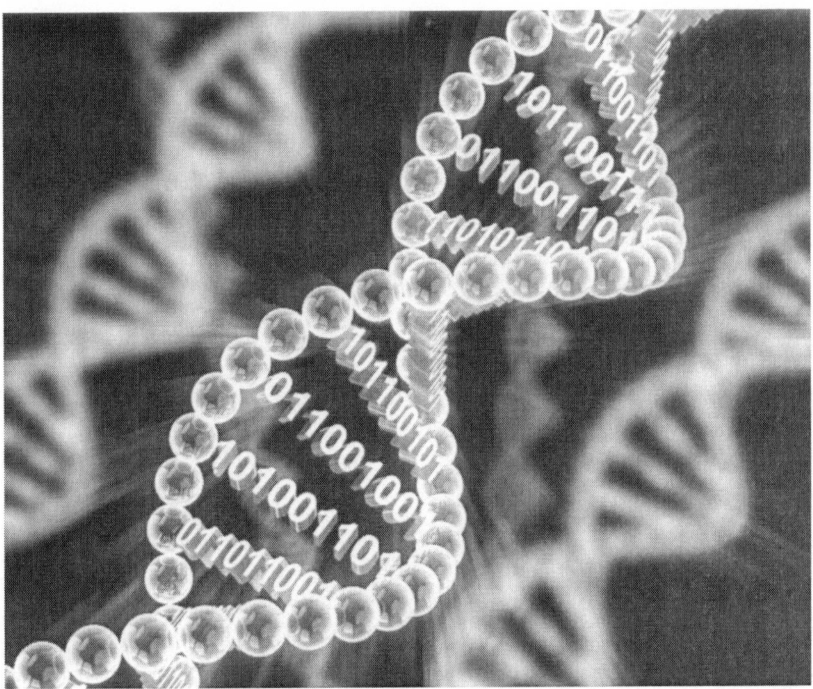

Using DNA for digital storage? *Courtesy iStock.com/ymgerman*

there are limits to the number of times a digital file can be migrated and converted. Bit rot is always a lurking danger. The software to render those ones and zeroes also has to be emulated in the newer system for it to be retrieved.

Migrating ones and zeroes back to an analog format is one option for conservation. In chapter 2, we quoted New York Public Library's chief reference librarian Henry Miller Lydenberg as saying in 1921: "Who knows that we will not some day soon be printing our records on thin strips of imperishable metal that will endure for all time."[12] The Digital Optical Technology System (DOTS) is a visual "eye-readable" method of storing digital files in analog form for no fewer than one hundred years on a strip of chemically inert metal, just as Lydenberg anticipated nearly a century ago. Digital data are converted to dots on the metal tape; the tape can also store visible text and images. DOTS includes a microfiche-scale human readable text at the beginning of the metal tape that provides instructions about how to construct a reader for the information. The tape is nonmagnetic, immune from electromagnetic fields, and can be stored in normal office environments or in temperature extremes from 15 degrees to 150 degrees Fahrenheit.[13]

Restoration is the final aspect of archival work. Memory institutions have worked hard over the years to restore analog news content in their own archives and to restore the content donated to them from news organizations themselves. Whether and how future digital news content might be restored to an original form is highly problematic, however. Just as newsreel or television film clip outtakes are not the same as the version of the content that was shown in the theater or aired on the nightly news, restoring a news website and its ads as they appeared at a particular point in time using a particular web browser or mobile device is all but impossible for all of the reasons laid out in chapter 8.

Vint Cerf, sometimes called the "father of the Internet," is now a vice president at Google. He has proposed a method of restoring digital information using the concept of "digital vellum." In a 2015 interview with British Broadcasting Corporation (BBC) science journalist Pallab Ghosh, Cerf explained that digital vellum would involve taking "an X-ray snapshot of the content and the application and the operating system together, with a description of the machine that it runs on, and preserv[ing] that for long periods of time. That digital snapshot will re-create the past, in the future. . . . The digital vellum idea is not just [a] physical medium, but an ecosystem which is able to remember what bits mean over long periods of time."[14]

DOTS thin alloy tape with microscopic analog capture of digital data and visible images. *Courtesy Group 47 Inc.*

Anticipating that there will continue to be technological developments in the creation and delivery of news, it would be foolish to assume that any archival process in use or under development today will be sufficient in the future. It is therefore crucial that the impact on the archival function for news content be considered whenever a new production and delivery form is introduced. It cannot be an afterthought as it always has been in the past. If we have learned anything from three hundred years of news work in the United States, it is that the archival storage function must be considered upfront, during the development of any new format, not after years or decades of content has been lost.

Whether it is holographic or virtual reality news storytelling, advanced information graphics, deeply sourced news application interactive databases, or some other form not yet envisioned, there will be new content that captures the news audience's attention. Without advanced planning for the capture and preservation of that content *as it is being created*, we will face the same problems we have with every other new form of news. Organizations such as the National Digital Stewardship Alliance and many others mentioned in this book are trying to develop best practices for effective content stewardship.[15] But unless the news organizations themselves embrace those efforts at the initiation of the news content production process, it will be impossible for memory institutions to make up for the losses that will occur.

Of course, there are legal and economic obstacles to such efforts. Most news websites and digital mobile content depend to some extent on sometimes proprietary content with copyright, licensing, and other legal strings attached. In his BBC interview, Cerf proposed that "the rights of preservation might need to be incorporated into our thinking about things like copyright and patents and licensing."[16] Even if the legalities can be addressed, the cost of keeping the equipment and information updated and working through the technical issues is daunting.

AVOIDING HISTORICAL AMNESIA

> The reason we know so little about the present is that it is always waiting to be understood—and reshaped—by our future.
>
> —Gregory Zinman, "The Archival Silences of Nam June Paik's Etude," 2016[17]

We began this book by asking the question, "Who needs yesterday's news?" Journalists, historians, genealogists, legal practitioners, business proprietors, artists, economists, and innumerable others refer to archival news in our current era, and such users will likely continue to need it in the future. The real question is, "How do we ensure that today's news will be preserved and accessible when it's needed tomorrow?"

Historian Abby Smith Rumsey puts the imperative to preserve knowledge, especially digital data, bluntly: "The primary challenge is moral and goes to the very core of our humanity: What do we owe other people, including people not yet born?"[18] Our central argument is that individual collectors and those in the news and information industries, memory institutions, government agencies, universities, research centers, and philanthropic organizations need to work together now to ensure that we pay the debt we owe to the future.

NOTES

1. Rick Prelinger, "Silence, Cacophony, Crosstalk: New Talking Points," (presentation at Orphans X: Sound, 10th Orphan Film Symposium, Culpeper, VA, April 7, 2016).

2. Bernard F. Reilly, "Toward a Rational and Sustainable Division of Labor for the Preservation of Knowledge," *Library Management* 37 nos. 4–5 (2016): 2.

3. Reilly, "Toward a Rational and Sustainable Division of Labor," 3.

4. Mario Tedeschini-Lalli, "Reinventing 'Past' in the Digital World," *Medium*, December 18, 2015, https://medium.com/thoughts-on-journalism/wait-a-moment-that-s-cnn-right-82c1fcaf57a0.

5. Tedeschini-Lalli, "Reinventing 'Past' in the Digital World."

6. "DNA Could Be Used to Store Data More Efficiently Than Computers, Scientists Find," *The Daily Telegraph*, August 17, 2015.

7. Lucas Mearian, "Superman Memory Crystals Could Store Data for Billions of Years," *Computerworld*, February 17, 2016.

8. "DNA Could Be Used"; Eliza Strickland, "Tech Companies Mull Storing Data in DNA," *IEEE Spectrum*, June 20, 2016.

9. Peter Bright, "Microsoft Experiments with DNA Storage: 1,000,000,000 TB in a Gram," *Ars Technica*, April 27, 2016, http://arstechnica.com/information-technology/2016/04/microsoft-experiments-with-dna-storage-1000000000-tb-in-a-gram/.

10. "Megabytes, Gigabytes, Terabytes—What Are They?" www.whatsabyte.com/.

11. Bright, "Microsoft."

12. "Times Files Saved by a New Method," *New York Times*, August 12, 1921.

13. "Group 47—What Is DOTS?" http://group47.com/what-is-dots/.

14. Cerf quote from Pallab Ghosh, "Google's Vint Cerf Warns of 'Digital Dark Age,'" *BBC News*, February 13, 2015, www.bbc.com/news/science-environment-31450389.

15. Abbey Potter, "Digital Library Federation to Host National Digital Stewardship Alliance," National Digital Stewardship Alliance news release, October 19, 2015.

16. Ghosh, "Google's Vint Cerf."

17. Gregory Zinman, "The Archival Silences of Nam June Paik's Etude," (presentation at Orphans X: Sound, 10th Orphan Film Symposium, Culpeper, VA, April 9, 2016).

18. Abby Smith Rumsey, "The Risk of Digital Oblivion," *Chronicle of Higher Education*, May 4, 2016, http://chronicle.com/article/The-Risk-of-Digital-Oblivion/236342.

EXTRA! EXTRA! READ MORE ABOUT IT

The histories of different types of media have been well documented over the years. We relied on these key media histories in researching this book. These works provided important context about the evolution of various media forms but, as we found, did little to examine each form's particular preservation issues. We hope that this book has addressed that oversight. For those interested in delving more deeply into the history of each of the media discussed, we provide this very selective reading list as a supplement to the many valuable sources we included in the endnotes of each chapter.

For more information about newspapers, several classic works will fill in the history of that industry's development. Michael Emery, Edwin Emery, and Nancy L. Roberts, *The American Press: An Interpretive History of the Mass Media* (Boston, MA: Allyn & Bacon, 1996) is a good starting point, as is Hazel Dicken-Garcia, *Journalistic Standards in Nineteenth-Century America* (Madison: University of Wisconsin Press, 1989). A more recent work is Christopher B. Daly, *Covering America: A Narrative History of a Nation's Journalism* (Amherst: University of Massachusetts Press, 2012).

Several key works on the history of photojournalism and visual journalism are Michael L. Carlebach, *The Origins of Photojournalism in America* (Washington, DC: Smithsonian Institution Press, 1992) and Joshua Brown, *Beyond the Lines: Pictorial Reporting, Everyday Life, and the Crisis of Gilded Age America* (Oakland, CA: University of California Press, 2006.) Get the story behind some of the most iconic photojournalism since 1942 in the compilation by Hal Buell, *Moments: The Pulitzer Prize–Winning Photographs* (New York: Black Dog and Levanthal, 2015).

Although there are a number of books about the history of British newsreels, our focus was on the United States. More information about the history of American newsreels at a pivotal point in time can be found in Kenneth R. M. Short, *World War II through the American Newsreels, 1942–1945: An Introduction and Guide to the Microfiches* (Oxford, UK: Oxford Microform Publications, 1985).

Those interested in radio and television's evolution should refer to Douglas Gomery, *A History of Broadcasting in the United States* (Hoboken, NJ: Wiley-Blackwell, 2008) or Robert L. Hilliard and Michael C. Keith, *The Broadcast Century and Beyond* (Burlington, MA: Focal Press, 2010).

Much of the history of digital news is still being written as the evolution of this medium unfolds. But the issue of the "digital black hole" has been the topic of books such as Abby Smith Rumsey, *When We Are No More: How Digital Memory Is Shaping the Future* (London: Bloomsbury Press, 2016). Solid analyses of the digital news production process can be found in Pablo J. Boczkowski, *Digitizing the News: Innovation in Online Newspapers* (Cambridge, MA: MIT Press, 2004) or Nikki Usher, *Making News at the New York Times* (Ann Arbor: University of Michigan Press, 2014).

INDEX

Page references for figures are italicized.

ABOUT THE AUTHORS

Kathleen A. Hansen is a professor in the School of Journalism and Mass Communication at the University of Minnesota–Twin Cities.

Nora Paul is director of the Minnesota Journalism Center in the School of Journalism and Mass Communication at the University of Minnesota–Twin Cities.